Cookery Books:

A Slice of the Pyrenees.

The Snail Cookbook.

Fiction:

Billy Ruffian's Courier.
Part one - Rites of Passage

Billy Ruffian's Courier.
Part two - Hawkshaw.

Billy Ruffian's Courier.
Part three - Baltic Exchange.

www.gunncomms.co.uk

Copyright © Walter Gunn 2015

The right of Walter Gunn to be identified as the author of this work has been asserted by him in accordance with the Copyright, Designs and Patents Act 1998.

All rights reserved. No part of this publication may be reproduced, stored in or introduced into a retrieval system, or transmitted, in any form, or by any means (electronic, mechanical, photocopying, recording or otherwise) without the prior written permission of the publisher. Any person who does any unauthorized act in relation to this publication may be liable to criminal prosecution and civil claims for damages.

This book is sold subject to the condition that it shall not, by way of trade or otherwise, be lent, re-sold, hired out, or otherwise circulated without the publisher's prior consent in any form of binding or cover other than in which it is published and without a similar condition including the condition being imposed on the subsequent purchase.

All characters in this publication other than those clearly in the public domain are fictitious and any resemblance to real persons, living or dead, is purely coincidental.

Walter Gunn
Billy Ruffian's Courier

Part 1 - rites of passage

This book is for:
Maude and her garden.

Also, many thanks to my friend Jo Markham whose attention to detail pointed out so many embarrassing spelling mistakes, typos and lapses of concentration. (How she and my wife Jen, sniggered.)

I must not forget to give special thanks to my good friend Val Turner for the loan of her dad - Ben Whitley.

Walter Gunn
Billy Ruffian's Courier

Part 1 - rites of passage

Billy Ruffian's Courier   Part 1 - rites of passage

Contents.

Chapter One - The Stoker and the Admiral............................	1.
Chapter Two - Billy's On The Move...	27.
Chapter Three - We Need to Keep Him Alive.......................	45.
Chapter Four - Roy Rogers the Singing Cowboy...................	71.
Chapter Five - The Killing Range..	90.
Chapter Six - A Freer Hand..	110.
Chapter Seven - The Letter..	114.
Chapter Eight - Alice Alacrity...	125.
Chapter Nine - Smelly Ben...	139.
Chapter Ten - The Protocol..	158.
Chapter Eleven - Part Frog...	179.
Chapter Twelve - The Hairy Cupid...	202.
Chapter Thirteen - A Fresh Identity for Bear Bait.................	230.
Chapter Fourteen - The Golden Mace.....................................	247.
Chapter Fifteen - To Bait the Bears...	259.
Chapter Sixteen - The Nineteenth Variation Bombshell......	272.
Chapter Seventeen - Quarr Abbey...	289.
Chapter Eighteen - All Flares Fired...	311.
Chapter Nineteen - Where a Gentle Grebe Waits..................	329.
Chapter Twenty - The School Report......................................	345.
Chapter Twenty One - Two Tokarevs and One Beretta.......	361.
Chapter Twenty Two - The Wet Deed.....................................	376.
Chapter Twenty Three - Anne's Favourite Game..................	394.
Appendix - Two Short Stories for Mo......................................	398.
The Hoopoe..	399.
Felicity..	403.
Ranks of the Royal Navy..	407.
Map of Portsmouth & Gosport...............................	408.
Map of the Solent & Isle of Wight..........................	409.
Glossary...	410.

Chapter One
The Stoker and the Admiral.

1961 - Port Swettenham - west coast of Malaya.
He had no idea how much pain he was going to feel in forty-three seconds; how much being shot in the back hurts, and that you feel like you're drowning when your lungs start to fill with blood.

Unwarranted and unbidden blows from the past years had piled up. In forty-three seconds and that final time-stretched instant of consciousness, he was to vow that if he survived there would have to be a change for the better. Conversely, if he did not pull through he would not be aware of it. In this brief moment to come the pragmatist in young John Sims Reeves would reckon either way there'd be an improvement. No matter, as it was, in one way or another, this young life was about to end.

*

Opera; this was his passion. He was enjoying himself. In this subject he could outrank an officer. 'She's called Tosca for the same reason Callas is called Callas.'

'I'm still in the dark... I don't get it.'

Saronged couples sway-strolled along the wide street bordering the old colonial dockside. Clatter of steaming woks, ladles brimming with stock, soup being skillfully wrapped in banana leaves and tied with raffia. Chatter mingled into the soft evening air. Sweet-scented wood smoke from the food stalls drifted over the table where the two men were eating.

'Okay, how about this, she's a diva... it's operatic tradition... surnames only for divas... come on, that's a hell of a clue!'

'Ah, are you saying, a diva is singing the role of a diva? Is that it?'

'Exactly so. Now my turn, perhaps you'll answer me something.'

'If I can... I don't know much about music though.'

'Not about music... change of subject. They were getting a bit close... a tads too near for comfort. Just how long would you have waited before giving me the nudge?'

The previous night an unlit gunboat had shadowed them, staying one hundred yards off their stern port quarter. The shielded gun on its foredeck pointed in their direction. Bright moonlight gave them a clear view. 'Indonesian,' the young officer said. 'Best put one up the spout in case they come closer.'

Sims, the marksman, stood next to him, snapped in a magazine and shoved the bolt home putting a round into the breech of his Lee Enfield .303. 'Probably better if I get the gunner first.' It wasn't a question, it was advice. This is how they worked together: each trusting the other's expertise.

'Can you see him through the slot?'

'He's wearing glasses... there's the occasional glint...

which eye shall I go for?' he said, smiling.

With the lights of Port Swettenham getting closer the gunboat opened its throttles. Kicking up a broad swathe of foaming phosphorescence, it headed away.

'Pretty close.'

'That doesn't really answer my question... how close?'

'I don't know... I suppose it depends on the moment.'

Sims, thinking about this answer, leant back tilting his chair on two legs and looked around at the crowded stalls, 'Some of these Malaysian girls are *so* gorgeous,' he said, glancing down the shadowy colonnade that lined the street to his right. A man flinched and ducked, another stepped out of the alley beside him, raised two arms and pointed them towards where they were sitting. Sims launched himself across the table and hit the man sitting opposite square in the chest with his shoulder.

Sprawled on the ground in a mess of Marmi soup, oblivious to the screams around him, the officer shouted, 'What the hell do you think you're doing?'

His forty-three seconds were up. 'Oh shit, that hurts... oh fuck that's so...' John Sims Reeves faded in mid sentence.

It took a few moments for the officer to realise the man pinning him down had stopped moving. Besides soup and noodles, something else warm and viscous was dripping onto his face.

'God, no, Sims... *Sims!*'

*

1 month later - Changi military hospital Singapore.
The sweating interviewing officer flicked through his

notes and Sims' record. He was there to assess the extent of Sims' injuries and whether his fitness would be of a standard to continue in the service. 'Reeves, you do realise you could reach the very top of your branch?'

'Wow, all the way to *Chief Stoker!* Dizzy heights... rarefied air there, sir. My future grandchildren will be so proud. I hardly know what to say.'

'Careful, Reeves, it's a vital job.'

'For someone maybe. But not for me it isn't, sir.'

'Why on earth not?'

Sims, already fed up with this interrogation, deviated: it had taken less than a minute. 'You may not find this relevant, sir, but haven't you noticed: all chief stokers are ugly. Tell me if you've ever seen a good looking one. It's as though one day they get promoted... overnight... ugly.'

'As a matter of fact, Reeves, I don't find it relevant, and I'm the one who's supposed to be asking the questions. *Reeves*, I'm trying to help you.'

'With respect, sir, that's like being given a hand up to the guillotine.'

'Have you no ambition at all? Are you as aimless as you appear? '

'Not aimless, just marking time, sir.'

'Until what?'

'Until I leave the navy and start a real life, sir.'

The officer again looked down at his notes and read the service record of Leading Stoker John Sims Reeves. 'It says here you've twice tried to purchase your discharge. Why do you think you were refused?'

'Beats me, I was eligible and I had the cash. Last time, they told me not to bother again.'

'They told me not to bother again, SIR!... you forgot to say SIR!' The officer was nearing retirement. At forty he was still only a sub-lieutenant. He was going nowhere. Insisting that ratings called him *'sir'* in every sentence: practically every clause, helped shore up his rock-bottom dignity - there appeared little of that left.

He mopped his dripping face and referred to his notes once more. 'Perhaps the navy thinks you're worth hanging on to, Reeves.'

'Can't see why, sir.' Just a little emphasis on the "sir".

'Nor can I... at last we agree on something. However, their reluctance to let you go might have something to do with you being a marksman, and saving the life of an officer... ... it says, wounded in action, shows bravery in extreme conditions.'

'Whoever wrote that ought to take up a career in journalism... it was hardly action, sir, we were eating dinner... and it wasn't bravery, it was ignorance.'

'Ignorance?'

'Absolutely, if I'd known how much it was going to hurt, Lieutenant James Fox-Eastleigh would sadly be no more... six feet under or if you like, just to keep things nautical, a full fathom five down, sir.'

'It also says here, LM(e) Reeves trespasses close to insolence.'

'Ah, marksman; hero; insolent; just the qualifications for a top of the line Chief Stoker. You missed incompetent, sir.'

'Reeves, I've about had enough of you, just because you're in a hospital bed does not mean I cannot or will not put you on a charge. Think carefully about what I've said concerning your advancement.'

Sims caught the eye of his favourite nurse - she came over. 'Excuse me, sir, I think LM(e) Reeves should rest now. He's been badly wounded.'

'Very well. I'm going to do my absolute best not to visit you again, Reeves. Ratings like yourself give the Royal Navy a bad name.'

'Thank you, sir. It sounds like you're going to recommend my release?'

'No I am *not!*'

The officer wiped his brow, collected his notes, and without asking Sims how his injury was healing, waddled out of the ward.

'Thanks, Su... two more minutes... strapped up or not, I swear I'd have belted him.'

'He's always the same, always... he's a real arse.'

Hearing Su's soft, clipped chinese voice calling a naval officer an arse, made Sims both laugh and wince at the same time.

'Are you alright?' she asked, leaning over him.

'No, *oh God, no.* I may require emergency remedial treatment... upper thighs definitely need a massage... I think a severe going over is on the cards.'

'Sims, you have a *back* wound,' she sighed.

'I'm no expert, but surely it would help wouldn't it? Come on, Su, have you no imagination? See it as a new and exciting form of physiotherapy.'

She looked around the ward: no matron lurking. 'Never happen... maybe... ...later,' she said, kissing him lightly on the forehead.

*

He had been ordered back to England to recuperate. 'I

shall miss you, Su.'

'Maybe you will come back when you're fit again,' she said, pulling the sheets over them as a cool breeze blew in through the open window.

'Hope so.'

*

6 months later - HMS Start Point - Chatham - Kent.
Sims had secrets. His records said he was intelligent - he kept this hidden under a wash of humour and indifference. His records did not mention he had financial assets and a passion for classical music - especially opera. Both these, he thought best to keep quiet about. Of the income from his late parent's and his late grandparent's houses, he had not thought it necessary to inform the Royal Navy or the Inland Revenue. His love of opera was not something to be openly confessed on a stokers' mess deck.

Nor was another secret; his father had been a lieutenant-commander in the war. Stokers and officers are presumed distant relatives on the evolutionary tree - both not to be tolerated by the other: both consider themselves occupying the loftier branches.

Sims had ambitions for life beyond the navy. His plan may have been a bit sketchy - limited in scope even. At present it amounted to no more than shedding his rather ridiculous uniform. Beyond that, things strategic were a bit vaguer - flimsy would have been an improvement. In three years or less he was going to be a free man, until then, however, squeezing the most zest out of his remaining time in Her Majesty's Royal Navy was to be his prime concern.

For the moment, life for Sims seemed to be on the up. He had recovered well, only days away from flying back out to the Far East to join the small frigate HMS *Urchin*. In his opinion, small ships were a ton better than big ones - less bull-shit, more relaxed. It was going to be a blissful, if not debauched, eighteen month commission that lay ahead.

His vision of things to come was crystal clear. In Singapore, there was every possibility he might catch up with Su again... he could smell the mouth watering aromas from the road-side food stalls. In Sembawang, he would eat vast amounts of Marmi soup and Nasi Goreng.

In the tropics dehydration is to be avoided. His remedy was straightforward; he intended to drink Tiger Tops lager in staggering quantities, or at least in quantities that would make him stagger. Health must come first he advocated, and thirst is the first sign of liquid deficiency. He pooh poohed such arguments claiming alcohol exacerbated dehydration. Naturally, his good sense said it was imperative to drink plenty.

Hong Kong - Wanchi district: Abalone soup; Eggs Foo Yung; San Miguel lager - more staggering to be done here. Fighting the Yanks - this would have to be done before midnight: they were not allowed ashore any later. More San Miguel beer - the price of which dropped dramatically after his American cousins were tucked up in bed. Fighting the Aussies - this could go on all night. Take note, it was this dubious criteria that proved, as far as Sims was concerned, that Australia had a proper navy.

In Japan he would dive head first into Saki and stuff he would rather remain ignorant as to its ingredients and making. There would be Bulgogi in Korea, though here, he would leave alone steamed silk worm pupae - he was of the opinion they tasted exactly like moths smell. Pupae aside, he was going to have *such* a ball.

Young Sims Reeves' senses were on high alert: primed and ready to be overloaded. No planning necessary, no carefully composed mission statement. He would follow his often bloodied nose. Except this time, if at all possible, he was going to avoid getting shot in the back.

*

Mt. Kinabalu - Borneo.
Humidity extreme, Lieutenant James Fox-Eastleigh and his escort slowly made their clammy and dripping way down the lower slopes of Mt. Kinabalu towards Jesselton. He'd received orders to return to HMS *Alacrity* without delay. His small party would have made more haste had it not been for the sacks of decomposing rebel heads being carried - they were beginning to smell abominably.

The escort were hill tribesmen and pragmatic. Heads weigh around fourteen pounds, they would give clear and irrefutable evidence when collecting the bounty - why bother with rest of the body?

Fox-Eastleigh was relieved to be returning. It had been a long and difficult anti-insurgence operation. More than once he had felt dangerously exposed without Sims' back-up.

His commanding officer met him on the gangway. 'Pack your kit straightaway, James, you're flying to RAF Changi this evening, and then back home to the UK.'

'Any idea why, sir?'

'No... need to know basis only.'

'Any news of Reeves, sir.'

'Yes, he's recovering reasonably well... been back home some time now... light duties on HMS *Start Point* in Chatham.'

'Thank God for that,' James breathed.

*

Tunworth House - Tunworth - Hampshire.
'Billy Ruffian, how on earth did he get that name?' asked the young tanned lieutenant.

'*How!* That's precisely what he is; that's how,' the commander sat opposite replied. 'He's a scrapper; never backs away from a fight. I can tell you there have been times that he's shown himself to be much more than a ruffian - given no mercy and taken no prisoners. Believe me, he has earned that nickname many times over.'

As if to gauge their interest, the speaker looked at the other two sat at the table, they sending back the right signals, prompted him to continue. 'Curiously maybe, his nickname has less to do with his pugnacity, and much more to do with his past and his passion. This table we're sat round is very much linked to his epithet,' he paused a moment. '*Come on*! Any guesses how?'

The commander, a good talker, knew how to hold and engage an audience. He pointed to the head of the table where there lay a large rectangular leather writing pad. 'This is what it says,' he said, getting up and walking to the far end. At the top of the pad and slightly narrower was a strip of thick steel with a row of three large rivets across the top. Out loud, he read the words embossed in gold in the leather:

*'This armour plating was cut from the hull
of the Bellerophon-class Battleship:
HMS Bellerophon.
Commissioned 20 February 1909.
On May 31st 1916 during the Battle of Jutland
HMS Bellerophon engaged the German fleet at
'Windy Corner' at which time she fired sixty-two
12" rounds without receiving a single hit herself.
This glorious Battleship was scrapped in 1923.'*

He now moved to the side of the table, pointed to a brass plaque set in its centre and read the words carved into that:

*'This table was made using timbers from HMS Bellerophon; an Arrogant-class 74 gun ship of the line. She was launched in 1786 and fought in three major fleet actions:
The Glorious First of June - The third Battle of Ushant
The Battle of the Nile
The Battle of Trafalgar
Off Rochefort in 1815, Napoleon went aboard
"the ship that had dogged his steps for
twenty years", to surrender to the British.
HMS Bellerophon was an historic ship. Those who served in her, affectionately called her: 'Billy Ruffian.'*

The commander sat down once more. 'There is also an old shanty called 'Billy Ruffian', which, should I have the time one day and you the misfortune, I'll sing for you.'

The lieutenant shifted in his chair and smiled, 'Interesting answer, but it doesn't explain his passion with the ship... with collectors of memorabilia isn't there quite often some link or other?'

'Ah, and there is one. Our Billy Ruffian was just

fourteen years old when he served on the *Bellerophon* at 'Windy Corner'. His bravery under fire was marked on his records as exceptional, and so, at such a young age, the path to the top was open to him. The experience marked him for life. He had learned an important lesson: to survive; you must fight. Gentlemen, Admiral Jessop *is* a battleship. He *is Bellerophon*. Therefore, he *is Billy Ruffian.*'

The other naval officer, a quiet and quiet spoken lieutenant-commander, asked, 'I've heard of him, naturally... never met him and know little of him. How long has he been in the Naval Intelligence Division?'

'For most of his career in one way or another. Our Billy Ruffian has fought for and helped shape the entire structure. *Bellerophon*, the ship that meant so much to him was eventually scrapped. He's going to fight with all he's got to see the Naval Intelligence Division isn't scrapped as well. Yes, he's a ruffian, but he's a very loyal one.'

'Is that what this meeting's about, NID's demise?' asked the lieutenant-commander.

'Better wait and see.'

*

On HMS *Start Point*, John Sims Reeves sat at the stokers' mess deck table listening to a most absurd conversation. It was 1200 and all talk inspired by the daily rum allowance of a third of a pint of grog - it was tot time. A time for daft stories and even dafter arguments. There was one rule only: a simple unwritten one, truth didn't matter, entertainment did. Sims knew he would miss this lot, they were the funniest and most disrespectful crews he'd ever sailed with.

Blackie Blackshire was in full flow. 'Sims, you missed this fuckin' bible basher... cheeky bugger came right down into the mess... started going on about how we should all keep away from naughty women, and how great God was and that... so Mick says to him: if God was so bleedin' clever, how come half my family have got bad backs and piles? Then Jeffers said: why have we only got two arms when four would have been much more useful?' Blackie paused till the laughter died down. 'He couldn't answer that could he?... he puts on this crappy holy voice, and says to Jeffers: God saw fit to give us two, my son, what on earth would we want four arms for? And Jeffers says: we could carry on doing the crossword while we was wiping our arses... that had him... completely fucked he was... got up and left without a word.'

The dozen or so stokers around the table were crying with laughter.

'He'd got a point though, four arms might be a bit awkward... I mean unless you had extra pockets in your trousers, where would you put your hands?'

'Yeh, I reckon with four sleeves the price of shirts'd go through the bleedin' roof.'

'If there were two on each side, which one would you salute with?' asked Mick.

'Don't be a cunt. There'd be special Admiralty Regulations. You'd probably use both.'

'Has half your family really got piles?'

'My sister's called Emma?' said Mick.

'What's that got to do with it?'

'It's short for Emma-roid.'

'You lying twat.'

And so the conversation and laughter went on...

'I knew a tiffy once with piles... used to poke em back up his arse with a toothbrush,' said Blackie.

'Must have made his eyes water.'

'Don't be a dick, he used the smooth end.'

'He use the same one for his teeth?'

'Course he did... he was a bleedin' Jock.'

Immersed in this ridiculous chat, the hum of the fans, pumps and machinery that shared the mess deck with the men, Sims sat there glowing. He'd not only downed his own tot, also by long standing tradition because he was leaving, he had sampled everyone else's. 'Three years and I'm out of this lot, bollocks to signing on for another twelve.'

'Don't blame you... think of it, another twelve years, and all that time without a tot,' said Mick.

'Without a tot!... what the fuck you talking about?'

'They're going to stop it.'

'Never!'

'Absolute gospel. Edith Summerskill - may she rot in hell - is trying to get it stopped. I read it in the paper... she reckons it's inappropriate for men in the modern armed forces to consume such large quantities of alcohol while on active service... she reckons it renders them in an unfit condition to fight.'

'That's bollocks that is. Give old paddy here a tot and he'll fight anybody... if there's nobody else around, he'll give himself a goin' over... in an unfit condition to fight, I've never heard such bollocks,' said Blackie.

'You're a lucky bugger, Sims... wish I was going out with you... Saturday night in the Union Jack Club Singapore, best entertainment in the whole world.'

Yet to have travelled further than Chatham, a junior stoker asked, 'What's the Union Jack Club?'

'I just told you. It's the best entertainment in the bleedin' world... Saturday nights they have this enormous talent competition... it's fuckin' priceless it is... packed to the gunwales... Gurkhas with their families too, they love it... you don't get many half-cut matelots trying to sing arias in Nepal, you see?'

'What does the winner get?'

'Pissed usually, like everybody else.'

The mid-day session came to an end. The tannoy sounded, "Both watches of the hands fall in," came the tinny voice over the loud speaker. Sims stood up. 'Well, I'm off then... see you around sometime.' He knew the chances of this were very unlikely. Great mates while on board a ship together, after that, new ship, new mates. That's the way it was, no life-long friendships, aboard ship acquaintances only. As much as he was looking forward to his new posting, he was getting fed up with this constant change. For some time Sims had felt unsettled: rootless.

He made his way over the gangway and onto the dockside, cautiously stepping over watering hoses, ship-to-shore power cables and other hazards that seemed strategically placed to trip up a young matelot with far too many rums under his belt. It was only ten minutes walk to the naval barracks next to the dockyard, and until his travel orders arrived that is where Sims was to be billeted.

Doing a passable imitation of someone in charge of his legs, he thought, I'm going to get my head down and sleep some of this lot off. With no official duties to do, Sims stepped through the entrance of the red brick building of the ratings' quarters, climbed the stone stairs to his mess, and lay on his bed. Matelots, used to living in the hum and clangor of a working ship are able to sleep anywhere and any time. With the added inducement of multiple tots of rum, he was asleep in seconds. His impeccable instincts woke him at supper time, he blearied his way to the dining hall, and then, on auto pilot, returned to his bed and slept right through to *'Call the hands'* next morning.

*

A tall, gaunt, elderly man entered the room. The three men at the table stood up as he did so. 'We have a crisis, gentlemen; a serious one.' Vice-Admiral John Jessop, standing at the head of the table, paused to let the sentence sink in. 'Be seated.'

He continued. 'I have spoken to most of you over the past few weeks, some I have told more than others, you all know the risks. We will, in future, only gather here and *never* at Admiralty House. I've had this place swept clean - there are no listening devices.' He looked at each of the men in turn. 'Our ship could be leaky.' He paused, 'I assume you've not introduced yourselves... I will do so now.'

'Lieutenant-Commander Maitland, this is Commander Stinton and Lieutenant Fox-Eastleigh.' Looking at Fox-Eastleigh, he said, 'Commander Stinton and Lieutenant-Commander Maitland are trusted Naval Intelligence

Officers.' Then shifting his gaze to the other two. 'As aide to the Commander-in-Chief Far East Fleet, Fox-Eastleigh here, has been on the fringes of naval intelligence business for some time. He did some sensitive work for us in the Far East, and did it very effectively. As far as we know, neither MI5 nor MI6 are aware of his being anything other than an aide... you'll see exactly where he fits in shortly.'

The three men nodded to each other and shook hands.

The old admiral waited, and then began, 'To business. For those of you who have not been fully briefed, listen carefully. I've called you to this place because security at "head office" cannot be trusted.'

He began his exposition, 'There are those in the Army and the Royal Air Force, who have long been jealous of the Royal Navy rightfully being known as The Senior Service. Also, within government circles, there is a desire, let us say a movement, to combine all three intelligence divisions into one super department. Now, the fact of the matter is this; these points of discord spell danger for the Naval Intelligence Division.'

He waited for the effect of what he'd said to register. 'If we value our title; our tradition, and the good of the country, the Naval Intelligence Division must remain independent of MI5 and MI6. It is for this reason I've seen it necessary to form this cabal within NID. Its function will be to try and ensure this amalgamation does not occur, and to ensure that we give no reason for the powers that be to think it necessary.'

After another short pause he carried on. 'Our existence is to remain completely hidden from all other Naval and Military Intelligence Services. You are only to report to me... is that understood?'

'Yes, sir,' all replied.

'There are to be no telephone reports or signals. Verbal reports will be carried out face-to-face. All documents are to be delivered by hand and to the hand of the intended recipient. I ask once again, is that understood?'

Again they nodded and replied, 'Yes, sir.'

'Lieutenant Fox-Eastleigh, for your information, we are still smarting from the affairs of that blasted picture salesman turned frogman; Buster Crabb, and that of the Krugers at the Portland Underwater Weapons Establishment,' Jessop said, angrily. 'With Portland we were partially to blame, we lacked due diligence. Though, in both cases I believe we were set-up by our own British intelligence agencies.' He took a deep breath. 'Recently, US intelligence has let it be known to MI5 that there are continued technical leaks to the Russians concerning HMS *Dreadnought*. These are coming directly from one of our bases... I have this information on good authority from forces friendly to NID... MI5 have not seen fit to inform us directly or, perhaps I should say, not at all. I can only guess the reason for that.'

There was a uneasy shuffling from the others at the table. Lieutenant Fox-Eastleigh raised his eyebrows, and let out a low and long, 'Christ!'

The exposition continued. 'The infighting that takes place within NID; MI5 and MI6 is well understood among international intelligence services. It is for this reason the Yanks are not prepared to reveal their sources and risk the exposure and lives of their field workers.' He continued, '*Dreadnought* is our first nuclear submarine, and the most advanced design in the world. Using the US designed reactor and drive system, its range and endurance will, by far, outstrip that of any conventional diesel-electric powered sub. Naturally, the Americans are not best pleased about these leaks. Both our countries have a strategic interest not to let the advantage slip away into enemy hands.'

The three other officers traded concerned glances. Russian espionage had been, and seemingly still was, taking place right under the nose of the Naval Intelligence Division. That there were still active cells in their establishments took some swallowing - a bitter pill.

Admiral Jessop coughed for attention, 'Gentlemen, you must all know that espionage never ceases. Portland was never going to be the end of Russian attempts to gain naval secrets. I must stress again that it is imperative to NID's survival that we clean up any cells operating from our submarine depots... and, we must do this ourselves.' He scanned his notes. 'Portsmouth and Gosport in particular are a major concern - HMS *Dolphin* is our main training and logistics centre for nuclear subs, and just a short distance away, housing the nuclear propulsion training centre, we have our nuclear engineering school HMS *Sultan*. It is my opinion the cells mentioned by the Yanks, are most likely to be operating in this area.'

With the air of a man about to enter battle, Billy Ruffian said, 'Gentlemen, if they get there first, MI5 will seize this opportunity as a way of delivering the Coup de Grâce to the Naval Intelligence Division. They will stick the knife in, twist the blade, and NID will be no more.' He paused once again. 'Somebody, or bodies, at the top of the British intelligence structure sees our lack of performance as an ideal way to further their agenda of getting us all under one roof, under one leadership... *theirs.*'

The old Admiral stood silent for a few moments. 'The opposition has long argued this under the guise of efficiency and cost cutting... events and NID's shortcomings have played into their hands. It seems, that the time is right for them to make a move.' Glancing at each of the others, he added, 'Understand this; to the right person, it is an opportunity to possess power unequalled by anyone in Great Britain... such power in the hands of one person is extremely dangerous. Unfortunately, there are those high-up in NID's organisation who would be happy for this to go forward.'

Finally, Billy Ruffian sat down at the head of the table.

'Our independence is really under threat, sir?' asked the commander.

'Yes, Stinton. Very much so I'm afraid. If we do not sort this out, the thin end of the marline spike will be inserted, and before we know where we are we'll find ourselves spliced with the Army - *God forbid.*'

'And a very unpleasant thought that is too,' said Stinton.

The admiral nodded. 'So gentlemen, I repeat, we need to take the initiative and root out any espionage cells on our patch. We must go through all submarine depots, Portsmouth, Chatham and Rosyth with a fine toothcomb. This cabal must get on top of them without MI5 or NID's assistance. They must be cleaned-up before any possibility of further leaks, or the active cell's dispersal.'

'How are we to be organised, sir?' asked Lieutenant-Commander Maitland.

'Chatham and Rosyth will be controlled by other members of the cabal. I am not at present going to reveal their identities. They are known to Commander Stinton who is to be our coordinator. The fewer people who know of them, the safer they are.'

'One more question, sir,' said Maitland, 'Is there anyone at the top of our lot who is on our side or aware of our existence?'

'Yes,' That was it, on that point, he was not going to give more. 'As for the organisation, you, Maitland, will control Portsmouth operations, and now you will see where Fox-Eastleigh fits in. The Aide to Commodore Sherwood, Commanding Officer of HMS *Dolphin*, is to be replaced by our man here,' he said, pointing to the young lieutenant.

'So where exactly will I operate from, sir?' asked Maitland.

'I want the Pompey team spread well apart. As Fox-Eastleigh will be active in *Dolphin*, it would not be wise to have you also located there. We need somewhere relatively quiet - a place where we can come and go freely without creating suspicion. On the Portsmouth side of the water, not far from the gunnery school at Whale Island, is the Seamanship School. This small establishment is administratively attached to HMS *Victory* barracks. However, it is remote from *Victory*, and it's staff are more or less autonomous... it is ideal for the job. You Lieutenant-Commander Maitland, are to be its new boss.'

Billy Ruffian surveyed the three officers in front of him. 'There remains one thing to resolve. To avoid suspicion, we cannot have you, Lieutenant-Commander, visiting *Dolphin* too regularly, and same is true for you, Lieutenant, with visits to Pompey. We need someone to act as courier, someone who can handle himself, a fast launch without the aid of additional crew, and most importantly, be competent with a side-arm. As members of the Special Boats Service are all known to MI5 and MI6, it cannot be one of their lot... this position is yet to be filled.'

'Sir?' said Fox-Eastleigh, 'I know the perfect man. I worked with him in the Far East, I was well-advised in trusting him with my life.'

'Sounds interesting.'

'There is one particular aspect that may give you doubts about him, sir.'

'Very well - out with it!'

'He's a stoker, sir,' said Fox-Eastleigh, close to apologetically, 'but he possesses a cool head in a spot of bother, and that, I can testify from my own experience. Also, and maybe unusually for an engineering rating, he is a first rate coxswain... a natural with twin engine fast launches. He is also an ex *Ganges* boy,' added Fox-Eastleigh. 'He *is* a marksman too, he represented the navy at the Inter-Services shoot. In the rifle event he won the .303 Deliberate Cup, and he was handy enough with a pistol to win that event as well.'

'Are you recommending him out of loyalty, Lieutenant?'

Lieutenant Fox-Eastleigh hesitated for a moment. 'Yes I am, sir, but his talents speak for themselves.'

'Well done, well done... loyalty is a commodity in short supply these days... *Ganges* boy eh? Gentlemen, unless there are any other suggestions,' he paused, and as no other name was proposed, he said, '*Ganges* swings it for him... stoker or not. We'll take a look at him. What's his name?'

'LM(e) John Sims Reeves, sir.'

'Stinton, I want you to find out where he is, countermand all existing orders and movements affecting him, and have him drafted to the Seamanship School posthaste. Maitland, there's no time to waste. You'll take over as Officer in Charge of the Seamanship School with immediate effect. As soon as Reeves arrives have his competence with the fast launches verified. If he proves satisfactory, I want you to go and see Sub-Lieutenant Hennerbury at Whale Island gunnery school and tell him you have a student for him... he'll understand what you mean. Tell him to put Reeves through his paces on the pistol range... Hennerbury will know exactly what we're looking for.'

'If I may, sir,' interrupted Fox-Eastleigh, 'I think you'll find he's serving on HMS *Start Point* in Chatham.'

'Straight away, Stinton... get on to him straight after this meeting.'

For a few moments Admiral Billy Ruffian sat silently in his seat at the head of the *Bellerophon* table. Finally, he stood up, 'That's all for now, gentlemen. We'll meet here in seven days time at 1100 hours. In the meantime, I need other proposals for the post of courier. If Reeves is not up to the mark we'll move him on.'

As the others readied themselves to leave they distinctly heard Billy Ruffian mutter, 'A stoker, a marksman, and a coxswain... damned hard to believe.'

*

At 1040 the bosun's whistle sounded on the tannoy, "LM(e) Reeves report to the Main Gate... LM(e) Reeves report to the Main Gate," it repeated. 'Great... my ticket's arrived... my draft chit's here... we're off... the grand tour starts *now!*' Sims said, to nobody in particular.

He entered the Guard Room alongside the main gate and made himself known to the duty Regulating Petty Officer. 'LM(e) Reeves reporting.'

'I can't see what you've got to smile at, lad. If I'd just had my Far East posting cancelled and was being sent to Pompey barracks instead, I think I'd be really choked.'

As with so many of his kind, this Regulating Petty Officer's day was made by handing out bad news. Sims, like most ordinary naval ratings, hated their breed; everything about them, and especially the stupid way they wore their hats so that the peak almost touched their noses. He now hated them even more and made a mental note that when he was finally back in civvy street, he'd find this bastard and give him the biggest kicking he'd ever had, and he himself had ever dished out. 'They must have made a mistake,' he croaked.

'No mistake, lad. This is your name and number, and you are posted by special order to the Seamanship School... though god knows why they would want a smelly stoker there, I can't imagine. But orders are orders,' he said, smirking.

A desperate Sims asked, 'Are you absolutely certain it's me?'

'Yes. Get your kit packed and report here 1100 sharp

tomorrow. You won't be going by train, you're going by Royal Naval transport, direct to Portsmouth... dust cart, I shouldn't wonder. Away you go,' he ordered.

Sims stomped back to his mess - he cursed in time with every step... 'Fuck, fuck, bollocks, shit, bollocks, fuck, fuck, bollocks.'

*

Stinton's car entered HMS *Victory* barracks and parked just inside the main gate. The Officer of the Watch, saluted him. 'We're expecting you, Commander.'

'Show me the office and fetch the driver, I want to get on with it as soon as possible,' snapped Stinton.

'He's ready and waiting, sir.'

Before entering the office Stinton turned to the Officer of the Watch, 'I'll do this on my own, Lieutenant.' He closed the door behind him.

'Hill, our records show you have the necessary security clearance for the job you are about to do. Tomorrow you are to take a staff car to HMS *Pembroke* barracks in Chatham. You are to be there for 1100 hours precisely.'

'Understood, sir.'

'This is a high security job, you will tell absolutely no one about this journey - you will not log the trip on the transport section's records. The car's mileometer will be reset on your return. You are to collect an LM(e) Reeves - he will be waiting at the main gate... you will tell him nothing about this conversation. Do you understand?'

'Yes, sir.'

'You will deliver him, post-haste, to the Seamanship School in Sultan Road. You will tell him to report to Lieutenant-Commander Maitland.'

'Yes, sir. With regard to refreshments, am I allowed to stop for a food break?'

'No, you will be supplied with packed lunches. A word of warning... under normal circumstances Reeves cannot be considered dangerous. He has, however, a record of occasionally not behaving himself when disappointed... in the past, he has gone absent without leave ... *AWOL*, Hill, *AWOL*.'

'I take it then, he *is* disappointed about something, sir?'

'Yes. Remember this, Hill, if you value your job and pension... you will deliver him safely, and you will keep your mouth shut, that is, firmly closed about all of this.'

Driver Hill did not like being threatened. Wary of this man and the instructions he was giving, he asked, 'Isn't this a job for a regulating branch escort, sir?'

'No. It's a job for *you*, and you'd do well to remember what I just said about your job and pension.'

***

Chapter Two
Billy's on the Move.

At 1058 Sims with kit bags reported to the main gate. On duty again was the slimy RPO who had taken so much pleasure in giving him the debauch-dashing news.

'LM(E) Reeves reporting for transport to Portsmouth.' A light sea-mist and drizzle blew in.

'Nothing here for you yet. Wait outside until it comes.' Then, with a little sneer, 'They say it's quite nice down there this time of the year. And by the way, make sure you give my love to *Big Sylvie*.' He referred to one of the most notorious prostitutes in Hampshire. Grinning all over his fat face, he turned and went into his office.

Sims, already teetering on the edge had now been pushed over. A line had been crossed, he was in free-fall. 'I'll be glad to... going by the pock marks on your face, you obviously knew her well, shall I tell her the antibiotics worked fine, or are you still suffering? ...is taking a leak still a right nightmare?... you know, like pissing broken glass. If it is, here's a tip; in future go for nice smelling sexy women... but, oh silly me, how would you know what they look like?... got your notebook?... write this down. They're the ones that don't look as if they've got a full-house of syph, gonorrhoea and crabs... don't apply their make-up by the half hundred weight, and don't smell like they've just crawled out of a kipper box... but, there again, I suppose the poor old regulating branch have to take what they can get, don't they?' Sims said, sympathetically.

Almost at the run, fat face stormed out of his office. Before he could get fully into stride screaming spit-flecked abuse at Sims, a naval staff car pulled up alongside them.

'I'll deal with you in a minute,' he slobbered.

The staff car driver shouted through the open passenger's window, 'I have to pick up an LM(e) Reeves and deliver him to Portsmouth; *no* delay.'

The RPO took root. Officers only; stokers never, absolutely never, warranted staff cars.

This was no time to hang around. Sims grabbed his kit bags, went to the back of the car and threw them in the boot. He then just as quickly slipped into the rear seat. The driver, sensing the urgency of Sims' predicament, started the engine, drove a little way further into the barracks, turned round and then drove smoothly past the still stunned RPO. Sims, for his part, gave him a sweet smile; his best shot at a royal wave, leaned out of the window, and said, 'Well done... an almost perfect imitation of an idiot... try opening your mouth just a teensie bit wider.'

The driver, hearing this comment, accelerated away. Half-way up the hill that led from the barracks to Chatham, Sims leaned over. 'Do you mind stopping and letting me sit up front... I only wanted to use the back seat to give that fat idiot the shits.'

The driver grinned. 'And you did a very good job of it... his face... you've never got a camera when you need one. I'd avoid going back there for a while if I were you.'

Sims got into the front seat and introduced himself.

'Mine's Derek... Derek the driver.'

'Ex-matelot?' Sims asked.

'Yeah... did twenty two years, got my pension... picked this job up almost straight away... joined at fifteen... ex Chief Bunting Tosser,' he said, using the naval slang term for a signalman.

'In that case, you must have been a *Ganges* boy... rough old place.'

'*Rough* doesn't come anywhere near it... first couple of weeks I was petrified of everybody and every bleedin' thing... *Jesus!* Thinking about climbing over that effin' mast on a frosty morning still makes me bum clench... probably changed all that now: softer world.'

'You are joking, of course?.. no effin' chance... HMS *Ganges* - the caring ship; number one priority, scare the crap out of all new entrants on their first day. "You're *going* to do the mast... bad weather no excuse". Same day, next lesson; how to scrape out and wash your knickers.'

Derek laughed, the car veered a little, 'Careful, lad, you'll have us off the road.'

'When I was there, a jock petty officer with eight pints under his belt tried to do a hand-stand on the button one night... fell the full 143 ft, bounced off the safety net and went straight through the post-office roof.'

'Good thing he was pissed then.'

'They didn't know it had happened 'til the postie opened up in the morning and found him laid across the weighing machine.'

'Christ! what'd he do?'

'You know what posties are like, sticklers for detail, and a bit thick... he checked his weight, stuck him in a post bag, and had him sent to Rosyth... second class of course, him being a jock.'

Derek laughed again and called him a liar.

'Well, the first bit's gospel any way.'

An easy flowing rapport formed. The miles eaten up as they chatted away. This lad does not seem to be as advertised, he thought.

'How come they sent a car for me?'

Until the picture cleared, he was going to lie. 'No idea. How come you're going to the Seamanship School?'

'Search me. Yesterday I was all set to fly out to the Far East, and the next thing I know, old shit face back there tells me I've been redrafted and to pack my things.'

'Big mystery, then?'

'Yeah. I'm starving... we stopping anywhere for food?'

'No, they've given us packed lunches.'

'Did they stick a tot in for me?'

'Bit of a bugger, but no. I could have helped you out with it.'

'No way... definitely forbidden. Anyway you're already all over the road.'

'Want to know something? That's *the* thing I miss most,' Derek said, wistfully. 'A tot a day... luxury. You know they're trying to stop it, don't you?'

'Yeah, that's why I'm out of it as soon as my time's up... that and the bull-shit.'

'What about RPOs?'

'Yeah, them too. What is it that makes some people go for a job like that?... I guess it's the same with coppers... haven't got any time for them either.'

'Come on, they're not all bad, lad... most of them... but not all.'

The traffic was light. The mileometer clicked steadily away.

'If the traffic stays okay, we should get there just after 1600 at the latest.'

More than the climate and the flesh-pots, there was another reason the Far East was preferred to Portsmouth: a person he once knew was there. 'Don't rush,' he said.

Sims, caught up in his thoughts, said little for the next few miles. Derek looked over, 'You've not got much to say, lad.'

'Yeah, well... you know what it's like, always kept in the dark... be nice to know what was going on for a change. What's the phrase?... need to know basis only. Tell me this; why does it always feel I'm the only bloke in the whole fucking world who *doesn't* need to know?

'This happened before, then?'

'Not exactly the same, no... has a similar feeling about it, though.'

'What happened?'

'On a surveillance job in the Far East... shot in the back... weeks in hospital, only just recovered... can't say more than that... they said they'd castrate me if I did. Funny thing, I'm quite fond of my bollocks, I feel there's still quite a lot of mileage left in them... so... ...nuff said.'

'For Christ's sake, lad, is that straight up?' Sims nodded. Derek's meeting with Commander Stinton all too fresh; he had instantly disliked Stinton and just as quickly taken to Sims. 'Well you can't have done anything wrong or they'd have sent an escort for you, and you'd have been hand-cuffed as well.' Derek paused while rounding a parked lorry. 'Had time to tell your folks yet?'

'Don't have those.'

'That's bad luck, lad. No relations at all?'

'Just a distant couple in France... they've never kept in touch though... haven't heard from them in donkey's.'

'Girl?'

'Not full time... did have... she's the main reason I don't want to go back to Pompey.'

Best not to pry further: Derek drove on. He and his wife had been unable to have children. He thought about Sims. Nice lad, typical matelot... good company... in time he'll sort himself out.

They left Petersfield and drove down the A3 past Butser Hill. 'It's nice at the top... me and my wife Maggie used to go walking up there when we were first going out together.'

'Been married long?'

'Thirty years... got hitched when I was twenty and she was eighteen.... couldn't have kids. First real girlfriend she was. She's an Isle of Wight girl... a real good sort.'

Sims wasn't sure if he meant she was a good sort because she came from The Island or despite it. *Best not to pry further...*

'We've got a place in Buckland... nice and close to work. Stones throw from the Seamanship School.'

Close to Horndean, they caught up with the traffic and the car pulled to a stop. Derek glanced over at Sims; he was asleep. Glad Maggie can't see him, she'd want to adopt him immediately - no questions asked.

Soon after they passed through Waterlooville, he woke Sims, 'Better show a leg, we'll be there in ten minutes or so. Arriving in a smart car like this we want you looking alive, lad.'

Sims sat up straight, stretched and rubbed his bleary eyes, 'Good of you, I needed that... didn't get a lot of kip last night... when do we get to *Victory*?'

'I'm only taking you as far as the Seamanship School. You're to report to Lieutenant-Commander Maitland... he's the new boss there.'

'Roger. Lieutenant-Commander Maitland. Okay, got it.'

In Sultan Road they drove to the far end near the dockyard and drew up alongside the school's main gate. Sims climbed out and removed his kit bags from the boot, 'Thanks... great trip... good to meet you... see you around, okay?'

'My surname's Hill... I'm based in *Victory* barracks; possible we might just bump into one another... let me know how things go. If you need me, just ask for Derek the driver Hill.'

'Sure... any relation to Graham?' asked Sims, and walked through the gates into the Seamanship School.

'Sod off... they all ask that,' shouted Derek after him, and watched him go. What did he say? "Something like this happened in the Far East"... shot in the back...

wonder what they've got lined up for him?... not likely to be in his best interest that's for sure.

*

Phillip Throagh was standing looking out of the window when the telephone rang. He had been acting as though one of the approaching cars might be his. He walked over to his desk and picked up the receiver, 'Throagh,' he said, pronouncing his name *throw*, he waited, giving no other information than that.

A quiet voice on the other end of the line said; 'I thought you might like to know there's been a meeting. It was supposed to be a debriefing about the Kuchin operation. I suspect it wasn't. Our contact says there's also been another at Billy's house. Our favourite aide, Fox-Eastleigh, is back from the Far East. He was there at Billy's.'

'Hmm. Keep your eye on them, get close, get as close as you can.' He put the phone down.

Throagh smoothed his fair red hair and thoughtfully twisted the ends of his similarly coloured moustache. Standing erect he took up a long stainless steel ruler from his desk and with it commenced rhythmically slapping his right calf. He painted an odd picture - a bristling cavalry officer in a pin-striped suit. If it had not been for this suit, if the ruler had been a riding crop and Throagh had been wearing riding boots, he might have even looked like one. This then, was the image he projected; one he was happy to let people accept as true - a devoted patriot, ready to charge into the valley of death. The truth was a little more bizarre. Throagh was no patriot. He was, however, a devout, aggressive homosexual who had never ridden a horse in his life.

He picked the telephone up again, dialled and waited, 'Billy's on the move, my lord... yes of course... no, no... leave it to me.'

'Go careful, Phillip, dear. We should meet soon.'

Phillip Throagh put the phone down and recommenced slapping his right calf.

Elizabeth Glass snatched the phone off her husband. He shrugged and returned to his study.

'Glass here,' she said, as if issuing a threat.

'It seems there's to be a fresh Naval Intelligence cell put into action in Portsmouth. It might be a precautionary measure on their behalf... maybe a fresh team, or it might not. Regardless, extra care is called for. I'll keep you informed.'

'Thank you. I'm due to meet our contacts again in a few days. Should I say anything... mention it to them?'

Phillip Throagh drummed his stubby fingers on the desk, 'Of course: *forewarned is forearmed.*'

'And, another thing,' she said. 'I was in London in the week... my account has not been credited lately. You're behind with your payments.'

'I'll see to it straight away.'

'Make sure you do,' she said, belligerently.

*

Lieutenant James Fox-Eastleigh's pride and joy was painted in the most fetching bluish metallic silver - he adored his open-topped 1947 two litre Sunbeam Talbot. All caring males know, or all males who care of such things, that cars are female, and as the first three letters of the registration number were MBL. with no great stretch of creativity, he had named her Mabel.

Having overcome such bitterness that remained, his many ex-girlfriends would have admitted that he was handsome. Yet for all his good looks, the young lieutenant never seemed to hang on to his conquests for much more than three weeks - the record though was two months. This was an isolated case and one that distorted statistics, the girl having had to accompany her parents to Germany for seven weeks out of the eight.

All of the ex's felt they were being two-timed - cheated on. In a strange way they would have felt less bitter if his bit on the side had been another woman, and not something that boasted four cylinders and dished out fifty six brake horse power: being side-lined by an automobile guaranteed a considerable strain on male female bonding. Lieutenant Fox-Eastleigh claimed that to keep it fully on-song, this particular model needed his constant attention. Besides, why should he worry? A good looking young naval lieutenant with a car like Mabel, could get all the girls any one man might like to handle.

It was a glorious day, and with the hood down he was happy to get out of London and move down to where the air was fresher and roads less congested - he could let *Mabel* have her head.

He drew to a halt outside the guard room of HMS *Dolphin.* The duty quartermaster saluted him. 'Can I help you, sir?'

'Thank you, Quartermaster, I'm Lieutenant Fox-Eastleigh, the new aide to Commodore Sherwood.'

'We're expecting you, sir. If you follow the road down to the end, the commodore's office is .....'

Fox-Eastleigh interrupted. 'No need for directions, I know where to go, thank you.'

'Do you need a hand with anything, sir?'

'No thanks, I can manage.'

'Nice car, sir.'

'Thank you, thank you. Yes, she is... never missed a beat all the way down.'

In a part of the old fort; Fort Blockhouse, the commodore's secretary showed the lieutenant into a large panelled room, 'Ah, you must be my new man... come in, come in,' said Commodore Sherwood.

'I am indeed, sir. Lieutenant Fox-Eastleigh reporting for duty.'

'Is that a Sunbeam Talbot you've got?' Without waiting for an answer, said, 'I saw you drive up... lovely car. Looks well looked after too. Perhaps you'll take me for a spin sometime?'

'I'd be delighted to, sir.' Pride guilty, he was, within reason, willing to show off Mabel to anyone who asked. Though on this occasion, doubts surfaced; could a man as tall as the commodore be comfortable in the front seat? However, he argued, if he could fit in a sub and command it, he'll manage Mabel somehow.

'First things first; best get yourself settled in the wardroom. I've made sure there's a decent cabin reserved for you. Off you go then. We'll talk tomorrow 0900 sharp.'

'Yes, sir. Thank you very much.'

He left the building and stood for a moment breathing in the fresh sea air unpolluted by London's fumes or the stench of rotting rebel heads. He felt good. It was going to be a challenging job. Deciding where to start was going to be the first difficulty he needed to address. At least, he thought, the boss seems a good sort. Straight forward, practical. And, he liked you too, Mabel. You've always brought me good luck.

It was a big break. For the development of his career, it had considerable muscle. Fox-Eastleigh knew he was punching high, it carried a daunting responsibility. There was one other niggling reservation; the moment they met, LM(e) John Sims Reeves would know exactly who was responsible for the cancellation of his Far Eastern tour. And, Sims , he well knew, had a sometimes dangerous way of speaking his mind and acting accordingly. Independent thinker; unusual in a lower deck rating... gets him into trouble... yes, independent thinker rather than just bolshie, that's why I chose him as my partner... why I'm still here... still alive, he thought.

*

'Posh car,' said the leading seaman meeting Sims inside the Seamanship School's gate.

'Yeah, finally, they're showing some respect for stokers... and, let me tell you, young dabtoe, it's not before time.'

'Less of the dabtoe. My name's Ben... Ben Whitley. I'm the other fast launch coxswain here. I guess you're LM(e) Reeves?'

'Right, apart from admirals and the pope, most people call me Sims.' Not quite understanding why Ben referred to himself as *the other*, he asked, rather confusingly, 'If you're *the other*, who's the other?'

Ben squinted at him, thinking at first that Sims was taking the piss. Then, realising he wasn't, he said. 'I'd better take you to Lieutenant-Commander Maitland and leave him to explain that *you* are.'

'Me?'

'Yep. Stick your kit in here,' he said, showing him a sparse but neat office. 'This is where we, the élite, hang out... come on, better go and find the boss.'

The small yard they crossed laid with old worn granite sets was surrounded on three sides with red brick and green painted wooden buildings. The fourth side opened onto a long jetty. Sims liked what he could see, the old school smelled of rope and tar: it had a quiet, comfortable, contented with its lot feel about it. 'Cosy,' he commented.

'Yeh, it's good here. Out of the way... we rarely get bothered by anyone. The boss is new though... only just arrived... doesn't seem a bad sort so far... early days.'

Through a small green door set into the green wooden wall, they entered a warm outer office. 'Wait here a mo,' said Ben, knocking on an oak door.

'Come in,' a well spoken voice said.

'I have LM(e) Reeves here for you, sir.'

'Ahh... good. Show him in please, Whitney.'

'It's Whitley, sir.'

'Ah... yes, yes, quite.'

'In you go, I'll catch up with you when you've finished, okay?'

Sims went into the office, stood to attention in front of the desk where his new boss was seated, he saluted.

'LM(e) Reeves reporting, sir.'

Maitland looked him over and thought, good build, plenty of muscle by the look of it. From what they say about them, he looks too fit to be a stoker. Out loud, he said, 'Well Reeves, any idea why you are here?'

'Not a clue, sir. One moment I was in Chatham due to be drafted to the Far East, and then all of a rush I was hurried down here. So, no. Not a clue, sir.'

'Well I hope you're not too disappointed. Been out there before have you?'

'Yes, sir. I've done two stints previously and, if I am to be permitted, sir, a much nicer climate in January, than Pompey's.'

'Quite, quite... I dare say. Now then, Reeves, this job although a little less exotic in location, is nevertheless an extremely interesting one. We are in short supply of ratings with your qualifications. We think ourselves very lucky to find a qualified diesel mechanic who is also a marksman and coxswain... ex *Ganges* boy, aren't you?'

'Yes, sir,' said Sims. In truth, he was thinking, *Christ!* this must be a first - an officer who has actually read my life story.

'Alongside our main duty of training midshipmen and seaman petty officers in the finer points of boat handling and ropemanship, here at the Seamanship School we are also tasked with securely delivering important, sensitive, and urgent documents to various establishments and ships around Portsmouth harbour and The Solent. To do this we have two fast, twin-engined motor launches, and to drive them, we have a general postie - that's ummm, Whitney, yes, that's right, Whitney...'

'I thinks it's Whitley, sir.'

'Yes, quite. As I was saying, we use Whitley for ordinary urgent mail, and for more sensitive or secret documents, we use a courier: *you* are to be the courier. This will be your main role here. There are lesser duties, Whitley will brief you on those. While you are with us you will have this special pass,' he said, handing Sims a small identification card. 'This informs whoever may ask, that you are on special duties and are free to come and go when you choose. The holder of this pass has many privileges, do not abuse them. Whitley will explain what you can now get away with while he is taking you and your kit to *Victory* barracks. Report here at 0900; Whitley is to give you a run round on what's what and where. Understood?'

'Absolutely, sir.' Sims saluted and left the office. What an interesting comment: Whitley will explain what you can now get away with, he thought, crossing the yard back to Ben's office.

Could be useful, thought Maitland, hope he passes muster tomorrow, we'll see how good he is with firearms.

Outside Ben was waiting, 'Did he give you your Special Duties pass?'

'Yeah. It sounds a bit good... what do you get for your money?'

'Plenty,' replied Ben, as they collected Sims's kit, 'for a kick off, you get your tot down here at the Seamanship School, and what's more, *NO WATER ADDED, IT'S NEATERS!* How about *that* for a kick off?'

'You are joking. Who swung that one?'

'Couldn't give a fuck, *who* - they just *did!*'

'What else? I mean, can we get into the wrens' quarters unchallenged?'

'Haven't tried that one yet... never thought of it.'

'Never thought of it!... you're not a bleedin' poof are you?'

'Only on Tuesdays and when my girl signs me off.'

'Okay, what about going ashore?... can you really just come and go as you like?'

'Absolutely. I tell you, this is the best job in the entire navy. We're treated like royalty, we've got our own private rooms so nobody disturbs us and we don't disturb them if we've got night runs to do. *And*, we can get our grub just about any time we choose.'

This was beginning to sound like it had the makings of a good posting to Sims, and helped by his over active imagination, just a bit of the disappointment he felt was starting to fade. But, for the moment, his mind fully occupied thinking up extra uses for this very valuable piece of card he was now in possession of. 'I might just go down town, and have a pint or two tonight... see how useful it really is... call it a test run.'

*

'Hello love, had a good day?' Maggie asked. Derek went into the kitchen and gave her a kiss. She moved over to the TV and turned the volume down a little. 'Good trip?'

'Not bad. I've had worse.'

'Supper'll be ready in a jiff... would you like a cuppa or something stronger?'

'I'll get myself a beer... might even have a chaser.'

'That's not like you... sit down... you've had a long day... I'll get them... chaser? What would you like?

whisky or neaters?'

The real stuff, neaters, was so hard to come by and even though he didn't like to dip into the last dregs, he buckled under, 'I'll go for the rum, love,'

He downed a good gulp of his beer and then took a healthy sip of his rum. He thought about Sims; Bass beer and Pusser's rum, the best combination on the face of the earth... I'm a lucky sod.

He said little as he watched Maggie move around the room getting supper ready. I'm a lucky sod, he thought again.

The niggle niggled, the lad wouldn't bugger off and leave him alone. After supper he opened another beer and poured a little more rum into his tot glass. Derek had been signals boss to the Home Fleet Commander-in-Chief. He, the silent, shadowy witness to the routine host of murky dealings smothered under armfuls of gold braid.

'You're a bit quiet, love... something on your mind?'

'Hmm, yeah... the lad I went to fetch today... I've never seen a staff car used to carry an ordinary matelot before... nice lad, you'd have liked him.'

'First time for everything, love... perhaps they were short of transport.'

'No... no, that's not possible. I was told not to log the journey... you never do that... every trip is always logged... *that's* a first. They're going to reset the mileometer... something not right about this; has a pong about it. Before I went to Chatham I was well and truly put in the picture by this commander... didn't like him, nasty bit of work. The lad's an orphan... been shot before. If he came a cropper, there'd be no one around to ask awkward questions.'

'Come on now, Derek, for God's sake. That's being just a bit too dark isn't it?'

'No, no I don't think so. I got the distinct feeling he knows something's up too.'

*

Billy Ruffian stalked round the room several times before stopping at the window. He turned, 'Stinton, our proposed courier, Fox-Eastleigh swears by him, he's supposed to be a coxswain and a damn good shot, however, even if Maitland gives the go ahead with the launches and Hennerbury passes him on the range, *we,* and this is the point, *we,* still do not know how he would handle himself in a tight situation. What is his true spirit, Stinton? Will he buckle under at the first hint of danger? *We* need that known, Stinton, *we* need it well understood. Our bait must last long enough to do the job. *We* cannot be seen sending a boy to do a man's job.'

'I think that's hardly the case, sir. Reeves was trained by the Korean Tigers. We both know what they're like: deadly, sir. And don't forget Fox-Eastleigh says the man has a cool head in a tight spot. So, all in all I'm not sure what you're suggesting we do, sir?'

'I suggest, Stinton, that we have someone rough him up a bit... see how he takes it. Tell them not to go too far, we need him serviceable. You know who to contact... get on to it, Stinton.'

'Yes, sir.'

***

Chapter Three
We Need to Keep Him Alive.

Walking briskly for his meeting with the Commodore, Lieutenant James Fox-Eastleigh mulled over his instructions from Billy Ruffian: hurry slowly, look like an aide, think like a detective, if necessary, behave like a killer.

Billy Ruffian's reasoning was equally clear-cut: if there were agents operating in our bases they were most likely to be members of civilian staff. He'd been ordered to check these out first. Agents needed time to establish themselves, this would, it was assumed, rule out naval personnel whose periods of duty in any one place were usually of too short duration. Fox-Eastleigh was not sure of Billy's logic, he decided to do his checks in parallel - the investigation might be less obvious if he didn't stay in one place too long; he would manoeuvre, dodge about, lay down a few smoke screens.

He stepped into the small but comfortable reception a couple of minutes before 0900.

'Good morning, sir,' said the wren who had shown him to the commodore's office the previous evening. 'Skipper's running a few minutes late this morning. He's down at the docks... should be here shortly.'

'Thanks... your name would be?'

'3rd Officer Harper, sir.'

'Any kind of christian name? he asked, his mind in overdrive; I must be going down with something... how come I didn't notice her yesterday? She's pretty damn gorgeous... perfect fit for Mabel's back seat.

'Christine,' and she added, smiling, 'that's a very nice car you've got, sir.'

'Yes, she is, isn't she?... My name's James, James Fox-Eastleigh.'

'Yes, I know, sir.'

He had never seen the point of delaying matters that involved the removal of undergarments. It might be put, young Fox-Eastleigh was never one to be caught going astern when he should be going ahead. He saw no professional conflict in running an adequate sex-life alongside counter espionage.

'Excuse me for asking, but how familiar with the surrounding countryside are you?'

'I know it very well, sir.' Aware there would be at least ten other wren officers who would want to get their hands on him and his car, she seamlessly added, 'There are a lot of good pubs if you know where to go.'

'Now, I know what you may think... this might sound like a bit of a cheek, seeing as we've only just introduced ourselves, but... I could need someone in the know to show me around? If it's a nice evening we could even let the hood down.'

Matters romantic took an inconvenient turn: before Christine Harper could take the first come, first served advantage, Commodore Sherwood strode into the room.

Sod it, thought this impeccably turned out and, according to her record, well brought up 3rd officer.

'Good morning, both of you. Are we ready for the

off, Lieutenant?' Without waiting for a reply, he strode up the stairs and into his office. 'Harper, Lieutenant Fox-Eastleigh and I have a lot to discuss... I don't wish to be disturbed, I'll call you if I need you.'

'Very good, sir,' she said, and left the office, but not without first exchanging glances with James and giving him a look that in any culture would be interpreted as; I will definitely see you later.

'Sit down, Lieutenant, first let me put you in the picture regarding what little I know. The precise details as to *where* are not important, it is enough to say that recently I met and had a long talk with Admiral Jessop. Naturally, I am as concerned about the CIA reports as he is. Due to the highly classified work we do here, security checks are, let us say, double checked by NID and MI5. After *Portland*, we're all nervous and, I suppose, the Yanks have every right to be as much so. The CIA seem to be better informed than our lot, so there's probably no smoke without fire. You have an important job to do, Lieutenant, what do you need from me?'

So, the commodore *had* been briefed: others were in the loop, thought James - it would make his job easier for sure. He was just a little uneasy that Billy had not told him who they were. How much the commodore knew was in question. He would not say more than was necessary.

'This task may take some time. Initially, I shall be looking for anomalies in staff behaviour at work and in their private lives. Most of this I assume will be a case of double checking. At the top of the list for scrutiny will be those staff who have access, via their work, to both here at *Dolphin* and HMS *Sultan*. I would also like a movement map of all documents drawn up... not just classified, routine documents as well. This should include where they are stored, and who might have direct, or indirect access to that storage.' He thought, I'll say nothing about Sims... that's enough for starters and leaned back in his chair.

Commodore Sherwood thrummed his fingers on the desk, 'If you don't object, I think Harper could deal with the documents map. She's exceptionally thorough and would handle the detail well.'

'Excellent, sir, when can we get started?'

'Right away... let's get Harper in now. The office next door is reserved for my aide - it will be ideal for you and Harper to work in unobserved by my visitors.'

It had not been necessary for him to rise to the rank of commodore to notice James's unqualified enthusiasm for the proposal, 'Absolutely first class, excellent idea, sir.' This job just gets better and better, he thought.

*

If Sims had listed a hundred places he did not wish to return to, Portsmouth would have sat somewhere between three and four - numbers one and two he would have reserved for the Persian Gulf or Benfleet in Essex; he was not sure which of the two would head the list. The thought of returning to The Golden Bell put him on edge - he'd had friends there; close ones. He couldn't be in town for any length of time and avoid doing so - someone was bound to find out he was back in Pompey.

We Need to Keep Him Alive.

He he had to face up to it. Sims walked the length of Charlotte Street and hesitated at number sixty: The Golden Bell. His nerves won; he walked past - the cause of his unease might still work there. This was harder than he thought it would be. His hesitance unnerved him: fear of entering a pub uncharted waters for Sims. 'Shit, I've got to do this,' he muttered and walked back.

He took a deep breath, pushed the side door open and entered. Although it had been a long time, his old haunt had not changed much; long 'L' shaped bar, cosy, chatter, and a cirrus wisp of cigarette smoke hanging two feet below the ceiling.

She saw him as soon as he walked in and straight away disappeared through the door at the rear of the bar. After a few minutes she returned: her purpose intent on ignoring him.

He leant on the polished wooden bar. It was a show of bravado. 'Any chance of some service down this end?' he said to the slim, dark haired girl acting as if he did not exist. Sims looked around, he nodded and smiled at Pearl the landlady.

The girl moved towards him; she drew level, and without facing him, or stopping, hissed, '*Sod off... Sims fucking Reeves.*' She collected a bottle from under the counter and walked back past him without saying a another word.

Pearl came over. 'Sims... long time, where've you been?'
'Far East, Chatham - now here for a while.'
'Usual boiler maker?'
'Please.'

Pearl pulled half a pint of mild into a pint mug, opened a bottle of brown ale, and slid them over to him. 'You don't deserve it... have this one on the house.'

'Thanks... you're looking well, Pearl.' She served another customer. The girl stayed at the other end of the bar - she had glanced at him a couple of times while he was talking to Pearl. Pearl came back. 'Mo seems a bit pissed off,' he said.

Pearl had been around: she rarely minced her words. 'Oh, Sims, for God's sake... you've got a fucking cheek, what do you expect?... how long's it been?... two years at least. You just disappeared... not a word to anyone. Pissed off! She has every right to be!'

He hadn't touched his beer. Pearl looked at him and shook her head. 'Have you any idea what you did to that girl?'

Sims on edge; cautious, 'How do you mean?' he glanced over towards Mo.

'*Men!* I bleedin' give up. Listen, when you two were together, it was always Sims this, Sims that... what you'd done, where you'd been together. She only ever talked about *you*. Sims, you tosser, she *adored* you... what you did was wrong; it wasn't nice... I've been through some rotten things in my life - it even upset me. And just so you really get the picture, you know... fully clued up, I was also a bit pissed-off you didn't say goodbye to me either.'

'Jesus,' he said, quietly.

'Do you know, after a week of you not turning up, she went to *Victory* Barracks to find out if you'd been in an accident or something. When they told her you'd been drafted out Far East, she came back here shattered... she *knew* you must have known about it for months. Sims, she *was* in a bad way - a terribly bad way... she's never mentioned your name since.'

'Oh Christ.' As he looked once more over at Mo, she met his gaze; if looks could kill, he would, at this point, be lying on the floor clutching a white lily to his chest.

'*Sims*! Don't tell me you didn't realise?'

His blood ran cold. 'No, I didn't, honestly... well, I mean... for fuck's sake there were the others, I wasn't the only one she was going out with, was I?' He felt sick.

'Okay, not when you first met her, *maybe*.' Pearl leaned over the bar and in a low voice added, 'After your first date, she dropped *the others* as you call them completely... there were only two or three that I know of anyway.' She leaned over the bar once more, and said, 'Sims, God knows why, but I always liked you... you are always welcome here, but, if you so much as think of taking up from where you left off, forget it. Try anything, and if she doesn't stab you, *I* fucking will.' As she moved off to serve a couple of Dutch sailors, Pearl turned and said, 'Oh, and by the way, she's married now... nice bloke.'

He left his pint untouched, and to avoid passing Mo, went out of the side door into the cold night air.

Pearl called out, 'Untouched boiler maker here, half-price, first come first served.'

Sims had felt sick. Leaning on a brick wall he threw-up into the gutter.

Walking along Charlotte Street a car drew up alongside. 'Is that you, Sims?' Derek the Driver called.

'Derek! I thought you were some old poofter kerb-crawling.'

'Get in,' said Derek, opening the door.

'You been drinking?... you smell a bit sickey.'

'No... ordered one... didn't even start it.'

'Must have been a bad one to make you puke at a distance, lad.'

'No, the beer was okay... it's me... just met the girl I didn't want to meet... seems like I really fucked that one up, mate.'

'Come and meet Maggie... it's only nine... we can have a chat... get it off your back. I'll give you a lift back when you want.'

'That's damn good of you... don't get me wrong, I'd like to meet Maggie, but not tonight, not smelling sickey. And, I'm more than a bit pissed-off... don't think I'd make very good company. If the offer's still open, I'll take you up on it some other time maybe.'

'Do you want a lift back to *Victory*?'

'No thanks, I think I need a drop of fresh air... I'll see you around... regards to Maggie.' Sims climbed out of the car, stood there until Derek had gone. As he started to walk back to *Victory* Barracks, he thought, Mo, my lovely, I'm so very, very sorry.

*

They watched him from some distance along the road. When he got into Derek's car they thought that night's opportunity lost. Sims then climbed out and walked towards them.

Billy had not told them his background. Their first error, already committed, was they had not asked for more information on Sims. They then made a series of others. Their second, was to assume that as a stoker he would be a push-over and thirdly, because he had just exited The Golden Bell they thought he'd been drinking - this was perhaps excusable: stokers do not usually go into pubs solely to eat crisps and put money in the Salvation Army collection box. The fourth was actually not their fault: how could they have possibly known Sims was dangerously pissed-off?

His mind clear: their body language equally so. 'Men on a mission,' he muttered. 'They're heavies. And, their timing's just right for us to meet by the alley. No bugger's mugging me.' *Right!* he thought, I'm going in first. They'll part to let me through, then come at me from behind. Before that happens, the guy on the left gets one in the throat. *Righty* goes in the gutter.

Sims tottered slightly: gave the impression he was three sheets to the wind and oblivious to their approach. One pace before he reached them he lashed out: lefty went down gagging - he would no longer be part of the affray. Sims instantly hooked his leg around Righty's knees and punch-shoved hard. Righty's training had taught him how to fall. As his arm came down to lessen his impact on the road, Sims kicked his elbow away: there was a crack from his arm and thud as his head made contact with asphalt. 'I have a motto,' Sims said. 'never use your fists until your feet are fucking bleeding.' He then kicked both men twice in the groin and twice in the head.

'Time to go,' he said, and turned down a side street.

*

'You're a bit quiet today... everything okay?' Ben asked,

walking down the pontoon to where the launches were moored.

He, more than sombre: the confrontation the previous night left him edgy - in all the times he'd used The Golden Bell and walked down Charlotte Street, he'd never been or felt threatened. In his bed he came to the conclusion they weren't ordinary muggers. This left him with the question of who they were. Hmm, this job might have a smelly side to it, he thought. Then, there were the facts of life Pearl had told him. They had bitten deep. He knew he'd screwed up. Things might not have been as he'd thought they were: always too quick off the mark. Maybe it hadn't been necessary for him to go to the Far East in a huff. The last thing he would have ever wanted to do was to hurt Mo - of the many girls he had met, Mo had hammered him, she had been the one he could, and often did, imagine getting hitched to. If Pearl's account was to be believed, it looked like he'd screwed her and her life up pretty badly. Sims' self-image did not stack up too good.

'I said, you're a bit quiet.'

'Yeah... just a bit knackered... not a good night... new room... new bed, no machinery noise... didn't sleep too well, that's all.' These were poor, see-through excuses; Ben knew it - matelots can sleep anywhere.

They stood alongside the black and white painted thirty-six foot launch. 'Have you driven one of these before?'

'A few times,' Sims replied.

'Take her out then... we'll go and play round the dockyard and then make a delivery to HMS *Vernon*.'

The engines coughed into life: twin exhausts gurgling

at the water line. Ben slipped the moorings and they slid away from the Seamanship School into the cold estuary waters. There was no horizon - sky and water met in wet dullness. In the distance, hardly distinguishable from the backdrop of mist, moth-balled cruisers and destroyers blended into the gloomy grey day. Reflecting his dark mood, Sims thought, headstones for long forgotten battles.

'Fuckin' taters, innit?' said Ben, rubbing his hands together and putting them back in his pockets, 'Roll on tot time.'

'Yeah.'

Ben put Sims through his paces. It soon became clear there was nothing he could teach him about boat handling. On their way back to the Seamanship School, he said, 'You've done this before. Sorry to have done it by the book... bit of an insult really... still, they're an expensive bit of kit... can't take chances... I'll give Maitland the thumbs up.'

'Yeah,' said Sims, not really listening.

'You sure you're all right?'

'Yeah.'

*

Next morning, Sims, still feeling smashed by recent events, walked across the narrow causeway that led to Whale Island.

'I have to report to Sub-Lieutenant Hennerbury... No.3 Range,' he said to the guard at the main gate.

'You are?' he asked looking Sims up and down and taking a particularly long look at his stoker's badge - stokers and guns; bad mix.

'LM(e) Reeves.'

The guard picked up one of three telephones and dialled. 'No.3 Range... Sub-Lieutenant Hennerbury... good morning, sir, there's an LM(e) Reeves here, says he has to report to you... very good, sir, I'll send him down straightaway.' He replace the phone carefully in its cradle and slowly turned to Sims, 'You're to go to No3. Range... and, you're late.'

Sims in no mood for this one, 'Let's get a couple of things straight. First, I told *you* No.3 Range, and second, If I am late it's because your two brain cells took so long to fathom out the phone. So, get this, I'm *not fucking late!*'

'Don't talk to me like that.'

'Why not? We're the same rank... so get knotted, and while you're at it, after you pulled your head from out of your arse, get stuffed.'

'I'm duty guard, I out-rank you. So don't talk to me like *that!*'

'And I've got one of these,' Sims said, showing him his special pass. 'So, once again, *get fucked!*' Blood moving and bubbling, Sims felt much better. 'Bloody wanker,' he said, loud enough for the guard to hear. Just for the moment, the confrontation put Mo and punch-ups to the back of his mind.

Long shiny black patent leather gaiters - Sims spotted Gunnery Officer Sub-Lieutenant Hennerbury immediately on entering the range.

'Are you Reeves?' he barked.

'Yes, sir.'

'God knows why they sent you here, lad. I wouldn't

trust a stoker with a blunt can opener... as for letting one hold *a gun*, that's worse than giving a mad woman a knife. Let's get this over with... come with me.'

They reached the small office and armoury, Hennerbury opened a cabinet that held an array of different makes of pistol. 'They tell me you've done a bit of pistol shooting before... that right?

'Yes, sir.'

'What sort?'

'Smith and Wesson, Enfield and, almost the same thing, an Albion, sir.'

'Which was your favourite?'

'The Albion, sir.'

'Good bloody God, an *Albion!* You cannot be serious, lad... why?'

'Well, of the three, sir, in my opinion and in my experience, it was the only one not to misfire, it has a nice light trigger pull, and a reliable auto-eject.'

'Ever use one in a competition?'

'Yes, sir... Bisley Inter Services.'

Hennerbury peered at Sims - something began to ring a bell, 'Hmm, how did you get on?'

'I won, sir.'

Yes, you did didn't you? thought Hennerbury, as he handed the pistol butt first to Sims. 'Let's see how you get on with it then... we'll start at twenty five yards.'

Sims couldn't be bothered to remind the officer he should have handed the gun to him with the breech open. He took the gun and with a practised action, snapped it open himself, spun the chamber, and checked the barrel was clear.

Bark reduced to growl, 'When were you last on a

range, lad?'

'Must be at least a year, sir.'

'Right. Face your target. Load six rounds. In your own time commence firing,' Hennerbury ordered.

Sims, taking his time, fired his six shots, and then ejected the spent cases. Hennerbury wound the handle that trundled the target back to them, unclipped the target, and with his back to Sims made the tally. 'Two bulls, three inners and a magpie... your first was a bit wild, lad.'

'I'm sorry about that, sir.'

'First time on a range for a year... nothing to be sorry about.'

'Thank you, sir.'

'Do you know why your here?'

'Not really, sir. I've just been drafted to the Seamanship School as a postie... although for some reason, they insist on calling me a courier.'

Hennerbury, his face pushed close to Sims' and rumbled, 'There *is* a difference, lad, posties don't carry guns, couriers do.'

Hennerbury placed a fresh box of shells on the firing point stand, put six targets in their holders and wound them down to the far end of the range.

'Get some practice on those, first...' he growled again, '... first, a couple of little tips: number one, if anyone on a range, no matter who, hands you a firearm with the breech shut, give them a bollocking... and if you're not on a range, make sure you shoot *them* first. Number two, on a technical point, you've got a good natural stance, but just place your left leg a little further forward... just an inch or two. It'll make a difference... better balance, lad.'

'About the open breech, sir. I did notice... I was being polite.' He thought "polite" better than couldn't give a fuck.

'There's no room for politeness when using guns... especially if you're a courier. When you've finished with all the targets, we'll move to fifteen yards and take six shots in six seconds. Get on with it.'

Hennerbury watched closely. He took notes as Sims fired at each target - each one being an improvement on the previous. When Sims had finished, he said, 'Not bad on the deliberate... you'll do. Let's do some rapid fire at six more.'

Sims, along with every other member of the lower deck, understood it as the eleventh commandment: thou shalt avoid gunnery officers at all cost or, at the very least, they should be given a wide berth. However, there being no criticism coming, no ear blistering castigation, the session with this one produced an odd feeling; Sims was uncomfortable with beginning to feel comfortable. Maybe he had impressed him, and *this one* in his own way, was prepared to say so: still, caution necessary.

'Reeves, I have to give Lieutenant-Commander Maitland a report on your performance... you did okay... clean up the empties. Don't let it go to your head.'

'I'll try not to, sir.'

Sub-Lieutenant Hennerbury mulled over how much he should say. It was plain that Reeves did not yet know the full extent of his job. Hennerbury had been given the code *student,* and though *he* knew what to expect,

We Need to Keep Him Alive.

it was unusual that the student didn't - Reeves had not been fully briefed. There's talent in this lad. Why hasn't anybody told him more?... he's in the dark ... very odd. If he knew what was what, he wouldn't have chosen an Albion - if he's to be in my navy team, he's worth giving all the help I can give, he said to himself.

Sims picked up the empty shell cases and without being asked put fresh targets back in their holders and wound them back to the butts at the far end of the range.

He's got good range discipline - doesn't need to be told what to do. Wonder what he'd be like on a combat range? Hennerbury thought. He said, 'Reeves, have you ever been on a combat range?'

'No, sir.'

'Have you ever tried a Browning 9mm Hi-Power?'

'No, sir.'

'Reeves, I want you to try one. We might as well do it right now,' he said, striding to the armourer's office.

He came back, waving the pistol in one hand, its magazine in the other, 'This is a dead standard model, and *this* is its magazine.' Hennerbury stood facing the butts. 'The magazine fits, thus, and safety catch, so. Hi-Powers are single action. To arm them after inserting the magazine, one pulls back the slide and releases it. Thereafter, loading is automatic. Therefore, for the job you'll be doing as courier, this is how Hi-Powers are normally carried; slide activated, hammer cocked and the safety catch on... the pistol is then termed *made ready*. All clear so far?'

'Yes, sir,' said Sims, itching to get his hands on this legendary pistol.

'One more thing, mind your grip, keep your hand as

low down the butt as is comfortable, otherwise it'll bite that bit of skin between your thumb and forefinger.' With that Hennerbury removed the magazine and placed it and the pistol on a nearby range stand.

'Your turn, lad.' He pronounced "lad"; led. 'Three at the first target and two at the others. Facing the target, load and make ready your weapon.'

Sims carried out the procedure he'd been shown. The gun felt reasonably well balanced - this his element, he was comfortable; at home.

'In your own time; thirteen rounds, *commence!*'

'Sims lined up on the target and applied a gentle pressure to the trigger, it was much stiffer than the Albion's. He relaxed, re-adjusted his grip and his stance, and fired, a fucking outer... this is going to take some getting used to, Sims thought. This was not what he wanted from his first shot. With constant adjustment to his technique, he continued firing. All the time, Hennerbury taking in every detail of his behaviour.

Thinking, adjusting and improving with every round, the sub-lieutenant noted.

Sims released the magazine and waited for Hennerbury's permission to check the targets closely.

'You look disappointed, lad.'

'Not as good as I'd hoped, sir.'

'Don't be so bloody daft... you've just moved from a push-bike to a Triumph Bonneville... it's going to take a little getting used to. This, Reeves, is a pretty good result.'

'I found the trigger pull heavy, and I'd like to have gripped it higher, sir.'

'Listen to me, lad, don't bother complaining, this is

the gun you're *going* to use - *no* arguments. I told you it was a bog standard model. Our chief armourer can make the trigger-pull as light as you like, and he can mod the hammer so you can hold it more-or-less where you like.'

'With all respect, sir, I'd feel happier with the Albion.'

'The Browning, lad, carries thirteen rounds... there are situations you might find the extra seven handy... might even be critical.'

'Me and the Albion only need one shot, sir.'

Hennerbury turned away so that Sims wouldn't see him smile. Cocky bugger. You'll see, I'll get him in the navy team... somebody with natural talent and confidence to match... just what we could do with.

'Reeves, did you like competition shooting?'

'Loved it, sir.'

'Why?'

Deadpan, Sims said, 'I'd have to think about that... just enjoyed it I suppose, sir... and, of course, it was a really good feeling thrashing the arses off people who think all stokers are prats.'

Hennerbury turned away once more. 'Wait here,' he said, and went into a small workshop. A few moments later he returned with a thin man dressed in a brown work coat. 'This is our chief armourer, Mr Les Goodwin. He's the best there is... listen to him carefully.'

'What did you think to the Browning, then?' he asked, glancing at Sims' targets.

'Early days yet, Mr Goodwin, the trigger pull is too heavy, so if possible, I'd like it at least as light as the Albion... if not just a little lighter. Also, holding so far down the butt made it feel unbalanced... almost as if it was slipping out of my hand with each shot. If you could do something about that I'd be really chuffed. Another thing, I heard an adjustable rear sight was an option? If so, I'd like one of them.'

Les Goodwin slightly raised his eyebrows, 'Anything else... a different colour maybe? We could do the barrel in a nice shade of pink and the butt in a matching cerise if you like.'

'Thanks for the offer... that'd be just a bit over the top, wrong for my complexion, don't you think?... the lads might think I was just a fairy with a pretty pistol... they're worse than a mad woman with a knife, you know.'

Goodwin laughed, and for the third time that morning Hennerbury found himself having to turn away - gunnery officers are supposed never to smile.

'It'll take a couple of weeks... we've got quite a bit on at the moment. You'll have to come down for a first fitting so's to speak. Seriously though, is there anything else you can think of... if there is, this is the time to ask.'

'I heard it's possible to have the grip modified to fit a shoulder stock. Any chance?'

'It might be possible,' Goodwin said, looking at Hennerbury for approval.

'Why do you ask, lad?' queried the sub-lieutenant.

'A bit of a gut feeling, sir... belt and braces maybe. For a start, I don't really understand why I'm here, why couriers need side arms, and then why it's best to have a Browning with its extra rounds. I'm now getting a feeling, it might come in handy, sir.'

'We'll see what we can do.' He turned to the armourer, 'I'll have a word later, Les.'

Les Goodwin walked off to his workshop, turned as

he entered the door, shrugged and thought, knows what he wants that one... knows his stuff... I bet he'd do a good gun justice... use it well.

While Hennerbury finished writing his report, Sims followed Les Goodwin into his workshop and to avoid the temptation of touching any of the immaculate array of tools, kept his hands firmly behind his back. Before Sims could say anything Hennerbury came in, 'Come outside, lad.' When out of earshot, he said, 'I shall talk to Lieutenant-Commander Maitland today. I shall tell him you passed muster well.'

'Thank you, sir.'

'Don't interrupt,' he snapped. 'I shall also tell him that you *are* to use the Browning, and when it's delivered, I want you down here at least three times a week for familiarisation exercises. In the meantime, you will use the Albion. *Understood*?'

'Yes, sir.'

'Get on with you back to the Seamanship School. I'll deliver the Albion and ammunition when I go to see Lieutenant-Commander Maitland.'

As Sims walked away Les Goodwin came out of his workshop and stood next to Hennerbury. They watched him go. 'Les, we'll have that cocky bugger in the navy team, you see. I know you'll do the best you can... I've a gut feeling he'll be worth it... we need to keep him *alive*, Les.' Les Goodwin nodded sincere assent.

It was high tide as he walked back across the causeway. A sharp wind off the choppy, green grey water knifed its way into Sims. The damp cold gave him an even greater sense of isolation. His mind returned to Mo and The Golden Bell. 'I'm going to have to talk to her. I can't leave it like this... she's got to know how things really were,' he muttered, and increased his pace.

*

'It seems they have a new recruit. You're going to be amused by this... what do you think?... of all things, he's a stoker... a leading stoker. Fox-Eastleigh's protector from Port Swettenham. So we have an untrained naval intelligence agent and a stoker. We'd better watch our step,' he said, laughing.

'Really, what is Billy playing at?... they *are* laying it on a plate for us, aren't they?... so kind of them.'

'Not only laying it on the plate; these turkeys are providing their own carving knife.'

'Oh I like that, I do like that,' he laughed. 'Well, better get the usual checks done on them again, let's see what mischief we can conjure for our *so* helpful friends. Get what you can, then we had better meet... their own carving knife, I do like that.'

'I thought you might, my lord,' said Throagh, and put the receiver down.

*

'How do you think it went?' Lieutenant-Commander Maitland asked Sims.

'Pretty good I should say, sir. Sub-Lieutenant Hennerbury says he'll come and give you the full report this afternoon.'

'Very well. In the meantime, I want you to spend some more time with your launch - there's a trip this afternoon to *Dolphin* and *Vernon* to do. I've spoken to Whitley, he'll show you where to park... you do the driving.'

'Yes, sir.'

Park! - hardly naval - wonder what navy he's from? thought Sims.

*

They cruised past the rows of grey warships tied up alongside the naval docks. Ben tapped him on the shoulder. 'Sims, I'm going to show you the most important perk of the whole job. What you do, is make yourself an advert like this,' Ben pulled a card out of the cockpit locker. On it, in big letters, was written:

Meet me tonight at 8 o'clock outside the entrance of South Parade Pier in Southsea.

'Now, when the weather's a bit better than this, the *Fanny Boats* come out... punters can't get enough of ships and matelots. Here's the routine; you cruise up from behind until you're alongside them - remember, from behind... they usually face rearwards, so they get plenty of time to see you coming. Take a good look for any prospects and if there are some, pick one out and show her the card. When you pull away, stuff on full power and put in a hard turn. It's dead impressive, works at least eighty per cent of the time if not more.'

'I reckon that comes under misuse of admiralty property?'

'If by admiralty property you mean *me*. As far as I'm concerned they can misuse me as much as they like, I'm not likely to complain am I?... quite like being misused.'

'Okay, but what if they don't turn up?'

'You have to buy your own beer,' he said, turning to

port and heading south.

Sims changed the subject, going on dates was not forefront in his mind at that moment, 'Thanks for giving me a good write up to Maitland yesterday.'

'No problem - just remember it at tot time.'

Later, as they approached the pontoons of the Seamanship School jetty, Ben pointed to a small freighter tied opposite, 'Latvian wood boat from Riga - she docks every twelve or fourteen days or so... she's a bleedin' nuisance... doesn't leave us much room to turn... thank fuck it's only in here for a couple of days at a time.'

They tied up the launch and went to their office - it was time to wrap up for the day.

'Fancy a pint tonight?' said Ben.

'Normally, yes. We'll have to make it another time - I've got something to do tonight that can't wait.'

*

He left it till late. Except for four locals playing crib the bar was empty. Mo came over to serve him; no hint of murder.

'Pearl's away tonight. What would you like, Sims, the usual?'

'Bugger the beer Mo, I need to talk to you, love.'

Mo, lips tight, 'She told me what you said to her the other night.' She paused for a while, looking at him, holding her breath. 'Did you *really* not know there were no others?' she said, quietly.

'No... no I didn't. I'd hoped... how do you know for sure?... you used to have.'

'Sims, we were together for six months, it was only

ever you... couldn't you bloody tell?'

'Mo, you have to believe me, I wish I *had* been able to... always useless at working stuff like this out... I guess I understand *things* better than people.'

She sighed. 'Sims, come down into the saloon for a moment, you're right, we do need to talk. *Jack,*' she called to one of the men playing crib, 'just shout if there's anything you need, I'll be serving in the saloon.'

They stood facing each other, her hands resting on the bar, fingers entwined. She said, 'You've lost weight. You look pale, Sims.'

'To tell the truth, I *feel* pale, love. Mo, listen, I never meant to hurt you. Please, listen to me, whatever you do, whatever you might have thought, you have to believe that.' As he said this, he reached to take her hands. She pulled them back: just a couple of inches.

'Mo, I promise I had never been happier than when I was with you.'

'Sims,' again she paused. 'More than anything, one thing I must know, did you love me?'

'Oh God, yes, and when I saw you the other night I realised I still do.' Mo looked down, then away and held her breath again.

'Life was so bright when we were together, even Pompey looked polished. You can have no idea how much I thought of you. I remember the time I was away for a few days. I phoned when I got back?... when you came to meet me... I could see it was you three hundred yards away; you bounce when you're in a hurry. Mo, you looked happy. *I* was happy, someone *wanted* to see me... when you saw me you smiled - no one makes up a smile like that. I knew then that I really loved you, Mo...

so very much.'

She looked at him eye-to-eye. Sims held her gaze. Jack called, 'Let's have some service up here.'

Mo returned and put her hands back on the counter - fingers untwined. 'But why didn't you say goodbye?'

'Pearl said I must have known for months - I didn't. They gave me less than a week's warning. It was only going to be a short trip, I wasn't supposed to be away for long - just a trip to crew a minesweeper back here; two or three months at most. A couple of days before I left, I was coming to see you. You were on the other side of Commercial Road, you waved... well, you looked like you were having fun with that other bloke.'

'That can't be what it was about! Is *that* what it was about, Sims? You *sod!* Oh you daft bugger. Oh you daft silly sod, John Sims Reeves! Until the other night, that was the last time I saw you... you never gave me a chance to explain anything, you sod. Sims, of course I *was* having fun. Didn't you ever notice, I made a point of always keeping you away from my family - they are not a nice lot, Sims. That *bloke* as you call him was my brother Pete, the only decent one among the whole bloody lot of them, we've always been close - it was his *twenty first sodding birthday!*'

'Oh Christ no, oh for fuck's sake don't say that.' Sims put his head in his hands. 'Oh for fuck's sake... what a fuck-up... oh God.'

'I hoped and hoped you'd return. Why were you away *so* long?'

With his head still in his hands, he mumbled, 'They flew me out to Singapore a couple of days later. To tell the truth, I didn't care *where* I went... I didn't know what to think... once I was there, there seemed no reason to come back. I swapped jobs with a bloke who needed to come home - I stayed on the *Alacrity*.' Sims looked up at her. 'Mo, that last day I was on my way to ask you...'

'Don't say it, *Sims - please* don't say it.'

She reached across and gently took his hands. Looking down at them, she said, 'Sims, at closing time, leave with the others. Give it a quarter of an hour, and then come back to the side door.'

He could see there was a dim light left on in the saloon bar. Sims tapped. 'It's unlocked.' She was standing by the fireside. In a whisper, she said, 'Come here.'

Mo put her arms round his neck and kissed him for a very long time.

She then softly made a simple, moving statement. 'I loved you so much, John Sims Reeves, and I think I always will. I know now, what it's like to be in love: I mean *really* in love - *you* did that for me.' She paused, 'I also know how much pain is felt when someone you love so much leaves you - you taught me that as well.'

They spent some time just holding each other. Then she kissed him. 'I'm going to go upstairs, have a bath, and wash the smoke out of my hair. When I'm done, I want you to come up.'

Before she left, Mo held him at arms length, looked at him for many moments, drew him back to her and kissed him again. 'Sims, my darling, tonight I want us to say goodbye to each other *properly*.'

***

Chapter Four
Roy Rogers the Singing Cowboy.

Billy Ruffian sat, elbows on the Bellerophon table, hands flatly arched each finger touching its mirror. Staring at the gap between his thumbs and forefingers, he might have been contemplating a past or future sandwich, 'Stinton, we have to move on. We've yet to receive their report on how Reeves took the roughing, but, time is getting short. There having been no other names put forward, what do you think to Fox-Eastleigh's man being brought in regardless? We always have the option of dumping him should we wish,' he said, now drumming each fingertip in turn against the other.

'I'll chase up our men, I'm surprised they haven't come back to us. As for Reeves, I've had some checks done on him, sir. Frankly, he seems to have what we're looking for and, *be* just what we're looking for. The fact that he is without close relatives could be useful too if things don't quite turn out right - nobody to make things awkward.'

Billy stopped thrumming, 'You say he's just what we're looking for, yet, give the impression you think he could be trouble. Do you expect trouble from him?'

'Well, not necessarily, sir, but when stones are being turned over, one never knows what to expect to find underneath them, does one, sir?'

'Hmm, I suppose so... anything else of interest?'

'Very much so. It seems he has a private income, and a bank account into which are made regular payments.'

'Couldn't this be an allotment from his naval pay?'

'No, sir. Definitely not, the payments amount to considerably more than he gets as a leading hand.'

'Anything else?'

'Yes, sir... he hasn't declared this extra income to either the Admiralty or to the Inland Revenue.'

'Let me get this clear, Stinton, do you think he's a bad lot or a good egg, then... which of them?'

'All in all, I think he's a pretty good choice, sir - the bank account and undeclared earnings might just give us some useful leverage should we need it.'

*

'Boss wants you in the office.'

Sims sat up straight, rubbed his eyes and stretched, 'Okay, Ben, I'm there.'

'You look a bit rough, good or bad night?'

'Both.'

'Ahh, good morning, Reeves, come in.'

'Good morning, sir.'

'Are you feeling alright, Reeves? You look a trifle second rate. You're not going down with something, are you?'

'I'm perfectly okay, sir,' he lied.

'Sit down. As you are aware, Sub-Lieutenant Hennerbury came yesterday, he... er... he seemed very interested in getting you into the navy firing squad.'

'Did you mean *firing* squad, sir?... perhaps it was shooting team.'

'Yes, quite... of course. As I was saying, he was more interested with your potential for the team than he was in giving his report. There again,' Maitland rambled, 'he wouldn't be interested in your inclusion, unless you *were* very good, would he?'

Sims shrugged, 'I wouldn't like to say, sir, nothing makes a lot of sense at the moment.'

'Quite... quite. Nevertheless, eventually, he did get round to saying you're as good a shot as any that has passed through his hands in many years. Reeves, coming from any gunnery officer that would be considered an excellent report, coming from *that* gunnery officer, it's quite extraordinary, well done, what do you think to that?'

'Thank you, sir.'

'You don't say much do you, Reeves?'

'Well, sir,' Sims thought for a few seconds, 'quite often when I'm asked a question, I assume an answer is required and I give one as honestly as I can. Then, not infrequently, I'm told not speak out of turn. It can be a bit confusing, sir, so I generally tend to keep responses short.'

Maitland studied Sims. To the point... not quite sarcastic... close though.... this is what Fox-Eastleigh meant... more to Reeves than meets the eye, he thought.

Sims soaked up the comfortable world that was Maitland's office; warm stove, clock ticking, nice desk and chairs - not someone from his navy. Seems decent, I'll keep on his good side. Sims suffered a career retarding habit of getting up the noses of people he didn't like - he saw it as a gift.

From a drawer in his desk Maitland took out a pistol, its belt and holster, and a box of ammunition. 'As well as trying to head hunt you, Sub-Lieutenant Hennerbury also dropped these off. Take possession, keep it loaded, and spare rounds with you on all duties.' He handed them over to Sims who filled the chamber, holstered the Albion, and put the spare rounds in their pouch.

'Now, we're going to be working quite closely together, Reeves,' as if to lay stress on the point, Maitland leaned forward. 'So please, when you are with me, allow yourself to be more than brief with your answers. Don't let these put you off,' he said, smiling and pointing at the two and a half gold rings on his sleeve. 'Officer or not, whatever's on your mind, feel free to say it.'

'Would that be because I've got the loaded gun, sir?'

'Quite. Now, Reeves, I'd like to give you freedom to join the navy team, however, I'm not sure you'll have the time. Does that bother you?'

'I have to confess I *would* like to be in it, but, if I'm the only courier, there's unlikely to be a stand-by to take over, is there, sir?'

Feeling his way, Maitland said, 'Certainly not in the short term.'

'How about long weekends and annual leave, sir? Do I get any of those?'

'You're going to be on call much of the time. Reeves, your job is an important and sensitive one. Leave is not going to be easy to arrange, I promise you I'll do my best. It may be that we can occasionally let you have time off in mid-week... how does that sound?'

'It's really okay being flat out, sir.' Mo caressed his

thoughts every time his mind unoccupied. He welcomed being busy.

Maitland picked up a package from the desk-top, 'A couple of other things; there's a delivery I want you to make to *Dolphin*. It's not sensitive, so you can have it signed for at the front desk in the strategic supplies section. To get people used to seeing you with a gun, like I said earlier, I think you'd better go fully booted and spurred, if you get my meaning. The second thing is, on Friday you're to come with me to a meeting. We leave here at 0900 sharp. You will wear respectable civilian clothing. Yes?'

'Absolutely, sir. Sir, do I carry the Albion?'

'Not this time, Reeves. And, now you've reminded me, Hennerbury tells me you're to be fitted with a specially modified Browning. When you've taken delivery, and until he thinks it no longer necessary, you're to go to the range at least three times a week - more, if time and duty allow.'

'I shall enjoy that, sir.'

'Good... quite. What did you think of the sub-lieutenant?'

'Given that he's a gunnery officer, and they're not the type I would usually go to the pub with for a fun evening, I think he's okay... straight.'

'Reeves, he's a good man.... knows his job... nobody better. He's worked with us for many years; listen to him.'

'Who's us, sir.'

'You'll find out on Friday.'

*

Their office windows steamed up, Ben smeared his hand over a pane and looked through the clear patch, 'I've just wet the tea, time for a cuppa?'

'Please... freezing out there. I've a delivery to make shortly, I need to adjust this first.'

'What *have* you got there?'

'It's an Albion, another perk... I get to shoot people.'

'Anyone in mind?'

'Baddies, I guess... which is my boat?'

'You've got the gun, you'd better have No. 1, it's the fastest by just a whisker.'

'Good man.'

Sims finished his tea and stood up, 'I'm off, then.'

Ben looked through his smear again, 'Don't forget your oilskins, there's going to be a lot of spray today.'

'Thanks, Mum,' said Sims, and left.

As soon as he was clear of the pontoon, he eased both throttles full ahead and listened to the note of the engines. *Nice,* he thought. A cold north west wind blew down the estuary thumping the icy choppy waters onto his starboard bow. Mum was right: wear your oilskins. He quickly passed the north dock wall, tucked himself as low as possible below the windscreen and headed south to HMS *Dolphin*.

'Hello, you're new,' said the wren in charge of reception, thoroughly approving of what had just walked in. She leaned across the counter and looked at the Albion in his holster, 'Do you always carry that blunderbuss with you?'

Sims glanced down at his flies. 'Really! Come now, madam, we've not been introduced, and already you're asking personal questions. What is it with you wrens?'

Wren Pam Somerton laughed.

'Somerton, leave him alone,' said a well spoken voice, from the adjoining office.

'Yes, ma'am.'

'I've this package to be signed for... anywhere I can get a cuppa?'

'If it wasn't for her,' she said quietly, 'I'd make you one myself... the Naafi's just round the corner.'

'Thanks... by the way, here's a little tip I picked-up in El Paso: it's no good carrying a gun if you're not prepared to use it. Now, tell me your name or I'll shoot you.'

'Pam... Pam Somerton.'

'What's yours?'

'Roy.'

'Roy, what?'

'Rogers.'

'What, the singing cowboy?'

'The very one,' said Sims, leaving the office, Pam Somerton smiling, and her, with a distinct feeling of better things to come.

He sat in the canteen cradling his hot tea cup and thinking about the previous night with Mo. He thought about the early hours of the morning and then their harrowing, haunting, parting.

To give themselves time to absorb what had happened, they agreed that Sims should not return to The Golden Bell immediately. He was distraught at the sadness he'd caused her and knackered from lack of sleep. In another place and at another time, Sims would already be lined up with Pam - things like that never took him long to sort out. For the moment he couldn't muster up the energy or interest - besides that, screwing up someone else was definitely not on the cards.

A gale on the brew: even the normally placid waters of the inner dock were disturbed. They swashed and slopped up and down between the joining gaps of the pontoons. He timed his steps over them for a down-swash. Gusts flapped his oilskins and buffeted him as he walked back to his launch; getting rougher, I'll be glad to hit the sack tonight.

*

Maitland drove through the main gates and out of the Seamanship School. 'You're very well turned out, Reeves.'

'Thank you, sir. We had a very good *sew sew* on the *Alacrity*. Rather than waste his talents, I got him to knock up a few suits.'

'I'm sorry, *sew sew*?'

'A Chinese tailor, sir.'

'Yes, of course.'

'Where are we headed, sir?'

'To a small place in between Alton and Basingstoke. We're going to the home of Admiral John Jessop.'

'Is this anything to do with me being a courier, sir?'

'It is indeed. Reeves, do you know what NID stands for?'

'Naval Intelligence Division. Although, I've heard it's said to mean No Intelligence Detected, sir.'

Maitland ignored the second of the possibilities,' And what do you know of the Naval Intelligence Division?'

'Not a lot, sir, only that they weren't up to speed at

Portland and took a lot of flak as a result, probably deserved it though... must have been asleep on watch.'

'Quite, quite,' Maitland paused. 'A fairly accurate assessment, Reeves, but today, one best kept to yourself. Admiral Jessop is among NID's top brass.'

'A conversation stopper you think, sir?'

'Quite the opposite, you and he might have had a very long conversation - you wouldn't have said much... he would have done most of the talking I feel... yes, it would have been decidedly one sided.'

Once again Sims thought this man Maitland was from a different navy... first *parking* then he didn't know what a *sew sew* was. 'Are you a NID officer, sir?'

'Yes... I am. Does it show?'

'I wouldn't know, you're the first one I've ever knowingly met, sir.'

'Are you sure... weren't you involved with some intelligence work in the Far East?'

'Not really, just a bit of support for someone, sir.'

Near Alton, Maitland said, 'Not far now, we take the A339 to Basingstoke just here. Do you know the area?'

'Not at all, sir.'

'It's quite nice. A couple of miles up the road, at Lasham, there's a very good gliding club. I learned to glide there a few years back... they're a good lot... pity we don't have more time... I'd call in and see a few folks I know there... never mind.'

As they passed the small road leading to the airfield, Sims noted the sign to Lasham Gliding Club, and thought, I'd like to learn to fly, I wouldn't mind getting my pilot's license... keep me busy for a while.

'You've gone quiet again, Reeves.'

'I'm fine, sir... really. Is it difficult... flying a glider?'

'If one has the time and money, just about anybody can learn.'

'I suppose it's a bit like sailing, only with a bit of *up* involved.'

'Quite, though you need to know a lot more about the weather... meteorology is very important.'

Not long after the sign to Lasham airfield, Maitland turned right towards the village of Upton Grey. In the village they turned left and minutes later they passed through the gates of Tunworth House.

'When we get inside, wait in the hall until you're called.'

Sims stood looking out of one of the large windows that flanked the front door. The clean, curving gravel drive wound through shrubberies and large herbaceous flower beds. It was a beautifully designed garden, and even so early in the year, the lawns were immaculate.

'Reeves, you can come in now,' said Maitland.

As soon as he entered the room he spotted Lieutenant Fox-Eastleigh. Hmmm... things are beginning to tie up. Sims frowned at the young lieutenant.

'I see you've recognised your sponsor, Reeves,' said Admiral Jessop. 'Stand where you are and let me have a damn good look at you.'

Billy Ruffian walked round Sims, eying him up and down.

'Good build, lad... ever play rugger?'

'Yes, sir.'

'Position?'

'Second row forward, sir.'

'Did you enjoy it?'

Sims hesitated, 'It was okay, sir.'

'But?'

'But, sir?'

'There was definitely a *but* in the air. What's the but, lad?'

Sims thought for a moment, and replied, 'I look at it this way, sir, if I were playing against a scratch team of wrens and *they* all decided to jump on me, I can see things about the manoeuvre that I might find enjoyable... when it's the 45th Commando that's doing the jumping, it can take the edge off the more pleasurable and aesthetic aspects of the game, sir.'

Lieutenant Fox-Eastleigh stiffened. Careful Sims, you don't know who you are dealing with.

Billy Ruffian stood in front of Sims. Being the taller of the two, he leaned, jutted his chin forward and looked Sims straight in the eyes, 'Would you like to reconsider your answer, Reeves?'

'No, sir. That *was* the but.'

'Good answer,' Billy Ruffian said, standing up straight once more. 'Wait outside again.'

'Well,' said Admiral Jessop, smiling, 'the boy says what he thinks... not scared to look me in the eye... his records suggest insolence. In my opinion, more honest than insolent... I like him. Well done, Fox-Eastleigh, if the rest you say about him holds, you may have given us a good man. Gentlemen, I need your opinion of Reeves - give it as straight as he did - you first, Stinton.'

'Sound; could be an asset... I'm for him.'

'Maitland.'

'I like what I've seen... skilled boat handling; Hennerbury speaks highly of him - wants him back in competitive shooting... I'm also for him.'

'No need to ask you what you think, Fox-Eastleigh. Go and fetch your man back in.'

'Yes, sir,' said Fox-Eastleigh, relieved.

Sims stood in front of the seated admiral. 'Reeves, a unanimous decision, it looks as though you're in.'

'With respect, sir, in what?'

'We'll take coffee now, after, Lieutenant Fox-Eastleigh will fill you in with some background to what we are doing.'

Sims wandered around the room looking at the battle trophies collected by the old admiral. He avoided Fox-Eastleigh. At this very moment, he felt like beating his head to a pulp. He knew the feeling would pass. He liked the man.

Sims read the plaque inset in the table. *Hell fire,* he thought, this wood is actually from the Bellerophon... Napoleon might have walked on it. He could hardly take it in; this historic piece of furniture was *not* in a museum somewhere. He slid his hand over the freshly polished surface and looked closer at the plaque. Sims noticed an odd detail: the slots of the screws were not full of wax, surely no one was going to clean those out every time the table was polished! That's taking bull-shit just too far.

After coffee, Fox-Eastleigh suggested they walked in the garden.

Sims did not trust himself to open the conversation.

'I suppose you have a few questions, Sims?'

He noted the familiar. 'Am I allowed to call you James, sir?'

'Not inside with the others.'

'I owe you a bunch, I know, but I was really looking forward to the Far East, now I'm in Pompey. It was a place I was trying to avoid. Wasn't there anyone else you could have chosen?'

'No. I'm sorry, but this is a sensitive matter we're involved in... extremely sensitive. I needed someone I could trust, someone I understood and who understood me. I thought you were still on light duties... didn't know you were in line for a Far East draft... I know how much you like it out there... but, you must understand, it wouldn't have made any difference to my choice. And, by the way, let's get one thing straight, it's me who owes you.'

'Fair enough. At least I'm getting some idea of why I'm here. Do you want to start briefing me?'

'What do you know of the Portland affair, the Krogers and Harry Houghton?'

'Not much... as I told Lieutenant-Commander Maitland earlier, our lot must have been half asleep... how can all that have been going on under their noses without noticing?'

'Sims, it was one affair after another, first Buster Crabb and then Portland - it was a huge embarrassment to NID. Let's take Crabb. Depending on who one listens to, Crabb was either a hero or about to defect to Russia. He was nevertheless, an MI6 recruit - that much is known for sure. In '56, when Nikita Khrushchev and Nikolai Bulganin visited Portsmouth on the cruiser *Ordzhonikidze,* It is said MI6 sent Crabb on an espionage mission to investigate *interesting technology*... there are conflicting opinions on exactly what he was going to look for. As you are aware, he died during the operation. Evidence is missing. His body *was* eventually found... though it was minus head and hands. The truth is, and maybe conveniently for someone, nobody could accurately identify him... also, someone, took all Crabb's belongings and even the page of the hotel register where he had written his name, so exactly what he was doing there we might never know. The point here is that MI6's responsibility is for overseas intelligence matters, and MI5's is strictly limited to operations within the United Kingdom. MI6 were deemed by MI5 to be operating outside their remit, while NID claimed it was a naval security matter and they were both poaching on their territory. MI6 tried to cover up their involvement, and behind the scenes, NID took the blame... With me so far?'

Sims nodded, 'Sounds like the left hand didn't want the right one to know what it was doing.'

'Hmm, just so. Now to the Portland spy ring. The Krogers, Harry Houghton and Ethel Gee, were passing secrets to the Russians. They used many varied methods even one using a bubble-gum machine salesman would you believe? Houghton, ex-navy master-at-arms, worked in the Underwater Weapons Establishment at Portland. He started a relationship with Ethel Gee - she had access to secret documents. Between them, they handed over to the Russians a frightening quantity of secrets detailing our first nuclear sub, HMS *Dreadnought*. Now, here's the point, Houghton was a heavy drinker and he'd been involved in selling medicines on the black market while working at the British embassy in Poland. He was a known security risk; *someone* should have picked him up. His ex-wife made a statement saying he brought secrets home... these claims were said to be an act of spite - and ignored. In my opinion, it wasn't incompetence that missed the risks posed by Houghton; he was tolerated. NID did not come out cleanly from this debacle... and here we are now, with more fears that there are other spy cells operating in our establishments. Should MI5 or MI6 find them first it will be the end of us - NID *will* be finished. Our group has been formed to stop this happening. Neither the larger Naval Intelligence Division, MI5 or MI6 know of our existence. There is something rotten in the state of intelligence.'

Sims sniffed and hrumphed, 'And you think just a small handful of people can cleanse it, James?'

Lieutenant Fox-Eastleigh pointedly ignored this question and continued the briefing.

'Maitland, myself and you, are to be the Portsmouth branch of the cabal; we have to do what we can - *undermanned or not*. I know you understand that none of what you hear today is to be repeated to anyone... I have complete trust in you. Time to go back inside I think.' Sims turned to go. Fox-Eastleigh caught hold of his arm, 'Sims, before we go, I must know, how is your health now?'

'Pretty good... James, don't worry about it.'

'I do though. They whisked me straight off to Borneo... didn't have time to come and see you, and say thank you.'

'Like I said, don't worry... it wasn't your fault. It was my decision.'

*

'Fully briefed, Reeves?'

'Enough to take in for one day, yes, sir.'

'Any questions?'

'Yes, sir. Who on earth cleared Houghton to work at Portland after his activities in Poland?'

'A very good question. One I hope to have the answer to one day.'

'With respect, sir, does that mean that you're not going to tell me, or that you think it was covered-up?'

At this question from Sims, there was a general, and considerable, unease around the table. Fox-Eastleigh closed his eyes; easy, Sims, easy.

'The latter,' said Jessop. 'Do you have any more questions like that, lad?'

'Yes, sir. How do we know the same person hasn't cleared other, supposedly clean, personnel at *Dolphin* or *Sultan*?'

'You have quickly nubbed our predicament - we don't... more questions?'

'No, sir. I think I understand.'

'Reeves, you are essentially our courier, but we also need you to keep your eyes wide open for anything non-standard, and should anybody try to intervene with a delivery, you are entitled to use your gun.'

'Can I have that in writing, sir?'

'No. I give you my word, in such a situation, I'll protect you. There are privileges that go with the job, you may come and go from *Victory* as you please, there will be no extra duties, free travel passes if required. Do you have a driving licence?'

'Yes, sir.'

'Good, there'll be a Land Rover at your disposal. If necessary, you may use your launch. Do not abuse these privileges. Do not tell anyone what you are doing. We'll adjourn for lunch now, and then it's back to Pompey for you and Lieutenant-Commander Maitland.'

*

'What did you think?' asked Maitland.

'Unforgivable, the eggs had been cooked too fast, *and* they were overdone, sir. Why is it that some cooks think eggs should have the texture of plastercine? My gran would have thrown them out of the window.'

For the first time, Sims heard Maitland laugh. 'Reeves, that is so special, you've been briefed on a matter that only a handful of people in the whole of Great Britain know of, and you complain about the eggs... I can't wait to tell F-E that one.'

'F-E, sir?'

'Fox-Eastleigh. He was quite concerned you were going to put your foot in it, you know. He thought you'd either end up with us, or in detention.'

'I suspected as much, sir, that's why I played it close to the limit.'

Maitland was quiet for a few miles or so. 'Reeves, what is so special about *Ganges*?

'Very simple, sir. It delivers very good sailors. Kids of fifteen leave home and go there for a year. It is also brutal. It seems brutality is key to producing the *right stuff,*' said Sims, remembering his own time there.

'Sounds awful.'

'It was. *Ganges* is built right on Shotley Point; just where the Orwell and Stour meet. The Point is perfectly positioned to catch the freezing wind straight off the North Sea. You would not believe how cold it was. In winter we'd be out sailing and we'd dip our arms in the water - it was warmer than the wind. It was so cold there, sir.'

'Good God,' said Maitland.

'At *Ganges*, a lot of us stopped believing in God. Do you know, sir, we had recruits from Borstal correction homes who said *Ganges* was far, far worse.'

'Sounds like an awful rite of passage, Reeves.'

Sims thought about this for some time. 'How many rites of passage does one get in a lifetime, sir?'

'I thought, just one. Why do you ask?'

'Sometimes, I think I've been through several, and now I'm just entering another,' he said, thinking about being shot in the back, Mo, the two heavies, Hennerbury and Admiral Jessop.

'So, you think during one's lifetime there could be many?'

'Yes... possibly... and should there be, I just hope there are some decent pauses in between.'

Maitland again drove in silence for a few miles. He decided he liked this lad sitting next to him. I can see why Fox-Eastleigh likes him, he thought.

'If you don't mind me saying, sir, you don't seem to know much about the navy.'

'I don't profess to... in fact I make a point of not bothering to. I enlisted, and then was commissioned as a cryptanalyst during the war - I worked at Bletchley Park on the enigma code... knew Alan Turing... genius, and the nicest of men... I haven't ever done much real navy work... I'm quite enjoying it at the Seamanship School.'

'Do you think we were lucky to find him? I mean, were clever people like him in short supply?'

'No...' Maitland said, almost to himself, '...although he *was* exceptional, there were lots of other very clever people around... what we lacked, were clever listeners.'

*

Stinton entered Billy's office, 'I've just received our roughing-up report. I'm not sure if it's good or bad news, sir.'

'Well, out with it, then.'

'The reason they were a little tardy with the news is quite straight forward. I'm afraid Reeves left them in a bit of a mess. One, has a massive swelling on his throat and is only now able to take solids, and the other will be out of action for some time with a broken elbow. It also seems both received groin and head injuries as a result of Reeves kicking them several times.'

'Hmm, good news, I think... looks like he's our man, Stinton. There wasn't a mark on him when he came here, I had assumed it had not taken place. And, the bad news?'

'Our men think they were set up. Reeves attacked them first. They think he had been warned, sir. They've threatened revenge.'

'Inform them that there was no tip-off and tell them if they cause trouble I will see to their future role in the Royal Navy, personally.' After a pause, he said, 'Reeves appears to have his wits about him, Stinton.'

'He does indeed, sir. He passes with flying colours.'

***

Chapter Five
The Killing Range.

Sims ambled up to Whale Island's main gate, 'No.3 Range, Sub-Lieutenant Hennerbury. Don't hang about, I might be late.'
Still smarting from their first meeting, 'You know where to go,' snarled the duty guard.

He pushed the door open; the range was empty. Sims sauntered over to Les Goodwin's workshop. 'Mr Goodwin, good morning... they tell me you've finished my Browning.'

'I have at that, lad... want a look see?'

'Too right... can't wait.'

Les Goodwin wiped his work bench clean, took a wooden case off the shelf and put it on the cleaned area. 'I've put a lot of hours into this one... made the case myself... hope you like it,' he said, stepping to one side so that Sims could have a proper look at it.

'If the gun is anywhere as good as this case, it's going to be perfect... that's a lovely grain. What sort of wood is that?' he asked, gently running his hand over the polished surface.

'Chilian Laurel... had it at home for years... brought it in specially. I'm glad you like it,' he said, proudly.

'This is too good for a gun... it's a bleedin' jewellery

box.'

Les Goodwin smiled as Sims tried to find the catch to open it.

'Don't want to moan or sound ungrateful, but I think I can see a teensy snag. How, when you're just about to be shot, do you get the gun out?'

Les put on a wise expression. 'Ahh lad, You've got a lot to learn. You only keep it in this when the Browning's not in its holster... you'd look pretty stupid wearing this on your belt.'

'Okay, let's say, I'd like to put it in its holster... how?'

'This is the clever bit... I've had this idea for ages about making a box like this... the sides are pivoted... push the sides in at the bottom... the top pivots out and the lid springs open. What do you think?'

'That is brilliant, Mr Goodwin.'

'Les,' he invited Sims to call him. ' Go on... open it.'

'No, no... Les, is your name, Mr Goodwin; mine's Sims.'

'Fuck off, and open it before I change my mind.'

Sims pressed the sides, the lid popped up, he lifted it wide open. Inside, the gun glistened in its carefully formed indent, spare magazines lay alongside, also in made to measure indents, Sims gasped. 'Jesus, Les, this is beautiful.'

'Just Les; Jesus Les was someone else, lad.'

Sims smiled - the old guy was okay - on the ball.

'Blued barrel... it's a Belgian model... just now and again we get hold of the odd gun or two from unofficial sources... we don't put them on our inventory... thought you might like this one.'

'Jesus Christ, Les,' Sims reached forward to take the

pistol out of its case.

'Better not touch it until Hennerbury gives the okay... talk of the devil, I hear the dainty sound of his jack-boots.'

'Morning, Les... morning, Reeves, have you seen it yet?'

'Morning, sir... seen but not touched, sir.'

'Well, what are you waiting for?.. we haven't got all day, lad. Come on, Les, let's go and give Reeves his first fitting... let's show him what a Browning's like that's been tweaked by a master, shall we?... you'd better bring along the belt and holster too... we'll get that nice and comfy while we're at it.'

Sims took the Browning out of the case and felt its remodelled grip, checked its balance, held it pointing down the range - it felt perfect.

'What do you think, lad?' asked Hennerbury.

'It's nothing like the one I fired before, sir... it's like a completely different model.'

'Make it ready then, and in your own time, two shots at each of the first five targets and three at the last.'

Sims loaded the magazine, the balance was slightly different, if anything, he felt it was better. He lined up on the first target and fired two shots in fairly rapid succession. Without turning round, he said, 'Can I look at those two sighters, sir?

'Go ahead... wind it back.'

Sims brought the target back and studied it for a moment - he was happy with the result, he knew what to do now, and he adjusted his stance as Hennerbury had advised on their first meeting. Hennerbury noticed this. *Good lad.*

'Can I go for the rest now, sir?'

'In your own time, Reeves, finish the target.'

'Lovely balance, Les... trigger's perfect,' and in the same manner as before, continued firing at the remainder of the targets. He released the magazine, and lay the pistol back in its case after having given it a loving wipe on his trousers.

'It's perfect, Les... don't do another thing with it... leave it just as it is.'

While Sims was talking to Les, Hennerbury wound back the targets and inspected them. 'Jesus Christ, Reeves, I don't care if you're busy or not, I'm getting you back into competition shooting - I'll talk to your CO again... Les, take a look at these.'

Les Goodwin, mouth slackly open, said, 'Bloody hell.'

'This must be the perfect pistol... there can't be a better one in the world,' Sims said, looking at the targets.

Hennerbury gave an unofficial smile, 'Les, I think a celebratory wet of tea is called for, how about putting the kettle on?'

Astonished at Sims' shooting and happy with the response to his workmanship, Les bubbled, 'I'm on my way.'

Firing ranges are not built for comfort. In Portsmouth in January, they are not the most inviting places to be. Sims however, in his excitement hardly noticed this insult. By contrast, the workshop was warm, its stove was alight and the tea hot.

'Reeves, the last time we met I asked you if you'd ever been on a combat range.'

'I remember, sir.'

'I want you down here three times a week at least. As far as target practice is concerned, you don't really need it... though it doesn't do any harm to keep in form. I think you need some time in combat situation... you may find it useful in the future... I haven't been instructed to do this, so it's best we keep it to ourselves... understood, lad?'

'Perfectly... why do you think it's necessary, sir?'

'I want to make sure you stay alive long enough to shoot for the navy.'

'Very nice of you to have my best interests at heart, sir.'

'What rifles have you fired?'

'At *Ganges*, I tried out a Lee Enfield .303 , Lanchester and Martini Mk3, sir.'

'What did you think to them?'

'Lanchester was an unreliable load of crap and had a mind of its own... tended to go off without being asked, Lee Enfield, reliable but very old fashioned... though I should think Les could make one shape up, and the Martini I thought was a great gun, sir.'

'How did you get to shoot a Martini... I mean, stoker... Martini... not a combination that normally springs to mind... come to that, lad, how did you get into shooting at all?'

'Well, sir, before the navy I shot all sorts... 12 bores, 4.10s, .22 and .177 air rifles... even a muzzle loader... But, I think it was the .177 that taught me accuracy... it was a little Diana, very light... you had to be steady... get your breathing right. Me and my mate we used to have competitions, we'd stick red matches into the ground, and try to set them alight.'

'Who used to win?'

'Well, I suppose I won most often... but he was good... he didn't make it easy for me.'

'Perhaps we could do with him as well, did he join the service?'

'No, sir, he became a jockey... too small for the navy... pity.'

'So, what happened at *Ganges*?'

'Quite early on they took us to the .22 range. We used old guns, and cards with ten targets on each, "Fire five rounds at the top left target on your card"... mine all missed, they were all in a tight group low down on the card, I was really pissed off... it was the one thing I thought I could do well at. After they checked the targets our instructor called my name out... I thought I was in for a real bollocking... it never came... they gave me a fresh target, told me to shoot one round at the top left... told me how to adjust my sights... and so on, and to cut a long story short, I took ten bulls out of ten... they were a bit surprised... to me, it seemed quite natural, I feel at ease with guns... always have done. After that I was allocated my own Martini, which our *Ganges* Les equivalent set up exclusively for me, and I was in the team. Since then, I've been shooting in comp's whenever I can... and that's about it, sir.'

'Do you fancy doing some rifle shooting here?'

'Absolutely, sir.'

'In good time... next time you're here, it's the combat range... Okay?'

'Definitely, sir. One more thing. It seems a touch ungrateful to ask, but the stock for the Browning, wasn't it possible?'

'I discussed the matter with Les... we were both of

the same opinion. There's no stock, because there's no point... not accurate enough at any distance... let them get close... draw them on, Reeves... wait until you can see the whites of their eyes, Reeves.'

'I get the point, sir.'

'I want you here tomorrow morning, I have a course at 09:00... make it 11:00 sharp.'

*

When he arrived the next day, Hennerbury's course was still in progress; he made straight for Les's workshop to see if he could scrounge a cup of tea.

'Where do you think you're going? Come here, Reeves, I want you to show this bunch of fairies what a reasonable shot can do.' Hennerbury turned to the all male group of midshipmen. 'Ladies and Gentlemen, this specimen here is a leading stoker. It is said that the only thing they're good at is getting pissed, playing with their plonkers, and polishing shovels. Occasionally they do so all at the same time. Their reputation is not so far off the truth, however, this one is a little different, and if we can get him to grip a pistol instead of his plonker, he's a pretty acceptable shot.'

Sims smiled, Hennerbury was reverting to type - it was so nice not to be on the receiving end. This was the kind of gunnery officer he understood: insulting, belligerent, obscene, and in every way conceivable; awful.

Hennerbury continued: 'You lot, who can only be a huge disappointment to your parents... you were supposed to point your pistols at the targets, not wave them around like tarts at a tupperware party.' He seemingly lived with the sole purpose of emasculating all those in his charge - it is what gunnery officers do. 'Reeves, get yourself ready. You lot, do you think you can manage to put ten single targets up, without getting them back to front?'

This is new, Sims thought, what's he up to?

'What our stoker is about to do is unorthodox... he's never done this before. Reeves, take a central shooting position between targets five and six... one shot at each of the ten targets... ten shots in ten seconds... make your gun ready... fire when you hear my whistle.'

Sims made ready, checked his arc of movement made sure his balance would be good, and stood waiting for the signal from Hennerbury. It came - Sims blasted ten shots, and at the end had around one and half seconds to spare.

'Wind those targets back and bring them to me... at the double!.. move!' he bellowed at the startled group.

Hennerbury inspected the targets and pinned each one onto a notice board. Take a look, Gentlemen, and promise me next time, you'll all buck up.'

The midshipmen crowded round the targets, and one of them, in awe, turned to Sims. 'That's really awfully good shooting.'

Hennerbury exploded. 'When you address a man as good a shot as Reeves is, and that man still has three rounds in his gun, you call him, sir... is that understood?'

'Yes, sir,' and turning to Sims, said, 'That's really awfully good shooting, *sir*.'

'You just remember that in future, lad,' said Sims, doing a remarkably good imitation of Hennerbury.

Sub-Lieutenant Hennerbury needed another reminder: gunnery officers should never smile.

To one side, he said to Hennerbury, 'I wasn't expecting to have to do that, sir.'

'So, what would you like an assailant to say, Reeves? Excuse me, sir, but, if you don't mind, I'd like to take a pot shot at you in a moment... I'll give you time to get ready, sir... Reeves, they are not going to give you any fucking warning - nor am I.'

Hennerbury turned to the midshipmen. 'I hope I never see you lot again... better get off to your sewing bee,' he then said to Sims, 'Combat range next... get your things... top your mags up... I haven't much time.'

*

'Now, don't slouch, stand up straight and listen to me carefully. Reeves, this is a killing range... targets show themselves briefly. You kill the guilty and spare the innocent... in the real world, get it wrong with the innocent and you have to live with that for the rest of your life... get it wrong with the guilty, and you don't have a rest of your life.'

'Understood, sir.'

'Make your gun ready... take two spare mags with you... when I give the command, go at the run.'

Sims waited.

'Go,' barked Hennerbury.

He ran in - firing left, right, crouching, rolling, firing, snap shooting. He stopped at the end of his run panting - not at all sure how he'd done.

'How did I score, sir?'

'Ninety percent... and don't feel that's okay, because it isn't... it means you're dead, Reeves. Listen; this is not a fucking competition where you walk away regardless of the score. In this game it has to be one hundred percent or you'll never walk again...' he gave Sims a close up of his teeth, '...got it, lad?'

'Yes, sir,' said Sims, taken aback.

'This time, I don't want you wandering down there as if you're some bleedin' poofter going down Commercial Road to get her hair done... act as if you mean it, Reeves... gee yourself up... focus! focus! *focus!* Let's see if you can do better this time. Les put heart and soul into that Browning, don't let him down... live up to his workmanship, Reeves... and don't let me down either.'

Sims was angry with himself. He had not taken on board that apart from James there were other people on his side, they wanted him to do well - for his sake, and for theirs too. The thought sobered him. He felt he had let them both down: had taken what they'd been doing for him for granted. He made his mind up that it would be the last time he did so. Sims might not have been aware of it at the time, but that day with Hennerbury was to be a significant stage in his current rite of passage. 'I'm ready, sir.'

'Okay, I want one hundred and ten percent from you this time, lad.'

Sims kept his anger in check. He felt an awful coldness inside, yet, he felt alive, time seemed to slow almost to a standstill. He ran into the street, left high - kill... left again - lower window - kill... right - child - don't shoot... right door - movement - kill. Like this, Sims carried on until he had one round left in his magazine, he rolled behind a low wall and snapped a fresh one in. Up, running and firing again he continued to the end of the range and sat there sweat dripping off his forehead - he knew he'd done well.

Sub-Lieutenant Hennerbury followed him up the range checking the results. He walked over, 'Why did you only fire twelve shots from your first magazine?'

'The low wall was a good place for someone else to hide as well as me, sir.'

Given that one hundred and ten percent is not possible, I'll award one hundred and five. Well done, lad.'

Sims hadn't told Hennerbury that his absence from ranges was because of his back wound. He could still feel a tightness under his right shoulder blade - he was satisfied that it hadn't affected his performance.

*

'Come in, Stinton,' said Admiral Jessop, 'if you've anything to report you don't want the others to hear, better say it now... they'll be here shortly.'

'Of course, sir. I've given it some thought to what I'm about to suggest, I think it would be a good thing to provide our courier with an alternative identity... a modified background if you like. If there should be an unexpected outcome to our endeavours, we can leave him as he is - an innocent naval rating, or a commissioned officer operating under cover: whichever suits our purpose, sir... doing this gives us a useful stand by.'

'Hmm... yes, it's a fair point... what do you suggest?'

'As we know, Reeves has no close relations... no one who can contradict whichever identity we choose to employ. I suggest we make him a lieutenant, sir... he's the right age... Lieutenant John Sims Reeves. Using the same name, solves a lot of problems with birth certificates etc, and as far as his ex-shipmates are concerned, he might always have worked undercover, we know he has been involved with Fox-Eastleigh before. If necessary, with a little manipulation, we can even account for his additional income... I think it might tie together quite well.'

'The more I hear of this, the more I like the idea. Well done... good thinking... get on to it directly after today's meeting... I'll sign the necessary.'

'Just one other thing, sir... it also ties up nicely with his background - his father was a lieutenant-commander... he was on the point of being promoted to commander and his first command, when he was killed on the *Penelope*.'

'How very interesting,' said Billy Ruffian.

*

Though it was a difficult time, he was glad to have been kept busy, the days and weeks had flown by. More and more of his time had been demanded on the range - two hours a day became four, and three days a week had become five. Hennerbury did not ease the pressure until he was completely at ease with Sims' performance. Gunnery officers are renowned for never being satisfied. Eventually though, even he had to admit Sims had achieved a level as good as any that had passed through his hands. It had been a difficult period for Hennerbury too. He had found it quite disorientating that he could enjoy the presence *and* be proud of a stroppy, cocky leading stoker.

His courier duties just about put paid to any free time he might have scraped together - he'd only managed a couple of visits to Covent Garden. Increasingly, Sims wanted to return to The Golden Bell and see Mo once more - if he were to have been honest with himself, he would admit harbouring a hope that she would change her mind, and they would get back together again.

*

In the mirror behind the bar, she caught sight of him coming in the side door. Mo quickly disappeared upstairs to pull herself together - they had to meet again, neither was sure how it would work.

'Mo not in?' Sims said, to Pearl.

'She must have nipped up top... how are things with you?... you've not been around lately... usual?'

'Please.'

'How long you in Pompey for?'

'God knows... indefinitely... maybe.'

Pearl looked at him for a few moments deciding whether to say what was on her mind. 'Sims, I think Mo's still soft on you... please don't mess her life up again.'

'It's over, Pearl, you have to believe that... we both have to move on... we're just good friends now... that's the truth.'

'She's looked so much happier lately... I don't ever want to see her so sad again.'

The door to the upstairs apartment opened and Mo came in. She walked straight over to them. 'Hello, you're a bit of a stranger.' She was trying too hard, a bit strained... not really Mo. Pearl didn't seem to notice. 'A bloke came in looking for you... he's taken to having the odd pint or two here on his way home... usually a bit earlier than this.'

'Did he say what he wanted?'

'No.' She moved off to serve a customer.

He was deep in thought when Mo called to him, 'Sims, talk of the devil... here he is now.'

'Derek, it's good to see you again... how are you... how's Maggie?'

'We're both fine... wondering when you're going to come and see us... where've you been?'

'Not where've I been, what have I been doing's more to the point... what would you like?'

'Boiler maker... old habits die hard... the bar girl's good, she'll probably remember.'

'Like a chaser?'

'Christ no... only at home... rarely when I'm out... gave them up years ago.'

Mo came to serve them. 'Boiler maker?'

'Please,' said Sims. 'His name's Derek... Mo, he's a friend of mine.'

'Not trustworthy then, I'll have to go a bit careful with him, will I?' Mo gave him a lovely smile.

Please don't smile like that, thought Sims, this is hard enough as it is.

'I can't stay long... got to pick Maggie up... Now then, no beating around the bush, when are you coming to see us?'

'Name the day.'

'Leave it out, it's just supper, not a bleedin' marriage, lad... Friday... 2000... you don't need to bring anything... just yourself will do.'

'You're on.'

'See you later then,' Derek downed his pint, and left.

Mo served Sims another, it was a busy night, no time to talk - he was relieved.

He sat at the bar trying not to watch Mo glide from customer to customer, slick movements; opening bottles; chit chat; pulling pints; puffing away a wisp of hair that fell over her eyes. This is too bloody difficult, damn near impossible, I'm going to have to leave soon, an hour's as much as I can take this time.

The bar thinned a little and Mo came over again, 'I can't believe I was so rude; I never asked,' she said, in a low voice, 'how's Gran and Grampy?' Sims had taken her to meet them one weekend, they liked her, they got on well, she liked them.

He had still not got over their deaths and it showed on his face. Mo put her hand to her mouth, 'Sims, they're not...?' Grief, that always vicious spectre; uncaring, forever hiding in the shadows ready to take him by surprise, caught him unawares. It bit him, rendered him without words - he could only nod. He saw Mo's eyes fill with tears. And before she could rush round the bar to him, he gave her a slight smile and quickly left. Knowing she would follow him, he ran along the street and turned down a side alley before she appeared. This first meeting after the night of their long goodbye had not been an easy one.

*

For an ordinary matelot, his tot of naval rum has water added to prevent it being stored - that way, it quickly goes sour. Sims and Ben received theirs without water. Typically, and totally against regulations, Sims had, each day, saved half of his rum ration and kept it hidden in his and Ben's office. Friday lunchtime he slipped the bottle into the inside pocket of his raincoat and left the Seamanship School - nobody was ever checked at the entrance; the same was not true of *Victory* barracks. He walked to Derek and Maggie's house in Buckland, knocked, and shortly a generously sized woman answered the door.

'Hello, my name's Sims... are you Margaret?'

'No, I'm Maggie,' she said, smiling at him, 'Hello love, you're a bit early... thought you were coming this evening... you are coming I take it?'

'Sure... looking forward to it... look, I can't stop... thought I'd deliver this for Derek,' he said, giving her the bottle. 'Bit risky taking it in and out of barracks.'

'He is going to love this... hardly any left in the house... you sure you can't stop for a bite?'

'Thanks, but no, I've to get on me bike... see you at eight.'

*

'Sims dropped this round for you this morning.'

'What a good lad... I was beginning to panic... my other's just about finished... wasn't sure if I'd be able to get more,' he said, looking lovingly at the bottle.

'Derek Hill! Since when is a bottle of Pusser's more important than giving me a kiss?... on second thoughts, you'd better not answer that.'

'Sorry, love,' he gave her a big kiss, and then gave an even bigger one to the bottle.

'Go careful, Derek Hill,' Maggie said, threateningly.

'Do you need a hand with anything, love?'

'No. Go in there, and get yourself and Sims a drink together... he'll be here in a minute.' With immaculate timing, as Derek had just poured a couple of rums, Sims knocked on the door.

'Come in, come in... hey lad, thanks for the Pusser's... shan't ask you where you got it... just glad to get it.'

'That's almost poetic... how yer doin'?'

'Fine, come and be officially introduced to Maggie.'

Sims went over to Maggie and gave her a kiss on each cheek.'

'Careful, lad, you'll get her all over excited.'

'What we on, Maggie?' asked Sims.

'Full roast.'

'First class.'

'Want a beer with your Pusser's?' Derek, handed Sims a glass of rum.

He took a firm grip on the glass. '*Alcohol*, never touch the stuff.'

There had been nothing minimalist about Maggie's portions - Sims was bloated and glowed from the effects of two or three bottles of beer chased by a similar number of rums.

'So, how have things turned out?'

'On the face of it, it's a pretty good number... I know now what I am officially - a courier. Unofficially, there's a lot more going on, but I'm not allowed to say what.'

'Couriers are usually trained specialists.'

'They're giving me lots of range time... combat range work is being done without my CO knowing.'

'Sounds a bit cloak and dagger,' said Maggie.

'I think there's plenty else I've not been told... I'm not sure everything's pukka.'

'Lad, ever since I picked you up in Chatham, I've not

liked what you might be into. I carry a lot of top brass around... I hear all sorts of things... it's unbelievable, you'd think I'd had my ears amputated or something... if I hear anything that might concern you, I'll let you know.' For the moment, he thought it best not to mention Commander Stinton's threats.

'Hey, steady on, I don't want you getting into to trouble on my behalf. You and Maggie have a nice set-up here... I wouldn't want to see anything happen.'

'Sims, lad, it's not a risk for Maggie and me if I listen in... if they're daft enough to talk business as if I wasn't there, that's their problem... and you're hardly going to tell, are you?'

'No, definitely not.'

'If I have anything for you or need to talk, I'll tell Mo.'

'I'll do the same.'

'Who's Mo?' asked Maggie.

'Barmaid at The Golden Bell... Sims' girlfriend.'

'Ex.'

'Didn't look ex to me.'

'She's married now... *ex*.'

'Is she why you didn't want to come back to Pompey?'

'Yeah... can we leave it at that?'

Maggie changed the subject, 'We've got a place on The Isle of Wight... know The Island at all?'

'A bit... I do the odd run there in the launch I drive... Whippingham's nice... love the church, looks as though it was made in Bavaria... delivered ready to assemble.'

'Our place's not far from Whippingham... mind you, you're not far from anywhere on The Island,' said Derek.

'The church was the idea of Prince Albert... Osborne

House is just up the road,' said Maggie, 'Do you fancy coming over and staying a while?'

'Yeah. If I get time off, I'd like that.'

'And, if you ever need a place to hole up... you know, hide... come here... there's the place on The Island too... we'll give you the keys to both places,' offered Derek.

'Hell fire... that's a bit extreme. It shouldn't come to that... should it?'

'You said yourself, something's not pukka.'

'Thank you very much. So good of you to put my mind at rest... I feel completely at ease now. No need to look over my shoulder.'

'You can never be too careful... where do you deliver to on The Island?'

'Amongst others; Saunders Roe.'

'They're building the new frigate *Arethusa* at Samuel White's aren't they?'

'Enough questions... you'll be touching on sensitive areas shortly.'

'What I heard from the back seat gossip is it's going to have some pretty advanced stuff fitted - electronics, that is.'

'So I've heard... time to go.'

'Derek! You've gone and frightened him off with all your prying,' Maggie said.

'Not at all, it's been a lovely evening... a taste of civilisation. Early run in the morning... gotta get in some shut-eye.'

'You can't have had much of a family life recently,' Maggie said.

'No. Not really.'

'One for the road, lad?'

'No thanks... after your assessment of my situation, I have an unexpected and quite strong urge to nip off and emigrate.'

It had started to drizzle. Walking back along the cold wet streets, he thought, in three years time, I won't be going back to an effin' barracks at night, I'll be going home, my own home... and that's a promise.

Before she turned the lights out, Maggie said, 'Nice lad, I can see why you like him... a bit touchy about his ex... what makes you think he's still after her?'

'It wasn't him, it was her... different smile for Sims than for the rest of us.'

'You sound jealous.'

'No... I just get the feeling it wouldn't take much for one absent husband to come home and find he hadn't got a wife any more.'

***

Chapter Six
A Freer Hand.

'I have something for Lieutenant Fox-Eastleigh... I need to deliver it to his hand.'

'I'll tell him you're here,' said Christine Harper.

'Reeves, come in. Coffee's just been made... like some?'

'Please, sir. That would go down rather well.'

Door shut, they reverted to first names. James cleared some space on his desk. 'Unexpected visit, what are you thinking? What's on your mind?'

'Touching base, that's all. Nothing intellectual, just basic stuff... essential, but basic.'

'Such as?'

'How is it that there is not a single female at the Seamanship School, and yet this place is absolutely *crawling* with talent?'

Fox-Eastleigh smiled: females or opera, this was just a prelude to the main question of the day. 'Luck of the draw I guess.'

'My arse it is, you've fixed this up, like you fixed me up with NID.'

'Beyond my powers... sad to admit it, but beyond my powers.'

Sims thought about this, 'Got yourself lined up yet?'

'Plenty to choose from. However, there are three exceptional ones.'

'I'd be content with half an unexceptional one at the moment. Things are getting pretty desperate... thinking of advertising.' Sims took a swill from his cup, 'On a slightly different tack, though, how are your enquiries going?'

So this is it, main subject arrives, 'Drawn a blank. Nothing, not a thing out of place... very frustrating. If there's a cell here, it's well hidden.'

'Do you think Billy's source is sound?'

'Yes... why not?'

'I suppose he could just be a bit twitchy after Portland... you know, spooking at shadows.'

'It's not impossible... though he doesn't strike me as being the jumpy type... and he'd be taking a huge risk just for an attack of nerves. No, I reckon he's pretty sure there's something going on. If secrets are still leaking, it is most likely to be here in this area... just well camouflaged.'

'Hmm.' Sims looked at his watch and stood up, 'Must be off... thanks for the coffee.'

Outside the strategic supplies office, he hesitated, then thought better of going inside and chatting up Pam Somerton; fun to chat with, too likeable to mess around. Recent happenings with Mo had lent him incipient morality - he hoped it would be fleeting and not incurable. Sims, unsettled by this peculiar turn of mind, said, 'Fuck it!' and moved on down to the docks and his launch.

Skirting a destroyer leaving harbour and half way back to the Seamanship School he thought, *camouflage*, *smoke screens.* He pulled the tightest turn his launch was capable of doing at high speed, and returned to *Dolphin*.

'I need to talk with the lieutenant again.'

James Fox-Eastleigh called, 'What is it, Reeves?'

Leaving the office, Christine Harper closed the door behind her. 'I was thinking about what you said about camo. Has it crossed your mind we might have been thrown a dummy... a smoke screen. What if the *reliable information* wasn't so reliable after all. How about Houghton and Gee having already given everything of importance to the Russians? How about if that fresh revelation of secrets being leaked has been put about to distract NID? If someone shafted them before, why not again? On past performance, they seem open for it. Remember what Billy told you; espionage never ceases, perhaps they've evolved new methods. On the other hand, maybe they're after something else, from somewhere else. How about that for a healthy chunk of paranoia?'

'It's possible, I suppose... go on, give me a for instance.'

Mindful of the supper at Derek and Maggie's and the question about the *Arethusa's* advanced technology, he sat looking at his former boss, sniffed, then said, 'Okay, what about on the Isle of Wight; Samuel White's are building the new *Arethusa*, it's stuffed to the gunwales full of new electronics. Then there's Saunders-Roe hovercraft... SR.N1 and SR.N2. I bet the whole world's itching for details of those. What if it's the Yanks who are after that technology and have given us a false scent to keep us busy over here, while they do the business over there? I don't see why we should trust the Yanks any more than the Russians.'

'Sims, it's true I may be guilty of looking too hard, and not thinking enough. But even so, I don't see how I can cover the Isle of Wight as well.'

'Then ask NID for help.'

'Billy won't want to increase the risk of the cabal's exposure. He's been pretty definite about that. No, I have to stick to my brief... do what I've been instructed to do, or they're likely to accuse me of clutching at straws because I've not found anything.'

'Okay, but you don't mind me suggesting these things?'

'On the contrary, I really welcome your help. You know I *always* have done.'

'Good. One final thing, is 3rd Officer Harper one of the exceptional ones?'

'Yes,' said Lieutenant James Fox-Eastleigh, his face lighting up and showing the first bit of enthusiasm since Sims had walked in. He leaned over his desk and dropped his voice, 'There's an even better one in the strategic supplies office... definitely the one to go for.'

Sims stood up to go. 'Nice to see you're focused on the things that really matter. Of course, with all this crumpet around, you could be forgiven for stretching things out here a bit... I'll keep quiet, shan't tell Billy. I'll be off then... be seeing you.' Sims may not have agreed, but he could see James' difficulty; Billy Ruffian definitely not to be messed with, short staffed, tight budget. I've got a freer hand than him, he thought, I'll use it... plenty of talent on The Island too, Good place to start.

***

Chapter Seven
The Letter.

Sims walking into the cobbled yard of the Seamanship School was met by Sub-Lieutenant Hennerbury coming out of Maitland's office. 'Good morning, Reeves.'

'Morning, sir, nice surprise to see you,' said Sims, saluting.

'Reeves, don't lie to me, nobody likes to see a gunnery officer, it's our job to be hated... just remember that. Now then, I've just had a word with Lieutenant-Commander Maitland... we've come to an agreement. He's only going to allow you to enter the pistol competition... so no rifle shooting for you, lad... it's a pity, but there it is.'

Sims was glad of the outcome but said just enough to sound disappointed. He had a lot on his plate at the moment, and also had a growing conviction that sometime soon down the line, he was going to need all the pistol shooting skills he could muster. 'That's a shame, sir, I thought we were doing quite well with the Martini.'

'We were doing quite good with the Lee Enfields as well. But as I said, it's a pity... better than nothing at all, wouldn't you say?'

'Absolutely, sir. If you don't mind me saying, Lieutenant-Commander Maitland seemed dead against any involvement at first, you must have put a pretty good

The Letter.

case forward.' Sims, wondered what sort of threat a sub-lieutenant can make to an officer two ranks higher.

'You could put it that way, lad. See you tomorrow 0900 sharp.'

'I'll be there, sir.'

'I know you will, lad. I just gave you an order.'

'Yes, sir... of course you did.'

Ben Whitley watched Hennerbury leave, and not until then did he come out of their office. 'Right bugger he is... told me I looked like a bag of crabs and I was to smarten myself up if I knew what was good for me... told me to get my haircut too... right bastard.'

'Rubbish, he's a kitten. You've just got to know how to handle him... it's called diplomacy. Something seamen don't understand. Stokers have a natural flair for the subject - it's as though we were specially selected by God, endowed with charm, Ben.'

'Fuck off. This letter was delivered for you this morning.'

Sims went into his office and opened it:

> My Darling Sims,
>
> I cannot tell you how awful I felt when I realised Gran and Grampy had passed away, you must feel so alone now.
>
> I have started this letter so many ways, in the end I had to return to the way I first started, 'My Darling Sims'. Though I can never change my mind about us, that's what you will always be to me. You know I'm a catholic and you know I have always been religious - my

> soul is God's, but my loyalty must be to Brian and his baby I'm carrying. Sims, I want you to know it has meant so much to me to understand you really loved me when we were together, my heart will always be yours. There's so much I owe you.

Sims had to sit down, any hopes he'd had that he and Mo would get back together again, now dashed. Jesus, she's having a baby... she's taken up religion again... so that's why she wouldn't take the crucifix off, he thought. Taking it very seriously... that's so strange, wonder what brought that on? Sims read on:

> You taught me so much, you made me laugh, those silly stories you used to tell, I loved them. More than anything, Sims, you made me believe in myself. There's not a day goes by without me thinking of something we did together. Do you remember the first day we met... you stared!

The memory was crystal clear, he'd never been to The Golden Bell before. Fed up with going to Commercial Road dives he decided to try a pub in the back streets. The girl behind the bar stopped him dead in his tracks.

'You're staring... you shouldn't stare; it's rude,' she said.

'No I'm not... well, if I am, it's your fault.'

'My fault, how come?'

'You're worth staring at... a bit gorgeous.'

Mo had moved off to serve a customer. She passed

Sims. 'You're still staring.'

'You're still a bit gorgeous.'

'Which bit?'

'Not one... lots of them... I should have said, bits.'

She stalled, not knowing what move to make from here. But as inevitable as gravity, the girl seemed to be making excuses to be at his end of the bar.

Sims went in for the kill. 'Some of the bits are... though not all by any means... just some... you've got a lovely smile, nice teeth, fabulous lips, a beautiful mouth and you move so nicely.'

Mo was smiling, 'Keep going.'

'Bright, dark eyes... in fact, you're not just a bit gorgeous, you're all-over lovely.'

'Is this your first time in The Golden Bell?'

'Yes.'

'Do please come again,' she said, flashing him another lovely smile.

'That smile is an absolute killer. Can I call you Mo like the others?'

'Only if you tell me your name.'

'Sims.'

'Not your *surname!* your christian name.'

'Sims.'

'Really? Is it really?'

'Yeah... really.'

'That's nice... I like that.'

'Mo, I'm going to have to go. I've got a navy to sort out.'

'You going to come back?'

'Absolutely... you bet.'

'Don't leave it too long then.'

The Letter.

A few hundred yards on his way back to the barracks, he stopped, turned around and went back to see Mo.

Mo, bright-eyed pleased, smiled, 'That was quick.'

'You said don't leave it too long; I didn't... here I am.'

Close to stalling again, 'Was it my eyes or smile dragged you back?'

'Both. Do you get much time off? If so, I'd like to join the queue to take you out.'

Mo quietly looked at Sims for a moment. 'If you're serious, I'll give you a special pass... no queuing necessary... I'm off sometimes Wednesdays, always Sundays.'

'Sunday's best for me, where shall we meet?'

'Outside here... twelve o'clock all right?'

'Fine. Mo, if I don't turn up, it's not because I've changed my mind. I'm with the Fleet Maintenance Unit... they don't seem to care about my social life... something about war readiness being more important... I get sent anywhere at the drop of a hat. Where would you like to go?'

'If it's fine, I'd really like to go to Spice Island, haven't been there for ages.'

'I like it there too... I'll catch up with you later... maybe before Sunday if I can get away.'

'Hope so,' she said, giving him a beautiful smile.

'Mo, that smile's a killer.'

'Hope so.'

Sims returned to the letter:

> On our first date when we went to Spice Island; how could I ever be the same again? You changed the way I thought about myself. The sun was

> nice and warm, but there was a chilly breeze and we sat on a bench huddled together inside your overcoat, you always glowed, Sims, and your coat smelled nice too. When I told you my family came from there way back, you asked me what they were. I said, probably whores and rogues. You said, you didn't think so. I'll never forget what you said next. You said, there's a never ending line of people waiting to do us down; stick the knife in even. We don't have to join them. If you think whores and rogues, that's what you'll get.
>
> Then you made up this lovely story. You pointed to an old building and said that it was once a spice warehouse and it had been owned by a nice and kind family...

Ben came back in to their office, 'No time for reading love letters... boss has a job for you... Isle of Wight... don't forget to fill up before you go.'

'Thanks, Mum.' He put the partially read letter away - he'd finish it later; somewhere quiet.

'Reeves, I have a packet for J. Samuel White Shipbuilders... Cowes... it's urgent... get it over there as soon as possible... for the chief designer... needs signing for... get back in good time, there may be something for *Dolphin* later.'

'Am I allowed to stop for a cuppa over there, sir?'

The Letter.

'Yes, of course... we all need to eat and drink.'

'So I can take a sandwich as well?'

'I suppose so, Reeves, yes.'

'I'll get a receipt then. So you can reimburse me, sir.'

'I suppose so, Reeves, yes,' said Maitland, realising he had been led into that by Sims from the very start.

*

The sea state roughened into choppiness by a gusty wind from the north, pitched and rolled his launch. Despite this, he kept the throttles wide open and leapt from wave crest to crest. Occasionally, crest to trough, his timing not good enough: thinking of Mo, jolting wet moments. Even so, Sims made fair time. Dropping his speed as he entered the Medina estuary in Cowes, he slid gently into the calmer waters of Samuel White's yard, moored at their jetty and spoke to Security, 'I've a packet to deliver to the design office, but much more important than that, where can I get a cup of tea and a sarnie?'

'The canteen's up there... they'll look after you, Jack,' the old guard said, grinning, 'those girls up there eat young matelots like you for breakfast.'

'Can't wait... I suppose I'd better deliver this first, so I can enjoy being eaten and they don't have to bolt their food... bad for digestion... and the design office?'

'Those offices there... the ones with Design Office written in big letters on them... we like to keep things like that secret here,' he said, shaking his head.

'I need this signing for by a senior designer,' said Sims, to a young draughtsman.

'Certainly, I'll get one. Do you always carry a gun?'

The Letter.

'Yes, even when I go down the pub... sleep with it under the pillow.'

'Is your job dangerous... why do you need one?' the kid asked in awe.

'What sort of question is that?... to shoot people of course!'

'Really, do you shoot many?'

'Couple a day on average.'

'*Why?*'

'Cos they ask fuckin' stupid questions, and don't go and get the chief fuckin' designer when I ask them to,' blasted Sims, who, after his trip, was hungry, blood sugar low, and wanted to get to the canteen.

'Geraldine, look what we've got here... a real sailor... he's got a gun too.'

Geraldine came out of the canteen kitchen at the run. 'Ooh... hello, love, do you always carry a dangerous weapon?'

She had led with her chin, 'Yep, and sometimes, like today, I carry a pistol as well.'

The few workmen taking their break laughed at this exchange. One of them said to Sims, 'You tell her, Jack, she's always asking personal questions... she asked Nobby here how often he used his riveter... that's going just a bit too far, innit?'

Geraldine turned to Sims. 'Best ignore them, they're nothing but a bunch of dirty minded, foul mouthed fuck-pigs... what can I get you, love?'

'Any chance of a bacon sarnie and a cuppa?'

He went and sat down by a window overlooking the Medina and reopened the letter from Mo:

The Letter.

> ...It was the first story you told me. You said that it was where my great, and then ever-so-many greats, grandparents had lived, and they had a beautiful daughter who had married a sailor and that I looked just like her, and just as beauty can pop up generation after generation, so can goodness.
>
> When I got home that night, I wrote it down word for word so that I can tell it to my children and grandchildren. They must never think they are descended from whores and rogues, or they might believe it.
>
> I have added my own bits to the story, I hope you don't mind. The girl and sailor had three children, two girls and a boy. They called the girls: Angelica and Anise, and the boy Coriander. And, of course, they all lived happily ever after.
>
> Ever since that day, I tell everybody who asks, my family comes from a long line of spice merchants.
>
> Sims, come and see me in The Golden Bell, I want to know you think well of me.
>
> All my love, forever,
> Mo xxx

He slipped the letter back in its envelope. She had made it clear on the night of their long goodbye: the door was closed on any chance of them getting back together again. This letter with the news of her pregnancy, had firmly bolted it. He'd had plenty of time to get used to the idea. He should now feel free to move on; a freedom he did not bend to exercise, though needed to.

Life's auspicious moments, and, for that matter, jokes, need good timing. Accidents may require that bit extra; exquisite precision. Move one way or the other, a millisecond earlier or later, no accident; things stay as they are. Should the reverse be true; to the left or right too early or tardily, everything may change - luck is a matter for Fate and her timing. This is how she would work today for Sims.

He sat for a while gazing across the water, watching the comings and goings on the opposite shore. He wasn't going to rush back to Pompey, the sea-state would shore up his excuses. Anyway, he'd made good time on the way over, so decided he'd stretch his legs with a walk down to the ferry that linked Cowes with East Cowes. He said goodbye to the girls, okayed leaving his launch moored where it was for a while, and strolled out of the yard.

In the mellow sunshine, Sims sat on a bench watching the ferry passengers come and go. He had intended to reread Mo's letter. Before he could do so, his eyes fell on a woman getting off the ferry - there was something familiar about her. She was not a pleasant sight; not a soft line about her. She had, Sims thought, been designed by a naval architect and then put together in a shipyard - riveted rather than riveting. But, he had seen her before, though not recently. A man who had been sitting on a nearby bench got up and went to meet her. I pity the poor bugger if that's his date, gotta be desperate, he thought. He watched them move a short distance away and lean on the railing overlooking the harbour. Fate's timing was impeccable, The couple were to be the victims of a silent, unscarring accident; an incident causing no immediate damage nor injury. If the breeze had not gusted at that moment and flapped the woman's coat open, Sims would not have seen the man slip something into the inside pocket of her overcoat. They exchanged a few words and parted. The woman then returned to the ferry and boarded it.

*

Later that evening he called in at The Golden Bell. Mo came down to the empty saloon bar where he was waiting.

She took his hand, 'Hello, love,' she said.

'Mo, congratulations on the forthcoming... just beginning to show... thanks for your letter... it was beautiful, I'm glad you remember the story.' He squeezed her hand and kissed it, 'Mo, we must always keep in touch, and if you're ever in trouble promise me you'll let me know... I'll do whatever I can... I promise.'

'I know you would... I'll always do the same for you.'

He kissed her on both wet cheeks, 'So, just good friends from now on, then?'

'No, darling. The very, very best of friends,' she corrected him, 'always.'

***

Chapter Eight
Alice Alacrity.

'You've got another delivery to make to The Island... Samuel White's again,' shouted Ben, from outside the office door. 'You got something going on over there?'

'Yeah, yeah, yeeaahhh. You should see the size of her onefers.'

'Really? what's she like?'

'You'd only be upset if I told you... best you stick to blokes.'

'Fuck off.'

*

Calm sea; good crossing time, 'I've come to get eaten by Geraldine again... Design Office still here? Or has it sunk?'

The old guard told him to, 'Sod off.'

He nipped up to the canteen and ordered his sarnie first, 'Be back in a sec,' he said, to Geraldine. Reception empty, nobody attending the front desk. Sims, impatient, waited for a while drumming his fingers. Enough's enough, he decided, he wasn't going to wait any longer, leapt over the counter and knocked on an office door.

Straight edge, parallel ruler and drawing pen, clearly

marked him down as either a poser or coming from the drawing office. 'Can I help you?' he asked.

'Yes, you sure can. Thought you were all on strike again or down the pub designing... I need this signing for... anyone in the design office will do.'

'I'm your man,' he said, taking the package. 'By the way, some of our best designs were born in a pub. Don't underestimate the creative stimulus of beer.'

'I'll make sure I remember that... my sarnie's getting cold... any chance of some hurry-up?'

While he was signing, someone came through a side door, walked across the office and out the other side. Sims recognised him immediately; Mr Desperate, Big Bertha's dubious date. 'Didn't he used to play for Portsmouth?'

'Not him, no. He's one of our electrical boffins. No, no, he wouldn't know one end of a football from another,' he said, smiling at the geometricity of his joke.

Geraldine had slipped an egg in with his bacon. 'Don't tell anyone... they'll all expect the same,' she said, smiling.

Time to escape: sarnie in hand he headed for his launch and the Seamanship School. It niggled him, try as he might, he still couldn't place where he'd seen Big Bertha before.

*

'Come on, Joss, it's too nice a day to stay inside, let's take our break in the sun.'

The two wren officers picked up their cups - the slightly more rounded of them, Joss, took with her a pack of biscuits. On the south side of Fort Blockhouse, they sat on a low wall overlooking The Solent.

'It feels like spring is really here at last,' Joss said, as she opened up the pack and offered one to her companion.

'No thanks,' said 2nd Officer Anne Sherwood, 'I've no appetite.' She watched a black and white launch entering the narrows between HMS *dolphin* and Spice Island at high speed.

'Are you feeling all right? You were a bit short with Somerton earlier. She may chat, but she's such a hard worker.'

'Perhaps, but she does gossip too much with the visitors.'

'You can't blame her for *that*... have you seen him?'

'Him... who?'

'One of the visitors, the courier.'

'No, I haven't. It makes no difference anyway, we've so much work on at the moment. The amount of extra reports we're having to prepare for the commodore's office is ridiculous... outrageous.'

'Anne, he's *your* father. Surely you can quietly drop a hint - perhaps threaten to disown him or something like that,' Joss said, smiling.

She at last smiled. They had been at school together and for ten years: best of friends - no secrets between them. It was a friendship they both valued and trusted. Anne had only been at the school six months when her mother died in a car accident - it was an awful time; a terrible time. Not long after, her father took a commission in the Baltic while she remained at school in England. She had wonderful grandparents, but it was Joss and her parents that made her life bearable. Joss had two brothers and two sisters, there was always so much going on. Weekends and holidays spent at their home opened Anne's eyes to a world she'd never known - a full family compliment, no members missing.

'Oh that it were as easy as that,' Anne said. 'I am sure it has something to do with his new aide. He's been in and out of our office more times than I care to think. He asks so many questions - he's more like an auditor than an aide.'

'Perhaps he's got his eye on you.'

'Well he can forget that. He's not my type. Nice enough, but not my type.'

'How many years have I known you? And for all they must amount to, I have to say, I'm at a loss to know what your type is.'

'Joss, I'm the daughter of a naval commodore, every suitor I've ever had has been more interested in their promotion prospects than they have been in me. You'll have to forgive me for being just a little suspicious of every sub-lieutenant, lieutenant or sub skipper who comes knocking.'

'You'll never get anyone if that's your attitude. What does it matter?... have some fun before you ditch them. Anyway, they can't be only interested in promotion - you're a bit of a dish you know. I see the way men look at you.'

Anne sighed, 'How do you *do* it? You happily charge from one boyfriend to another without a pause, and you're never at a loss for offers. How *do* you do it?'

'Perhaps it's because I don't look so fierce when I'm being chatted-up. God, Anne, with that scowl, they're bound to go into a quick retreat. Also, I have the benefit of being brought up with two brothers; I understand men... though to be honest, there's not a lot to understand, they're pretty basic creatures really.'

'You make it sound so easy,' said Anne, miserably.

'It is, you need a bit of tutoring, for that we need a longer chat than this tea break will allow. What about going out for a drink tonight? You could do with a break.'

'To tell the truth, at this very moment I don't feel like it, but I know you're right, and I know once I'm out I shall be fine. A good whiskey and a stiff one at that is just what I need.'

Joss sniggered, 'Perhaps you don't need tutoring after all. I've been trying to tell you that for ages.'

'For God's sake! What is your mind like?'

'Normal, healthy, and very satisfied,' she said, with a distant grin. 'And just for the record, I'm rather glad you're not interested in Lieutenant Fox-Eastleigh - I think he's lovely, I might have a go at him myself.'

'Come on, you, we've got work to do,' Anne said, rising from the wall and brushing down her skirt, 'We'll work out the arrangements over lunch.' She stopped, 'No... on second thoughts we can make them now - how about coming for supper and a drink at home this evening? I can phone Mrs Calver in a minute.'

The whiff of food, appetite whetted, 'Now that *would* be nice, Jean Calver, best cook in Hampshire... probably the whole world.'

'That's it settled then,' said Anne, as they walked back into their office.

*

'Mrs Calver, that was super - I couldn't eat another morsel.'

'Jocelyn Mortimer, I've known you since you were hardly more than a morsel yourself - and *I'm* pretty sure you could.'

Jean Calver, the closest thing to a mother that Anne knew. In her sixties now, grey haired, cheerful, perhaps slightly more weighty than she would like or admit to - the cause obvious, she was the very best of cooks. Hell Head House was as much her home as anybody's. Anne and her father would not dream of making decisions about the place without consulting her - she was entirely one of the family. Often she ate with them. Just as often she took her meals in the kitchen where she could watch the television in peace.

'It's a lovely evening, why don't you and Jocelyn go for a walk while I clear up?'

'Don't you want a hand with the dishes?'

'No, my love, you look as if you could do with some fresh air. Go on, out with you both and let me get on.'

Outside, Joss said, 'There, Mrs Calver says so too - I told you, you're looking a bit off colour. Are you sure nothing's the matter?'

It was a short walk down the lane at the end of the drive. Then, they walked in silence down a narrow path that led to the foreshore.

'Come on, speak to me. This is why I came this evening - *remember?*'

'Christ, I'm so absolutely fed up with everything. Nothing feels right at the moment. For God's sake, I don't think I'm a lot different from most other women,' she hesitated. 'I don't want to end up an spinster like my great aunt, but, if I'm going to get married, it has to be the *right* man. You know, someone whose ambitions don't make me feel like a damn step ladder.'

They walked along the shore line to a small sheltered bluff where a heap of timber had piled up; flotsam from the last spring tide. Using a few of the drier logs they made a bench and sat down. A few hundred yards up-river, the liquid, plaintive call of a curlew sounded. They both looked up. Joss pointed. 'Is that the bird there?'

'No, that's a whimbrel, very similar... straighter beak... the one that made the call was a curlew. This one's probably on passage to Scotland.'

They sat quietly listening to the curlew's call.

'Do you ever think of leaving the Wrens, Joss?'

'Oh yes... of course. And I will do, as soon as I snatch the right man up. I rather like the idea of having a family. I'm in no great rush, though, but when he arrives I'll be off like a shot. Why do you ask?'

'More and more often recently I've been thinking of leaving. It's not just the work load, I feel there's much more *I* can do, much more *I* can offer. I think above all, I want to be valued for what I am, and not because I'm a commodore's daughter. Look, you were always ahead of me at school and in exam results, yet, I'm the second officer while you're still a third, and the only reason for that is my father's rank. That is not *fair*... it is not, *just*. I feel pretty damn guilty. Guilty, because I'm senior to you and don't deserve to be... guilty because I know when the day comes to leave, he's going to be so upset.'

'Surely he understands you'd leave the service if you got married?'

'Yes, I suppose so - but that's not likely to happen is it? I know he *would* like to see me married with children. He suggested I had my portrait taken for the deb' spot in the *'Horse and Hound'* or *'The Field'*. How completely awful: *'2nd Officer Anne Sherwood WRNS, daughter of Commodore Robert Sherwood and the late Alice Sherwood of Hell Head House Hampshire'*. It's a marriage meat market for privileged, brainless, tarts. You can have me if you've enough money: this brood mare is ripe for breeding. Come and get me now while wrinkle free stocks last.

I want no part of it: it's hardly better than prostitution. I love my father dearly, but it's not a route I'm going down, and *that's that.*'

A side to Anne she'd not heard before, 'Wow, strong, strong stuff,' was all Joss could think of saying.

*

It was a bright spring morning with no wind to stir the surface; the tide just starting to ebb; the water laying like wet lino. Even with its engines full ahead, the twin wakes from Sims' launch seemed subdued and quickly gave up their turbulence.

A quarter of a mile off his port bow a slack sailed ketch wallowed without steerage. From its exhaust came a few puffs of black smoke.

'No wind, *and* her engine's knackered.'

At two hundred yards he could see a young woman in the cockpit. 'Hmm, perhaps I ought to see if they need a hand.'

At twenty five yards, Sims could see she was a delight. He threw both controls full astern, then set them at stop and came to rest. 'Do you need a hand?' he called to the woman.

'Maybe... I think so,' she replied, and spoke to a person trying to start the engine.

Sims eased his throttles forward, cruised to within a yard of their stern and read the name; *Alice Alacrity.*

Any person who has just spent half-an-hour cranking the starting handle of an old diesel engine in a confined space, knows they have every right to be snappy. It was plain the man who came up into the cockpit knew his rights, and if pushed, might not be responsible for his language or actions.

Sims, with his mind firmly fixed on the girl, tried to appear polite, cultured, and anything else that might grab her attention. 'I'm on my way to HMS *Dolphin*, sir. I can give you a tow if you like.' Then, with absolutely no authority to do so, he said, 'It really is no bother, and I'm sure they wouldn't object to you mooring there until you've fixed things.' And without the vaguest idea of who the commander of HMS *Dolphin* was, said, '*Dolphin's* a submarine base and its skipper's a submariner... they're a good bunch, all-round much easier to get on with than surface sailors.'

The man looked at Sims for a few seconds; started to say something; changed his mind and paused, then, 'I'm glad to hear it, young man. A lift is exactly what we need.'

Sims was now in command. 'What we'll do is this, I'll take your bow rope and we'll tow line-astern for the main part of the tow... it will be quicker like that. Then, when we're fifty to a hundred yards or so off the entrance we'll stop. Put your fenders out; I'll come alongside, we'll tie bow to bow and stern to stern, then I'll manoeuvre you into the inner dock where there's usually some free parking.'

Near the entrance, Sims slipped the other boat free and went alongside the ketch as planned. The two boats drifted in the growing current while being tied together. The ebb tide was gathering pace. The man and the girl both looked concerned as they rapidly approached a large buoy. Sims casually finished checking the bow and stern ropes, stepped into his cockpit and in one smooth movement, shoved the port throttle fully forward, the other full astern, and pushed the wheel hard over to starboard. With the engines roaring, the props churning, he spun both boats on their shared axis. Then with both throttles full ahead he piloted them away from hazard.

Fractionally before they were facing the harbour entrance once more, Sims centred the wheel, and eased both engines to slow ahead. The two boats cruised gently into HMS *Dolphin* and the inner dock. Again he spun them and placed *Alice Alacrity* perfectly positioned alongside a vacant pontoon.

Sims climbed over the deck of the ketch and on to the pontoon to speak to the yacht's owner. 'If you'd like to come with me, I'll explain the problem to security. You'd better leave the young lady to explain what the boat's doing here.'

'Do you think my daughter will be safe amongst these rough sailors?'

'I didn't realise she was your daughter, sir... yes, of course, submariners are a pretty harmless bunch. All that time underwater and the pressurised hulls... affects their brains you understand. They sense they should be interested in the other sex, but sadly, they no longer can remember why. That's why most of them look confused and slightly puzzled most of the time. It's as though they've been lobotomised... quite tragic really.'

The skipper of the yacht looked intently at Sims. It was as though he was trying to suppress a smile; his daughter thought, *you are digging yourself such a hole!* Sims, though, was enjoying himself, determined that this distraction was well worth pursuing. 'Before we go to security, perhaps you would be kind enough to write your name, address and phone number. I'm a bit overdue, and it would be handy for me when I explain to my CO I helped out in an emergency... there's also the question of salvage rights,' he said, not having a clue how such rights worked.

The man handed him his address:

Owner of ketch, 'Alice Alacrity'.
Commodore Robert Sherwood RN.
Commanding Officer HMS Dolphin,
Gosport. Hants.

'Well, that was a very convenient chance encounter then, sir,' said Sims, saluting the commodore, 'I think, we can forget about the salvage.'

'What is your name, LM(e)?'

'John Sims Reeves, sir,'

'I have a question for you, Reeves. Where on earth did you learn to handle a launch like that?'

'Sir, I was a *Ganges* boy... a coxswain too.'

'Surely you only sailed cutters, whalers and dinghies there.'

'Yes, that's true. But boats are boats, and if they're fitted with twin six cylinder Fodens, they're easier to handle than something that just relies on the wind.'

On the tow back he had seen Sims looking *Alice* over, 'Another question, young man,' the commodore said, closely watching Sims' reaction, 'What do you think of *Alice Alacrity*?'

'She's really very smart, sir... beautiful. Just what you should expect of an old wooden ketch... special craftsmanship you don't see these days, decks and fittings look original - not overdone, they're exactly right. If I were ever to own a yacht, I wouldn't complain if it was just like her. And, I was thinking as I towed you here, for some reason the name seems to be appropriate, *Alice Alacrity*, it's charming... spirited. I might be a little biased in this matter, sir, my last commission in the Far East was with HMS *Alacrity*... I loved nearly every moment of it.'

'Only nearly every moment?'

'In a typhoon, carrying buckets of molten white metal down the engine room ladder so we could pour new big end bearings, is not a pass-time one looks forward to, sir.' He didn't mention being shot in the back.

The commodore, hrumphed, 'That, I can understand.' He added, 'I'm glad you like the name. Alice was a charming woman... spirited as well. Well, we have a common background, lad, HMS *Alacrity* happens to have been my last ship before I joined the submarine service. I met Alice while I was serving on *Alacrity* in Hong Kong... a very beautiful and very charming lady.'

The girl had watched Sims fixedly during the towing home and then through the entire exchange between him and her father. She stayed apart from them in the cockpit. Her father seemed to be enjoying the conversation, and the launch driver was at ease with him. She now turned and without saying anything to Sims, went down into the cabin.

'Last question, and I'll let you go,' said the commodore. 'Do you like sailing?'

'Yes, very much so, sir.'

'Hmm. You'd better be off.'

'Before I go, sir... about your engine. It's possible you have an air-lock; the fuel pipes from the pump sometimes age-harden and crack... it may only be minute... enough to cause a problem, though... it also may be that a fuel pipe union has loosened with time, then let air in. Does it smell more of diesel than before?'

'It does a bit, yes.'

'It's probably one or the other of those things.'

'Thank you very much for your help, young man, I shall get a tiffy to have a look at it. I shall also call your CO and tell him to go easy on you... you really had better get off now,' he said, and shook Sims' hand.

2nd Officer Anne Sherwood had returned to the cockpit and witnessed the end of the conversation and the handshake. Sims saluted the commodore, climbed back into his launch and started the engines. He released his bow and stern ropes, said goodbye to Anne, and left the inner dock.

Her father climbed down into the cockpit of *Alice*, he and Anne watched Sims leave. 'Damn fine sailor, that boy... handles that launch like a dream... got guts too... didn't bat an eyelid when he read my address.' His daughter, still watching Sims leaving the dock, remained silent.

The work load in her department was a strain, and for weeks, Anne had not slept well. That night, she found it even more difficult to settle, it was nearly three o'clock before she finally fell asleep. She put it down to the bright moonlight.

***

Chapter Nine
Smelly Ben.

'Come in, Reeves. How are you today?' Maitland asked, pleasantly, 'It's a lovely day, what can I do for you?'

'It *is* a nice day isn't it?... and it's very nice of you to ask how I am, sir... I've been, as you know, very busy lately; flat out... couriering... then there's also been all the range work. I've hardly had any time to myself. Private things are beginning to pile up, things I need to attend to, do you think I could have the afternoon off, sir?'

'I don't see why not... I don't have anything urgent,' Maitland said, looking at his schedule, 'I can't see a problem... by all means... we'll see you tomorrow then?'

'Yes, sir... on the dot, and thank you, sir... I'll go as soon as I've had my tot, sir.'

'Quite... ...Reeves, are you sure there's such a word as *couriering*?'

'Well my grandmother was French, and my grandfather said, according to her, you could stick a gerund on just about anything... she often did. To tell the truth I don't think she ever really got the hang of them. She'd almost get there, and then she'd go and spoil it by saying things like; you look very happing today, or are you seriousing?... quite confusing at times, sir.'

'Quite.' Not until Sims had gone did Maitland realise he had avoided answering his question.

Smelly Ben.

Sims downed his tot in one. 'I'm off for the afternoon,' he said, to Ben, 'think I'll pop into The Golden Bell on the way back to the barracks.'

'Have one for me will you?'

'Did you say on, or for?'

'For... definitely for.'

Mo and Pearl both came to serve him. 'Hello, sexies,' he leaned over the bar and gave each of them a kiss. Pearl moved off to serve a customer. Still leaning over the bar he looked down at Mo's roundness, 'How's things down there, honey?'

'Fine, no problems thanks. How are you keeping, my love?'

'Not bad... keeping busy... you know?'

'Got yourself a girl yet?'

'No.' He looked around the bar, 'Not many in today,' he said, changing the subject.

'Come on, Sims, a good looking bloke like you shouldn't have to go begging you know.'

Looking at her middle again, he said, 'I wish I had something like that to occupy *my* mind... give it time... it'll happen.' The girl on the ketch he thought not worth mentioning. She would only blur the stats. On a scale of one to ten, the chances of pulling that one were remote: bordering on minus twenty.

Sims leant back on his stool and glanced down into the saloon bar - he came close to losing his balance. It was *her!* - battleship woman; Big Bertha!

'Careful, darling, how many have you had?'

'Calling me *darling* does not help... love... Sims... are

okay. I've still got your letter...'

'What about sod or daft bugger?'

'Those are better... them I can handle. Mo, don't look now, have you seen Big Bertha down in the saloon bar before?'

She took her time, walked to the end of the bar, rearranged some glasses and came back. 'Yeah, she comes in every time the wood boat docks... who she is, I haven't a clue... he's one of the crew.'

'*Christ*, he must be bleedin' desperate... mind you, his wife's probably a hod carrier.'

Mo chuckled, 'If he's after a woman, he's got a bit of a problem there.'

'Why?'

'So's she.'

'How do you mean?'

'She's heavy duty, Sims... can't you tell?'

'She's bleedin' ugly I'll grant you... that doesn't mean much does it?... could be a right goer.'

Pearl came over to see what they were talking about.

'Sims wants to know, how we know, that Big Bertha down in the saloon is a strap-on merchant... can you help him?'

'Do you fancy her then?... go for the domineering types eh?'

'Honey-bunch, I'll try anything once... as long as it doesn't involve electric cattle prods or women that wear tweed upholstery... both probably put her way off-limits... come on, how can you tell?'

'Oh, *she's* easy... only just short of having a set of bollocks to scratch... though, looking at her, she probably tries,' Pearl said, with the wisdom of someone who had dealt with every type of human variance. 'The really difficult ones are those that look completely normal until they get really close, then you can see they don't act quite standard... I've worked in nearly every bar in Commercial Road, including the Albany and the Railway Cellars... it doesn't take long, you soon are able to spot them more or less straight away... I'll give you another lesson later... come on, girl, we've got customers waiting.'

Sims sat alone trying to place Big Bertha. He knew he'd seen her before other than on The Island. He didn't have that much contact with civilians so decided it had to be something to do with the navy. It definitely wouldn't have been in the Far East - tweeds not appropriate, he thought. Royal Navy and Latvian boat... might as well call it Russian... not a good mix.

Bertha got up, said something to her partner, and left The Golden Bell through the side door. Mo went over to the table to clear away the glasses. Sims saw the man speak to her, she nodded, came back to the bar, poured a double whiskey and took it back to the table.

When she next came to Sims, he asked her, 'He can speak enough English to order a drink then?'

'No trouble, his English is really quite good... often chats when he's in here on his own... says he comes from Riga.'

'Yeah, I can believe that, his boat's called, the *Rihards Vāgners* from Riga... went there on a cultural visit once... dead hole, should rename it Riga Mortis.'

'You said once that Richard Wagner was like gonorrhoea, alright in small doses... bloody hell, Sims, you could be a vulgar bugger at times.'

'Don't I remember,' he said, distantly.

She went to the other end of the bar; served, and was chatted up by two bib and braced dockyard workers. She looked back at Sims and thought, Come on my darling, you've got to try.

Sims decided he would return to the Seamanship School. He'd wait there to see this Latvian guy return on board. He bought a pie, said goodbye to the girls, and wandered back. First job is to get rid of Ben... don't want him asking awkward questions, he thought.

*

'You've returned early, Reeves... I thought we weren't seeing you until the morning.'

'That's right, sir... I was just about to start my dinner and I remembered there are a couple of maintenance jobs that need doing on the launch... duty first, sir... I can eat some other day... perhaps an afternoon off another week, sir.'

'Quite,' said a non-committal Lieutenant-Commander Maitland, who was now wary of Sims' ability to lead a conversation just where he wanted it to go, 'Quite... yes... we'll see.'

In their office, Ben jibed, 'You're keen... grovelling git... given the afternoon off, and then come back here instead.'

'You know me, Royal Navy first, personal interests second. Duty above everything and all that shite... I hope you've got some runs to do this after'.'

'Why?'

'I want the office to myself.'

Smelly Ben.

'Why?'

'Well,' Sims scanned around as if someone might be listening. 'Look it's like this, you have personal odour problems, Ben,... this is why you have to buy your own beer on dates.'

'Fuck off... I don't smell.'

'Listen, it takes a special kind of friend to tell someone they... how can I put this gently?... let's see, well... *stink*, seems to fit the bill.'

'You're winding me up.'

'I'm not. *You* don't notice it because normally you're in your boat and your stench is diluted by clean estuary air... at close quarters let me tell you, it's pretty vile... haven't you ever had a date faint, just when you've gone in for the kill?... of course you have... Ben, that wasn't submission... it's called unconsciousness... hypoxia; lack of oxygen... you must be careful, you could be fined for a public odour offence... you smell like an out-fall.'

'One day, Reeves, I'm going to flatten your bollocks.'

'Ben, violence is not the answer... soap and water is all that's needed.'

'Oh fuck off... I can't stand this. I've got work to do... I'm getting out of here... keep the office... it's all yours.'

'You see, even you can't stand it... open the windows before you go, please... don't bother shutting the door.' *Mission accomplished,* he thought, as Ben stomped out.

From the office window Sims had a good view of the freighter and the immediate dock. He busied himself cleaning the Browning, checking its magazines and polishing the box that Les Goodwin had made - it had become a treasured possession and he had taken to giving it the occasional light smear of beeswax polish. When I leave the navy, and if I ever get married, I'll give this case to my wife to keep her jewels in. In this frame of idle speculation as to who she might be, what she might look like, and what size brassiere she might need, he cleaned the gun and watched the dockside.

It was close to about high tide. On deck activity suggested the *Rihards Vāgners* was readying for sea. He had been in the office no more than an hour when he saw Big Bertha's partner return. The man walked across the gangway without acknowledging the busy crew. He stepped through a door in the superstructure and out of sight. Not the slightest interest in what's going on on deck... crew ignored him... speaks good English... he's no crew member, thought Sims.

Within ten minutes of Bertha's contact returning, the '*Rihards Vāgners*' from Riga left the dock. So, she collects stuff from British warship designer and delivers it to the Russians. My guess is she's a collector, and a postman. I'll keep this quiet for now... don't want to embarrass myself... Russians and Royal Navy, definitely not a good mix.

Around half past two that night Sims woke with a start, 'HMS *Sultan*... fucking *Sultan*... that's where I've seen her before... not quite as weighty then... but that's where... definitely,' he said out loud. 'She was some part of the education office, definitely.'

It took him more than an hour to get back to sleep. Matey, next stop for you sits on the other side of the estu-

Smelly Ben.

ary.

*

Wren Pam Somerton gave more than a hint of a smile to him as he entered the office. Leaning over the counter she said, 'Still got the new gun?'

2nd Officer Anne Sherwood heard this exchange. Though she couldn't immediately put a face to it, she recognised the voice and moved closer to the dividing partition of the office she shared with Joss. Joss moved closer too - listening to Pam chat up visitors could be fun, part of the day's entertainment.

'Yep,' he replied, not giving away much.

'Unusual choice,' she said, still leaning over with her forearms still resting on the counter.

'What is?'

'Not *is*, *was*... the Albion, it was an unusual choice.'

'Might have been a logical one... they're a good gun.'

'The other day I remembered where I'd seen you before... younger then.'

'Well of course I was. You see, Pam, it's like this, darling, *before* is in the past. So, I'd have to be bleedin' younger, wouldn't I.'

'You're avoiding the issue... I've seen you before.'

'Gun-fight at OK Corral?'

'Not exactly, though come to think of it, it was a shoot-out... Bisley... the Inter-services Competition.'

'Are you sure it was me?'

'Yes... but you weren't called Roy Rogers then... I know I'm right, I was on the scoring staff.'

'Then I hope you managed to.'

'Managed to, what?'

'Score.'

'God, I walked head first into that didn't I, Roy?'

Leaning over the counter towards her, his face just inches from hers, he replied, 'Yep,' and then said, 'I have to hand this envelope to Second Officer Sherwood personally. Is she here?'

'Yes, yes... in a minute... you said the Albion was a logical choice.'

'It was, and in competitions, might still be.'

'Actually, I'm a pretty good pistol shot, I think the Smith & Wesson has it hands-down over that old thing you were using.'

'*You* didn't win though, did you?'

'Okay, I'll give you that - that's fifteen love. But, I still don't get why you chose it... Come on, it doesn't allow pre-cocking... you have to pull right through the action every time you shoot. With S&Ws you pre-cock and then only need the lightest of touches on the trigger to fire. The Albion must put you at a terrible disadvantage.'

'I still won though, didn't I?'

'That's not the point, *Roy!* How much better would you have been with a decent gun?'

'Now, listen, Roy Rogers here is going to tell you how it is. I won because I was using the Albion, not despite it. There are a couple of very good reasons why I always liked to use one, both of them important if you want to stay alive, or win competitions. Do you want me to go on?'

'Quickly then, yes.'

'I'm only bothering to tell you this because you're a pistol shooter and you score... first, Smith & Wessons occasionally miss-fire, the Albion never does. Second, any disadvantage I might have been at, disappeared when we had to deliver six shots in six seconds. That's where I had everything going for me - no time for pre-cocking here. This is where I was in my element. S&W shooters don't ever really get used to the full pull-through. I got a maximum, they didn't. I knew if I stayed in touch till that point, I'd clinch it. And *that*, my darling, is exactly how it worked, and why I chose what I chose. There is a third point, the Albion is slightly heavier and just that bit more stable on target.'

'Good God!... that's pretty good thinking... who told you that?'

'No-one... if you think about it, it's bloody obvious.'

'You also won the .303 cup on four hundred yard range. So, what strategy did you use there then?... it was an equal field... everybody was using Lee Enfields.'

'No strategy, no tactics. I'm just bleedin' brilliant... game set and match I think.'

'Big head.'

'Isn't it time you fetched your boss?'

'Yes, okay.'

Anne and Joss quickly sat down at their desks and looked engrossed in their work.

'Excuse me, ma'am, there's an envelope to sign for from *Victory*,' said Pam.

'I'll be there in a moment,' Anne said, 'On second thoughts, send him in will you?'

'Very good, ma'am.'

Anne visibly stiffened as Sims walked into the office. Joss looked up to see what this crack shot looked like... It's the courier... very nice, she thought, even better close up.

'Good morning, ma'ams,' he greeted them both, and then, addressing Anne, he said, 'Did your father get the engine fixed?'

'Yes,' Anne replied, tersely.

'Was the problem what I suggested, ma'am?'

'I don't know... you have a package for me to sign for?'

Sims handed her the package and receipt form.

Anne signed, he asked, 'Tell me, is there regular transport between here and *Sultan,* ma'am?'

'I don't know,' she flustered, 'possibly... ask at the main gate for God's sake.'

'Thank you, ma'am... you're *so* kind.'

'I hope you're not being insolent, LM(e).'

Christ Anne, give him a chance... he's only being pleasant, Joss thought.

'Insolent, ma'am... perish the thought... God forbid, no... I should hate to think you thought so,' he said, laying it on thick.

'I think you'd better leave, *now!'* said Anne, becoming quite flushed.

When Sims left reception, Pam Somerton came into the office to watch him walk up the road towards the main gate. 'He was only a kid when he won at Bisley... cool as a cucumber... upset such a lot of pro's.'

'Very well, Wren Somerton... we *are* busy you know.'

Pam left the office, humming.

'You've met before, then?' said Joss.
'Yes, he towed us back in when *Alice's* engine failed.'
'You don't seem to think much of him.'

'No, I don't... he had the cheek to think Father was a civilian... he even suggested he might claim salvage rights. Can you believe that?'

'What did he do when he found out this civilian was a commodore and the commanding officer of the base he'd just towed you in to?'

'Nothing really... tried to brush it off, and then said he'd forget about the salvage.'

Joss laughed, 'I'm sorry, but that's so funny... not a nice spot to find himself in... took some guts I reckon.'

'What was really annoying, was that Father thought so too. They stood side by side discussing *Alice,* just like old friends. Joss, my father's a *commodore*, he's a *stoker* for God's sake!... surely there have to be several degrees of separation, don't there?'

'He seems a nice sort of person... perhaps the commodore's a better judge of character than his daughter.'

'It's not about *his* character, there's Father's position to consider... stokers and commodores shouldn't mix... they're not equal.'

'Come off it, Anne, it's not that long ago you were saying how guilty you felt because I was brighter than you, and yet you were senior to me... that it was only because you're a commodore's daughter... because of your father's rank, you said. How do you know the stoker isn't brighter than all of us? How do you know he's only where he is because he hasn't had our social leg-up?... you can't have it both ways,' she said, slightly miffed at her friend's double standards.

Anne's argument had been found wanting - she had been caught out and she didn't like it. Joss's comments only appeared to make her resent him more.

Smelly Ben.

*

A baffled Sims walked deep in thought towards the main gate - he couldn't fathom what he'd done to make that woman so hostile. He changed his plan, there was no real mileage in going to *Sultan*, who the hell would he ask?... what would he ask? No, he'd go and talk with Lieutenant Fox-Eastleigh. The problem was, how to pose the question without blowing the gaff?

'LM(e) Reeves would like a word. Have you time?' said Christine Harper.

'Come in, Reeves,' called Fox-Eastleigh, and when Christine had left the room, he asked, 'What's on your mind, Sims?'

'I'm trying to place someone, someone who might work at *Sultan*... maybe something to do with education... built like a light cruiser... rigged in tweeds... working title; Big Bertha... I think she was there when I did the LM(e)'s course a couple of years back... any ideas?'

'Come on, what do you know?'

'I don't know anything yet.'

'I think you do... or at least suspect something.'

'Billy Ruffian said keep your eyes open... I've been doing exactly that... can you or can you not, put a name to the person?'

'Your description sounds very much like a Mrs Glass... nuclear school course coordinator between *Dolphin* and *Sultan*. She's been checked... all above board... MI5 gave her a clean bill of health before she went to *Sultan*.'

'She's absolutely Pukka then?'

'Married. Husband's a local councillor, no children,

small house, no fast living... seems model.'

'Married!... wonders will never... I can understand the no kids though.'

'How do you mean?'

Not sure how much to reveal, he hesitated.

'How do you mean, Sims? What do you know?... why is she interesting?... not for a moment do I think you'd comply, but I think you know me better than to order you to spill the beans.'

They had been through a lot together; old loyalties crept in - keeping his old colleague in the dark was not pukkah. 'I find it difficult to believe that MI5 would miss the fact that she's a lesbian. But it's not *that* that's particularly interesting, it's the fact that they haven't seen fit to inform the risk factor to NID.'

'Good God, Sims, how long have you known this?'

'Not long... and that's the truth... she needs watching.'

'You know more,' he put forward.

'Yes.'

'Are you going to tell me?'

'I have a feeling... I can't substantiate it... it's not just MI5 I'm unhappy about... NID must be either incredibly incompetent, or someone knows about her and isn't telling... there are so many things that don't make sense.'

'Give me a for instance.'

'Look, James, neither you nor I are trained agents... I know what Billy Ruffian said; secrecy and all that. In my mind, it doesn't stack-up... if they were really intent on having a Ruski clear-out down here... no disrespect meant... you'd think they'd come in mob-handed... use professionals.'

'Between you and me, the same thought had crossed

my mind.'

'While we're on the subject... the same goes for some of the jobs we did in the Far East... it didn't strike me till much later... if things had gone wrong, they could have denied all knowledge... maybe it's one of the ways NID operates when on unsafe ground.'

'Things did go wrong for you.'

'I meant really wrong... as in, if I'd been killed.'

James sat looking out of the window, 'What to do?... what to do?'

'Well, I'd say for the moment we keep quiet... you watch her this side, I'll watch her mine... build a solid case before we say anything... then decide who to tell... and you know, finding *that* person might not be so easy as all that.'

'What you say makes sense... possibly treasonable... but sense... you really think the cabal is shaky?'

'Yes, I do... think of it, why Maitland?... he's a really nice guy... but he's a cryptanalyst, a code-breaker, not a heavy... why?... for the very same reason we're here perhaps.'

'I think you're way ahead of me, Sims... I may have been a bit slow.'

'I wouldn't say that... I've been lucky that's all... in the right place at the right time.'

'Are you going to tell me what else you've discovered?'

'No... for the moment, it's a no-go area... when I know where I'm going, I'll give you the low down.'

Fox-Eastleigh looked at Sims trying to understand his reticence to talk.

'If you won't tell me what, will you tell me *why* not?'

Smelly Ben.

'Okay, I said that things don't stack-up... make sense... I think it's worse than that... things are crappy, they *stink*... if we're being set-up, it's better you're able to stay in the clear... reveal your findings...'

'Your findings you mean,' Fox-Eastleigh interrupted.

'...and take any points coming,' Sims continued. 'If there's any nasty business, it's most likely to be on my side of the water... I'm a better shot than you remember?'

'I'm not letting you take another bullet for me... you can forget that.'

'There's not a lot you can do about it... no deal,' he was in full flow now. 'Have you ever thought why you were asked to join the cabal?... Let me tell you what I think. Billy said you were unknown - that's bollocks in my opinion... you *were* known all right, and you were asked because he could be pretty sure you'd ask for me... we'd been partners, remember? So, Maitland, you and me... green as grass... and another thing, I'm pretty sure Hennerbury at Whale Island doesn't think it's kosher either.'

'Who's he?'

'Gunnery officer in charge of the ranges there... he occasionally trains NID personnel on firearms... he's taken it on his own back to put me through the combat range at least three times a bloody week... won't let me get away with the slightest lapse of concentration... he wants me in the navy pistol team... Maitland's agreed... why the combat drill? The navy team doesn't do combat work... I'll tell you why, Hennerbury knows something's up, and he's after keeping me alive long enough to compete... he keeps drilling into me; draw them on, Reeves, draw them on... wait until you can see the whites of their eyes... James, you don't fucking well need to know *that* on a twenty-five yard competition range... I think, Billy Ruffian has his back to the wall... for some reason, he'll do anything to achieve whatever it is he's trying to do... and that, I doubt, has anything to do with the good of the country... I think there's a very good chance that we're pawns in some personal vendetta, or inter intelligence service shoot-out... roll-up... roll-up... see who can put a bullet in the back of John Sims Reeves... *again.*'

'Sims, for god's sake, you don't think it was one of our lot who shot you before, do you?'

'At the moment, James, I'd believe anything... the bloody surgeon wouldn't let me have the bullet, would he?... why not?'

'Good question. You made a reasonable request.'

'He said, it had been sent away for analysis... my arse it had... I mean, God give me strength, all Billy Ruffian asked before enlisting me into the cabal was a few questions about rugby, and that's all... they must be taking the piss.'

'How long have you been mulling this over?'

'Virtually from day one. I've spent hours going over everything, and the only conclusion I can come to is it's either been designed this way for a purpose, or they're out of control... shooting blind... both equally fucking dangerous for us... and as I said, I don't see why you need to be involved... live by the old saying, James; act green; keep clean, and never be late for your tot... hand in your notice... get the hell out of it while you can.'

'And that, Sims, is the only flaw I can see in your reasoning... I *am* involved... we both are... we've both been recruited by NID... they're not going to let go I think... as for handing in my notice... to quote you... no deal, we're in this together.'

'So, you do give *some* credence to *some* of what I've said?'

'I give credence to an awful lot of it unfortunately,' Fox-Eastleigh paused, 'Sims, I think we need to appear to be operating normally... like you said, build a strong case... I'll tell you what I find out about Glass... will you do the same?'

'Probably not... I'd better be off.'

The two men shook hands and before Sims left, James said, 'Go careful, my friend.'

Lieutenant James Fox-Eastleigh sat quietly thinking, he'd had a shock, nothing much useful surfaced apart from the thought, I'm not really cut out for this life... you know where you are with cars like *Mabel*.

*

He walked down to his launch. A sub was in the process of leaving port; the commodore was seeing it off and taking the salute - this meant Sims would have to wait until it was well out of the way, he sauntered down to *Alice Alacrity*. She is a lovely piece of kit, he thought.

'Good morning, LM(e), I thought I recognised you and your launch... remind me of your name again.'

Sims shot round. He'd been quietly absorbed studying at *Alice's* stern design, and not aware of the commodore's approach. He saluted, 'Good morning, sir... LM(e) John Sims Reeves, sir.'

'Well, Reeves, your engine diagnosis was right on the button... so, what's caught your interest about *Alice* today?'

'Just about everything, sir... I think she's lovely... not just saying that to please, I really do... the last time I looked at her I hadn't really taken in her beautiful stern... canoe shaped... it's looks just so right... does she sail well?'

'Oh yes indeed... always well behaved... rough seas never a problem with *Alice*.' He gave Sims a long regard, 'I'll tell you what, lad, I have a regatta coming up shortly... fancy helping to crew her? We'll have a shakedown trial first of course.'

'I'd like that very much... count me in, sir. I'd like nothing better, ... how will I know when?'

'I still have your CO's number... I'll also leave a message with my daughter.'

For fuck's sake, no! thought Sims, maybe if I'm lucky it might not come to that!

***

Chapter Ten
The Protocol.

'Anne?'

'What is it *now*?'

'Would you like me to call you ma'am?'

'I'm sorry... and no I wouldn't. What were you going to say?'

'I thought you were about to bite your nails.'

'Was I?'

'You're a bag of nerves, you're so strung up at the moment, whatever's wrong?'

'I don't know... nothing I can put my finger on... not a single thing... oh, every damn thing.'

'Anne, I'm going to give you some advice. You need a man, pick one, and do the business.'

'The business?'

'You know... *it*. You'll feel a different person, it'll relax you no end.'

'You just pick a man, and that's it?'

'It's better than resorting to artificial means.'

'Artificial means! That's obscene.'

'Oh I agree completely. There's nothing better than the real thing.'

'But, anybody, a complete stranger?'

'No, not a *complete* stranger. I've usually done a little

background research, and if they look okay, I start the process.'

'*Process!* Do these men know what's going to happen?'

'Not initially. I hunt them down - you know, stalk them - then I pounce. I like a clean kill, they don't usually know what's hit them.'

'*Christ!*'

'Having said that, I can see the end to my hunting days... I've definitely decided to go for James Fox-Eastleigh... the more I see of him the more I like him.'

'Isn't he a bit obsessed with his car?'

'That doesn't matter, it will keep him busy while I'm having his babies.'

'*Joss!* you've not even had a date with him yet.'

'Try and understand this; he doesn't stand a chance. I know how these things work.'

*

'Hi, gorgeous... just this pack... nothing to sign for.'

'Hold your horses, Roy,' said Pam, smiling, 'boss wants to see you.'

Joss looked up as he entered the office and sauntered over to Anne's desk, 'You wanted to see me, ma'am?' he asked politely.

Without looking up, she said, '*I* don't want to see you at all... my father says get here for 1000 sharp... Saturday... I'm glad to say I won't be there.' And still without looking up, she added, 'Well? What are you waiting for?... you can go.'

A counter sentiment almost delivered: Sims thought better of it, and left the office without even saying good morning to Joss.

'That wasn't fair of you... he doesn't have the rank to talk back to you... that really was using your rank to unfair advantage... it was disgusting behaviour... I'm ashamed of you, ma'am.'

This quite shook Anne. Joss never called her ma'am unless they were in the company of senior officers. 'I'm so sorry... God what's wrong with me at the moment... everything is so annoying, especially *him!*'

'That gives you no right to take it out on someone who is not in a position to respond... and don't say sorry to me, it's him you should apologise to... it was grossly unfair... the poor man looked baffled... perplexed... at a loss,' and with that, Joss Mortimer left the office, adding as she went, 'I'll take lunch on my own today, thank you.'

Anne got up from her desk and hurried after her. 'What's the matter?... don't go... please don't act this way.'

'What way?... unreasonable?... well perhaps now you understand how it feels... how he felt... it was disgusting behaviour, I meant what I said, I'll take lunch on my own.' With this she walked off alone.

Anne felt as if she was at the bottom of a very deep pit and with no way of climbing out. Her ill humour made worse by Joss not speaking to her for the rest of the day: she said almost as little the next morning.

*

He was glad of the diversion. Sailing *Alice Alacrity* might be a good distraction. There was the uncertainty of all that was going on around him with NID and the other British intelligence services. He wasn't sure if he had said too much to James. Were his reasonings even correct? He felt they were, and if that was so, what would be NID's next move? It was pretty obvious Big Bertha Glass and the Soviets were up to no good. Who the hell could he trust enough to tell?

Just as baffling to him, but perhaps slightly less dangerous, was Anne's attitude towards him. Why she hated him so much was an utter mystery. He had gone over every moment he'd been in her company and could not put his finger on a single time, anything, that he had done or said, where she might have had legitimate grounds for being able to take exception to him or his behaviour. The bigger tragedy was, she was the first girl he had seen since Mo who had really attracted him. She was, as he had often recently thought, an absolute dream. She was also, in awful balance, an absolute bitch. Despite this, he knew only too well he had well and truly fallen for her. He also knew it was a trip going nowhere, and just as some greater hand had flicked the romance switch on, he was going to have to wait until it decided to turn itself off. He came to the conclusion that life is perverse - there's Mo who loves me and has married someone else, and this woman who treats me like a nasty smell... as if I have less charm than a rotting rat. Sims considered he had every right to be glad of the diversion.

He was there on the jetty before the commodore and any other crew that might be coming. He boarded *Alice* and set about discovering how everything was put together: which rope did what, how to raise the mainsail. He had the impression that *Alice* was not sailed regularly and put this down to the commodore being a busy man. Sims went to the bows and clambered out on to the bowsprit to inspect the rigging there.

'All in order, Reeves?' called the commodore, from the jetty above.

'Looks okay, sir... I'll be able to tell better when we start hoisting things.'

'Just the two of us today... Anne is on duty... first I'll show you how to start the engine... she's a cantankerous old bugger,' he said, unlocking the cabin hatch and going below. He took a can of *Easystart* from a locker and shook it. 'Dammit it's empty... she never starts without it.'

Sims decided to say what he thought about the *Easystart*. 'Probably a blessing in disguise, sir... diesels get addicted to that stuff... hooked on it... does more harm than good.'

'Forgive me, lad, here I am trying to tell you how these things function when I don't really understand myself. You're the engineer... the ball's in your court... glad to have you on board.'

'Sometimes it's no more than a knack... cranking it over to a good speed, and timing exactly the right point when to release the decompression lever.' He took hold of the starting handle and engaged it. 'It's a warmish day... might go first time,' he said, winding the engine over, going faster and faster with every turn. He let go the decompression lever, the engine coughed into life and then quickly settled into a steady thumping rhythm.

'Excellent, really excellent, just what *Alice* needs, someone who can start her bloody engine... consider yourself a permanent member of the crew, young man,...

Right! on deck... let's get out to sea.'

Clear of the harbour, Commodore Sherwood sampled the breeze, 'I like to hoist and set the jibs and mizzen first... once they're set, *Alice* will almost look after herself while we raise the main... you see to the bow end, I'll see to the mizzen,.. that done, we can turn that infernal engine noise off... go to it then, lad.'

Sims went to the bows, unfurled the jib and raised the foresail, went back to the cockpit and hauled them tight. He was ecstatic: a sixty-two foot, twenty-five ton yacht and a stiff breeze, life has its moments, and when they come they can be so good.

'In a wind like this, I often sail just on jibs and mizzen.'

'We are going to raise the main aren't we, sir?... this *is* a shake-down.'

'Of course,' he answered bringing *Alice* into wind, 'I was just making the point that it can be a relaxing way to sail on one's own.'

Between them the two men raised the main's gaff and set the topping lift. The commodore re-took the helm and got them under way once more. *Alice* responded. She heeled, she leapt, pitched and sliced through the rolling waves. She was in her element: a fresh wind, strong waters, mistress of the celadon sea.

They practised changing tack until they were so slick they knew they couldn't improve. They practised wearing, smoothly taking the wind from one side of the stern to the other, until that also had been perfected. The two men hardly needed to talk - they too were in *their* element.

'We'll do some turns round a buoy? Need them nice and tight for the race.'

'Ready when you are, sir'.

He aimed for a large buoy two-hundred yards away. *Alice* was fairly racing now. 'Stand by... ready about... aft main, check fore,' he shouted, shoving the tiller hard over.

Sims let fly the jib and foresail, and hauled in the main, ducking under the heavy boom as it swung through onto the other tack. He rapidly set both fore sails. *Alice* was in full flow again. It wasn't a bad effort, just two or three yards past the buoy when they turned. 'We can do better than that,' said the commodore, echoing Sims's thoughts.

They repeated the manoeuvre at least a dozen times until the commodore was satisfied. 'Come on, lad, your turn on the helm... get the feel of her.'

Sims took over. He felt *Alice's* response to his commands. He played with her sail settings: tweaked the balance of the mizzen. This is all he had wanted to do since he'd first stepped on board. 'Can I have a go round the buoy, sir?'

'By all means... never can tell when we might need another skipper... just remember she weighs twenty five tons... she carries a lot of momentum.'

Sims aimed directly at the buoy. The commodore watched. God, this is going to be tight. Nevertheless, he'd made his decision; the helm had been handed over, all he could do now was look on and hold both his counsel and breath. No sooner had *Alice's* bowsprit reached the buoy than Sims threw over the tiller - *Alice* rounded it clearing the buoy by a few inches.

'That was close, lad... only missed it by inches.'

He, a touch miffed: 'Races are often won by inches, sir... and with respect, we didn't miss it - we cleared it, and with inches to spare.'

As equally impressed with Sims standing up for himself as he was with his skill, he said, 'I stand corrected, young man.'

'This time when we go about I'll haul the mizzen over as far to windward as I can... try and get her bum round a bit quicker.'

'She has a bum, has she, lad?'

'Oh, definitely; *stern's* far too harsh for a back-end as shapely as *Alice's*, don't you think?'

'I do indeed... bum it is then,' he said, smiling.

From so many years before, she returned, sat on his lap and whispered in his ear. The real Alice would have liked that, he thought.

After half a dozen more goes round the buoy it was plainly evident Sims was placing *Alice* exactly where he wanted. 'Take her back home, lad, we've done well, *really* well.'

Moored back at the pontoon, Sims asked, 'Do I have your permission to come and give a complete check-over of the rigging? I would also like to add some gear to the mizzen so we can get its boom further to windward when we go about... should give us a faster turn.'

'And her bum round quicker, of course.'

'Exactly, sir.'

Anne arrived and looked down on the two men working

together, 'Had a good day, Father?' She did not acknowledge Sims.

'Excellent, excellent... come on down.' He then turned to Sims, 'No problem with coming on board... always maintenance needed on these old boats... by all means try your idea for the mizzen.'

She came up to them, and still ignoring Sims, kissed her father.

'Thanks once again, lad... it felt like the good old days when I was a real sailor... a great day's sailing... regatta next week... how do you feel?'

'Starving. I hadn't given food a thought out there, but I need to get back if I'm to catch supper at *Victory*.'

'Why don't you come to Hell Head for a bite?'

Anne closed her eyes with horror: a gesture made too obvious to miss. 'Another time maybe... I have a few things I need to do back at base... but thanks for the offer, sir.'

The commodore put his hand out and the two men shook hands. 'Get along with you then, lad... and thanks again.'

They drove home to Hell Head House. She, unable to resist asking, 'How was the stoker?'

'Damn good... started the engine first go... I swear within ten minutes he knew *Alice* inside out... natural sailor... make a damn good skipper... took her so close to the turn buoy I could see individual barnacles... best day's sailing I've had for years,' he said, oblivious to the notion he might have offended her.

She frowned, 'Is there anything he's not good at?'

'Yes. He says he's useless at navigation... never been

taught... I'm going to make it a point of coaching him... it's possibly the only thing I'm better at... I've got to have the upper hand somewhere,' he said, smiling. 'He told me off too.'

'Don't you think he's a bit arrogant?... telling you off.'

'Good God no... he was right... he was standing up for his judgement... proper thing to do... I'm sure he would not have said anything if there'd been company... no, not arrogance... we were two sailors enjoying a fine day's sailing.'

*

On the eve of the regatta, Sims slept on board *Alice;* they were to leave at 0600. He was still fast asleep when the commodore and Anne arrived.

'Are you there, Reeves?' called the commodore down the hatch that led to the saloon.

Sims, mid-dream, bleary eyed, sat up. 'Yes, sir, coming right away... just need to put some clothes on.' He took the steps to the cockpit two at a time.

'Bad night, young Reeves?'

'No, sir, completely the opposite... best night's sleep for ages... morning, ma'am.' Anne shammed not hearing him and loosened a couple of mainsail furlings.

'Wake yourself up with some of this coffee, then we'll head off.'

Sat in the cockpit drinking, the commander said, 'I'm going to introduce a rule of order while we are on *Alice* - I thought I'd call it the *Alice Alacrity* protocol. It goes like this: unless we are in the presence of other naval personnel, we will call each other by our first names. Also, the person at the helm will be regarded as skipper. I believe we will be a better team if we adhere to these two simple rules. Sims, you may refer to me as Robert, Rob or Bob... the choice is yours.'

Anne did not respond, neither did she look like she approved.

'Sims, start the engine if you would.'

It took him two tries to get it going: he emerged through the hatch, 'That's got the blood moving,.. it's a good thing to let it run for a minute or two to warm up. And, if I might make a suggestion about the engine, I reckon it would be a good idea to have it converted to electric start. As that would require a battery, you might as well have glow plugs fitted... then, even Anne could start her.'

She glowered at him.

'Excellent idea... even I might be able to do it as well... have thought about it... never enough time.' Anne moved forward and stood in the bows; her back to them. 'Do you want to take her out, Anne?' the commodore called.

'No, I'll do the bow rope.'

He let go the stern rope and *Alice* slid out of the harbour. There being very little breeze, they sailed the first half-hour on engine alone. With improving airs, all the sails were hoisted, and with Anne at the helm, they made Cowes harbour in just under two and a half hours.

During the passage, Sims watched her closely. She knew what she was doing, she had *Alice* trimmed nicely and, for the conditions, setting a good pace. He went to check the main mast, leaving her and the commodore in the cockpit. He glanced back, she had been watching him. She held his gaze for a second or two, frowned, then looked away. She looked at him once more, then away again. She's impossible to work out... best give her up as a bad job.

Back in the cockpit, he and the commodore chatted about every manner of boating matters. Sims told him he had sailed in a Brigantine, and how sailing it between Hong Kong and Green Island he had been at the wheel. 'There was no wind at all on the harbour side of the island so we were on engine power. We could see the wind whipping up the waves on the far side of the narrow channel that ran between both islands. We cut the engine about half way through and just let our momentum take us on. It was simply magic. As we reached the wind, the flying jib snapped taught, and then the next, and the next, until all the sails were full. As each sail filled in turn, you felt this one hundred and ten foot boat surge and heel. I shall never forget it,' said Sims, vividly painting this far eastern echo. Even Anne seemed to be listening.

'I remember a brigantine like that when I was there... now... for the life of me, what was it's name?'

'There were two. Both owned by the same man... an American... great guy. One wasn't used for sailing... just took people staying at the Hong Kong Hilton for trips round the island. That was the *Wan Fu*. It was the other, that was rigged to sail; the *Laura 2*... fabulous boat.

'That's it... that's so... you're absolutely right, lad.'

'The best bit's yet to come; after we'd passed through the channel, the owner took it under full sail; twelve of them, straight through Aberdeen harbour right past the Sea Palace Restaurant. The whole place was seething with sampans and junks... boats of all kinds... great sailor that guy... never hit one of them.'

'How on earth did you get to sail on her? Were you crew?'

'No, a guest... a friend... it's a long story,' Sims said. Nonchalance nicely exaggerated, he went forward to the bows and inspected the outer jib. It was not doing enough work, it could do with a little more tension. Despite having set his mind not to talk to her unless spoken to, he called, 'Do you want the jib a little tighter?'

'*No*. I know what I'm doing.' These six words amounted to all she said to Sims on the entire journey to Cowes.

The commodore took the helm for the final leg into harbour and mooring alongside their allotted pontoon. Then, with *Alice* secured, he asked, 'Do you want to come with Anne and myself to get the race course and boat numbers?'

'I'll stay here and tidy up a bit... I want her looking her best.'

'*You* want! It's *our* boat, Reeves,' she snapped.

Not for the first time during the trip had Commodore Sherwood given his daughter such an exasperated look. It was pretty clear that he was as much at a loss as Sims for her crabby, waspish conduct.

He watched them walk away along the jetty. Out of sight, he thought, *sod her*, and began organising things just as he wanted them.

Three men walked towards *Alice*. They drew abreast, the middle aged of the trio stopped. Staring at the old ketch, he quipped, 'Looks like it was built by one-armed, one-legged lumberjacks... must be owned by some right bozos.' The younger two men laughed. Sims, though in the saloon, had heard the comment, and the laughter - he leapt into the cockpit and then on to the pontoon. Jabbing the man who had spoken on the chest, he said, 'Take that back?'

'What are you going to do if he doesn't?' said one of the younger men.

'I'll fucking well make him, that's what.' A dangerous time for someone, Sims was losing it: getting angrier by the second. A small group of spectators gathered. The three men felt a scrotum tightening inkling all was not going well; this was not to be a walk-over. Joining the group of onlookers, Anne and her father heard the final bit of the exchange. Sims was outnumbered, the commodore pushed forward. 'Sims, take it easy... let it rest.'

Sims stuck out his arm and held him back. 'Please stay out of this, sir.' The youngest of the three men took this opportunity to make a grab at him. This was a mistake, Sims, a blur, pushed the man's arm high with his left hand, and smashed his right fist into the man's side just below his ribs; he dropped to his knees and rolled to the ground gasping for breath. It had been a devastating blow. A split second later, without giving him time to react, he had elbowed the other man hard in the stomach. He doubled up, Sims kneed him in the face sending him sprawling into a tangle of mooring ropes, and finally dropping into the water.

'Now,' Sims said, 'I will not have you call my friends bozos, and I will not have you say disrespectful things about a very precious old boat that I happen to love. Apologise *now* or you'll end up like your scabby mate down there,' Sims moved towards him; the man backed away. 'Apologise *NOW*,' he shouted.

'Can't you take a joke, mate?'

'Don't... call... me... *mate!* And, this is the last time I shall say it. Apologise to my friends *now!*' Sims said this with a devastating quiet menace; he moved another pace forward.

'I'm very sorry,' he blurted.

'Don't look at me, look at them when you say it, and say it *LOUDER!*'

The man turned towards Anne and her father, 'I'm very, very sorry,' he said.

'Now piss off,' and pointing at the man still groaning on the pontoon. 'You might need to have him checked over in hospital.'

There was an instant round of applause to this conclusion. A man stepped forward. 'They've been a bloody nuisance all week,' he said, shaking Sims by the hand.

Through all of this, Anne had stood opened mouthed. This was the first time she had witnessed what an angry, and supremely fit young man can do when pushed too far.

The three of them returned to *Alice*.

'Thank you, lad. Three of them; you were a bit outnumbered, son.'

'Two and a slob,' Sims corrected him. 'As you could see... no problem.'

'You could have let it pass.'

'Forget it, sir. I'm not going to stand-by and let them insult Anne, you or *Alice*... ...ever. I only hope I haven't caused you any trouble.'

A couple in their late thirties paused on the jetty beside *Alice's* cockpit. He called over to Sims, 'Well done... just what they deserved... if you need a witness, call me... here's my card,' he said, handing it over.

The woman with him smiled. 'My gosh, that was a truly super punch... felled ox came to mind... byeee.' As the pair moved off, she took a long look back at Sims.

'No need to worry about trouble. There are enough witnesses to confirm they threw the first punch... I bet he's regretting doing so too... it was a hell of a hit, lad.'

'My immutable law of the street... if getting involved is inevitable; get involved hard and quick.'

*

Anne watched and listened to him talking with her father. For weeks now, she had struggled with an undeniable truth. Since the first moment she had seen him, she was aware of a simple, and possibly primitive, fact, she was deeply attracted by Sims, and this, she had vowed, could not be allowed to develop. Her father's position; her rank; their family's social standing, all said to her the liaison between herself and a stoker was impossible. Not to be tolerated.

Nature though, had conspired against her. Her resolve had been severely dented. It was not his violence that had done this, it was the adamant defence of her, and her father's name. She could not reason how she knew, she was simply convinced he might have had a dozen men to confront and it would have made not a scrap of difference to the decision he took. She would need to redouble her resolve. She looked at him. Anne knew this was going to be difficult.

'We bought some sandwiches while we were away... hungry?'

'Could eat a Maltese donkey... I'm always starving after a punch-up.'

'I hope you never hit me like that, son... at my age, I'd be in traction for a month at least.'

'No chance of that happening. I make a point of never hitting my friends or for that matter, female enemies,' he said, without looking at Anne.

'They've given us number thirty three in a thirty three yacht race... hope it's not an omen,' the commodore said. 'Three laps of a triangular course... we'll take a lap each at the helm... we'll draw straws... should take about two hours... race starts at 1200,' looking at his watch, he said, 'and it's about two hours to the off... we'll set out at 1100... how do you feel, Sims?'

'Fine... really looking forward to it... I'll make a bet we're not last.'

'How much?'

'A pint.'

'What, a whole one? That's a bit steep. I hope you honour your bets, lad?'

'Never.'

'Can we get on with the draw?' said Anne, with exaggerated disinterest.

'Okay, short straw chooses last and so on...' he broke three matches, each of different length, shuffled them and offered first choice to Anne, then Sims. 'Show your hands.'

Anne drew the longest. 'I'll take the middle leg.'

Sims had drawn the second. 'I'll take the last lap.'

'Me to start then.'

'I have a suggestion.'

'Go ahead.'

'With thirty-odd boats milling around, whoever's at the helm is going to be busy; I think the other two ought to keep an eye on sail trim... let the helm concentrate on position.'

'Good idea... do you have a problem with that, Anne?'

'No,' she said, sounding bored.

At 1100 precisely, the commodore called for the engine to be started, and they headed out to the race area. As soon as they were clear of the harbour, Anne took the helm from her father. 'See to the fore's, Sims, I'll do the mizzen.' He and Sims then raised the main sail.

Anne returned control back to the commodore and sat with him in the cockpit. Sims, never satisfied, tweaked, pulled, tightened, occasionally slackened, and then re-tightened the sails. With each adjustment he noted the effect it had on *Alice's* speed.

'Relax, lad, and come down here.' When Sims had sat down, the commodore said, 'Start-line north-south, wind north-west. Let's go through the start flags and basic race rules. The class flag goes up five minutes before the start. At four minutes to go, the class flag is joined by flag 'papa'. One minute to go, down comes 'papa'. When they drop the class flag, that's the start.'

'Flag 'papa' is a square blue flag with a small white square in the centre,' Anne said, sarcastically, and quite unnecessarily, to Sims.

'Christ! I know *that!* I have sailed before you know,' he replied, shaking his head.

'As I was saying,' the commodore gave an irked, exasperated look at Anne, 'broadly, boats on the starboard tack have right of way, and the overtaking boat has to give way to the slower. Any questions?'

'No, if I think of any I'll ask.'

Anne had nothing to say.

'It's going to be busy, be vocal - sing out if you spot a problem.

First the five, and then the four minute flag had been hoisted, then 'papa' was dropped. With one minute to go, the commodore had *Alice* in a good position to the north of the start line. With the wind just off the stern starboard quarter, *Alice* was almost running free, and lying about a third of the way down the field.

Sims shouted, 'There's the start,' and the helm was thrown over - *Alice* crossed the line. 'Great start,' said Sims, punching the air. They changed tack and headed north east to the second buoy. Sims was everywhere; in the cockpit, bows, midships - he constantly worked. Back in the cockpit, he said, 'I reckon we were about tenth over the line. It really was a belter of a start... tenth is going to be hard work hanging on to now things are settling down.'

Boyish enthusiasm had taken over. 'Keep up the good work, Sims, *Alice* has never gone so fast,' shouted the commodore. She gained another place during his lap, and when they had rounded the last buoy to begin the second lap, Anne took over the helm.

Sims could see straight away that even under hectic race conditions, Anne had little problem handling *Alice* like an expert. She showed intelligence, she was alert, and in command. She took each turn-buoy as if it was something she did every day of her life.

Sims wanted her to do well. He did not let up once in his drive to get the best out of *Alice's* rig. Anne handed over to him - she had gained two more places. 'That was pretty impressive,' he said, with unaffected and genuine admiration. She ignored him.

During the first leg, the wind backed and became more westerly. He was not making ground on the yachts in front. 'Anne, back off a bit on the outer jib,' he called. Anne did not respond. He waited - still no response from her; she had turned her head away. He waited minutes more - they were now losing too much ground. 'Ma'am... please!' There was a quiet quality in his voice that reached deep inside her, somewhere where she was not completely in control. She eased the jib as he had asked. He had called her *ma'am*, it was as if he had stepped away from her. There was now an even greater separation between them, a distance she had sought, and now it was there, she felt it to be regretted.

Throughout the remaining part of the race, Sims only referred to Anne as *ma'am*. By the time he had made the penultimate buoy, the wind had backed even further. 'It's a bit of a gamble, but I'm going to tack much further out, and if it backs even more we'll get a good run home.'

He turned for the finish line; there was only one boat

he could possibly take. He tried everything he knew to get more speed out of *Alice*. He wasn't going to make it, the other boat was better positioned.

Anne responded immediately to every call he made, she felt guilty, they might have been better placed if she had been more responsive.

Sims had done well, it was *so* close, but they were pipped by just a few yards. He turned for Cowes disappointed in his performance.

'Don't look so glum, *Alice* has never done so well,' called the commodore, and came down into the cockpit to take them back to their pontoon in Cowes harbour.

***

Chapter Eleven
Part Frog.

They ate only snacks during the race, and so, after mooring, securing the sails, tidying up loose ends, they were hungry. Sims walked into town to buy whatever food he could find while Anne and her father went to the clubhouse to get the official results. He needed to be on his own, he blamed himself for his poor showing during his turn at the helm. Getting himself to admit if Anne had not ignored him they could have just possibly beaten the boat in front, was not possible. However, what could not be denied, in her eyes, he was not, and never would be, a welcome member of the crew; he would think seriously about whether he sailed on *Alice* again.

Commodore Sherwood had said that it was Sims' hard work that was, in part, responsible for their being placed somewhere among the top eight yachts. This made him feel marginally better. Anne's father had gone even further on the trip back to Cowes, he had said, loud enough for her to hear, 'When Anne and I did our stints at the helm, we had you doing everything possible to help us, I'm not sure you got the same from us.' After mulling this over, Sims brightened - *Alice* had done well; they had done well, better than he thought they would.

Part Frog.

In a lighter mood, Sims returned with a bag of eggs, butter, bread and cheese - he would have bought bacon but after inspection: best left on the slab, it looked dry.

At the club house, *Alice,* the oldest boat in the race, had been loaded with compliments. Anne was on the verge of deciding to apologise to Sims; she chose not to. If she were to do this, she reasoned, it might put the final nail in her weakening resolve. Instead, she would make a last ditch effort.

Tied up on the opposite side of their pontoon was a neat sloop sailing under French colours. On it there was a neat French girl who had watched Sims' approach closely. As he stepped into the cockpit, Bob Sherwood shook his hand, and with a wide grin, said, 'Sixth place; seventh across the line... one of the boats in front was penalised, so we jumped a place, didn't the old girl do well?... that must cheer you up!... wish we had some champagne!'

'Absolutely. As we weren't last, the pint you owe me will have to do... we ought to raise the stakes for the next one. And, we'll haul her out of the water... clean her hull... might be good for a place or two more.'

They relaxed in the cockpit chatting and commenting on the other yachts.

'Nice looking boat... wonder what make it is?' said Sims.

'Nice looking girl too... had her eye on you all the way down the jetty.'

Anne was jealous, and after this comment from her father, she dived in with anger. Sims would be punished: made to demonstrate his ignorance. She spitefully said, and instantly regretted having done so, 'Why doesn't Sims go and ask them?'

'Okay,' Sims went over the pontoon. 'Bonjour à tous. Un beau bateau là! C'est quelle marque de bateau?'

'You have a slight southern accent,' said the skipper of the sloop, in impeccable English.

'Demeng instead of demain,' replied Sims, smiling.

The skipper laughed. 'Exactameng, come on board.'

Bob Sherwood turned to his daughter. 'You deserve that. What you tried to do just now was far, far beneath you.'

She looked away.

After an extensive chatting up, Sims returned to *Alice* carrying a bottle of Madiran. 'You don't see this very often... it can be very good. You'd better have it, I'll get shafted if I take it into *Victory*.'

'I'll take it home and we'll drink it when you come to supper.'

Behind her father's back, Anne pretended to stick her fingers down her throat: retching

He ignored her. 'They're about to leave for Hamble, otherwise I might have stayed a little longer.'

'I thought we'd lost you for good... she looked as though she was about to eat you alive.'

'Which one: Marie-Claude? or her mum?'

'Didn't take you long to get her name.'

'I didn't have to ask... she told me they'd be back here in a couple of days... might pop over.'

'Ahh, the sweet scent of romance,' Bob Sherwood said.

That frown: that jealousy again, 'Did you tell her what you did for a living?' She said, going below into the main cabin.

Best a change of subject, so he said, 'As to the matter of departures, it's slack water... hadn't we better head off ourselves? Looks good out there, a stiff westerly blowing... Gosport before opening time.'

'Good idea. *Anne*, on deck sharp and help make ready for sea - Sims you're skipper.'

Sizing up the wind, state of the tide and river traffic, he looked around the estuary. 'Listen up - we're going out under sail: no engines, no noise, no fumes... jibs and mizzen first... mid channel... mainsail.'

She bit: 'You're just showing off to... to that half-woman, half-man, Marie-Claude,' hissed Anne.

Sims smiled. 'Maybe, but I'll tell you this, there's nothing half-woman about her, and *I* know, I got really close... close enough to check. That's why I shall be back over here in a couple of days.'

Bob Sherwood smiled at this riposte: well done, Sims.

He made another quick survey of the surrounding river. 'Robert, you sort out the jibs, I'll look after the mizzen. Ma'am, you take both foresheets and leave them slack until I give the order.'

Ma'am. She flinched.

With everything ready, Sims ordered, 'Let go bows and bear-off.'

As the bows of *Alice* moved away a few feet from the pontoon, Sims slipped the stern rope. 'Aft with the sheets, ma'am... check, that's enough.'

The breeze filled the jibs and pushed the bows out towards mid-stream. Sims tightened the mizzen and with constant small adjustments to it's tension, steered *Alice* in this manner until she had enough way on to respond to the tiller.

Commodore Sherwood watched this demonstration of Sims' mastery of a boat he hardly knew: this lad's a natural skipper, he thought, absolutely natural.

'Ma'am, secure the fore sheets and come and take the tiller while I help with the main sail... there's a ferry coming in, keep to the west bank... take her fairly close to Victoria pier and the parade. Aim to keep that buoy ahead close to our port side. Once we're clear of the breakwater we'll head for home.'

Together, he and Bob Sherwood hoisted and set the main. Sims returned and took the tiller from Anne. Still well inside the harbour, *Alice Alacrity* was under full sail and gathering speed. They cruised towards the harbour mouth: watchers waved and whistled, a ripple of applause ran down the quayside. Commodore Bob Sherwood leant against the main mast with a look of contentment on his face - his *Alice* was being applauded.

'With this wind we should easily get to Pompey in an hour and half or less. When we're clear, what do you think to '*goose-winging*' all the way home?'

'Great idea,' said Sims, exhilarated. 'And when we're set fair, how about I make some omelettes? I've got eggs, cheese, bread and butter, what about it?'

Sims took *Alice* half a mile clear of the Royal Yacht Squadron, and then with the main sail set to starboard, and the jibs and mizzen to port, headed goose-winging for home.

The following wind and sea played with *Alice,* trying to yaw her first one way and then the other - the swell lifting her stern, overtaking her and then lifting her bows and dipping her stern. It didn't take Sims long to master the knack of using the rudder in the opposite sense to normal when a particularly large swell pushed *Alice* from behind.

'This is so good,' he shouted to Commodore Sherwood, 'come and have a go - *Alice* loves it - she's alive.'

Sims went below to the galley, Anne sat near her father. He was not happy about her behaviour on the trip; he gave her a look that she recognised as saying, I'm not going to be argued with. 'Anne, do not refuse his offer. No matter how awful they might turn out, say thank you, and eat it.'

Sims poked his head out of the hatch, 'The pan's heating up... I'll do them one at a time... who wants the first?'

'Anne will take number one.'

A few minutes later Sims reappeared. 'A three egg, cheese omelette and a chunk of bread and butter.' He called up her failed attempt to embarrass him with the French party, 'Bon appétite, duck.'... *duck*: calculated to perfection.

Anne created an inflection with her "thank you" precisely as she intended; I am not grateful, I eat this under duress and I am not your *duck*.

Sims slipped down to the galley, punched the air and muttered, 'Bon appétite, duck... lovely... bleedin' bull's eye.'

Between steering and coveting Anne's very acceptable looking plate, her father said, 'Try and show just a *bit* more enthusiasm.'

Sims returned, 'Take this, I'll take the tiller while you're eating.'

'What about you... where's yours?'

'Eat it while it's hot. I'll have mine when you've finished.'

Anne was, like them all, very hungry. Pushing her resentment to one side she tried a fork-full, and then, pushing it aside for a second time, she admitted to herself that it wasn't bad. In fact it was very good.

Her father was much more expansive. After almost shovelling down half, he said, 'This is super - who taught you to make omelettes like this.'

'My gran. She used to say; the French have six hundred and twenty five ways of cooking eggs and the English one: 'orrible.'

'She's French, is she, Sims?'

'Was.' The slightest flick: the faintest wisp of shadow passed over his face.

Anne who had been looking at him turned away. To acknowledge he was capable of feelings would be decidedly detrimental to her determined rejection of him.

'When I've cooked mine, there'll still be enough eggs for another... we can split it three ways if you like.'

'Go and get yours in the pan, lad, you deserve it... we'll draw lots for the biggest portion of the last one... though, I could just pull rank.'

Omelettes finished, plates wiped clean with fresh bread and void for the moment sated, they sat enjoying the fast run back to Gosport. Sims' background intrigued the commodore. 'You say your grandmother was French.'

'More or less. Her passport said French... she always thought of herself as Pyrenean. She would say; the Pyrenees are unique, and until they carved it up in 1659, we existed without government, and without a monarchy. We were unique within Europe, if not the whole world. She, being Pyrenean, naturally, spoke French and Spanish, and could get by in Catalan. She was also fluent in a local Béarnaise Occitan patois. She was a very clever person... and I'm part frog.'

'She taught you French?'

'Oh yeah, yeah, we'd speak it at home most of the time, and in the summer we used to visit her relatives. I picked up a lot of it there too playing with the local kids... the Pyrenees are really special.' He leaned towards Anne, 'It was good to have had the chance to meet Marie-Claude and get some practise in. As I said, I'll have to see if I can get back over to Cowes in a couple of days.'

Anne, frowning, pretended to be looking out to sea.

'I hope you're not feeling squeamish after the omelette? A slight sea like this can get some people with weak constitutions really going.'

'I don't suffer from sea-sickness, *ever*,' she snapped.

He thought the line of conversation getting heated. Bob Sherwood stepped in, 'Your grandmother... did you learn any of the others she spoke?'

'I get by pretty good in Spanish, and I know a few words of Catalan.'

Lieutenant Fox-Eastleigh was waiting when Sims brought *Alice Alacrity* alongside the jetty in the inner basin of HMS *Dolphin*. Sims leaped ashore and made fast the bows, then the stern. *Alice* protocol now suspended, he said, 'Would you like fore and aft springs, sir?'

'Yes, I think we'd better - see to it will you.' He then called to his aide, 'Is it urgent Fox-Eastleigh?'

'I'm afraid so, sir. We have a boat returning to base

with a sick man on board. She'll be here in fifty minutes by my reckoning.'

The Commodore turned to Sims, 'Well done, Reeves, a first class effort. Would you mind putting *Alice* shipshape before you leave?'

'Of course not, sir.'

There was much to do. Sims got down to the job of cheesing down loose ropes, coiling others, furling the main, mizzen and foresails, carefully lashing the gaffs to the booms, and securing the fenders. It was satisfying work after a good day's sailing. He did not bother asking Anne to help. She could not have made it clearer: he was an affront to her, everything her class stood for, his presence on board *Alice* was untenable.

He squared up *Alice's* deck to his satisfaction. He took the cushions from the cockpit down to the main saloon. Anne was there. Flustered by his presence in the small space, she blurted, 'The dishes need doing, Reeves, perhaps your grandmother taught you to wash up as well.'

It may have been that Anne did not expect Sims to react. It may just have been an ill considered, deliberate provocation to ruffle the waters. Whatever, she did not anticipate getting such an instant and strong reaction.

He was furious: he'd had enough of her constant dribble of vitriol. 'Leave my family, and especially my grandmother, out of it.' He rounded on her with such force that Anne took a step backward in surprise. 'What she achieved, she managed without the assistance of class and the benefit of being a commodore's daughter. She did it by sheer brilliance and hard graft; something you would know nothing about. And, what's more, everything she did, she did with kindness... she hadn't one, one hundredth of your nastiness.'

Uncharacteristically weakly, Anne said, 'You can't talk to me like that... I'm an officer... your superior.'

'I don't need the protection of the protocol to say what I'm going to say, ma'am,' he said, moving closer to her. 'It's been a fantastic day's sailing, brilliant weather and we've done really well,' he paused for a moment. 'Didn't you see the look on your dad's face when we were applauded? For Christ's sake he was proud and happy. What on earth did he do to deserve an unremitting bitch like you for a daughter?... today *should* have been pleasant, most *might* have even found it fun. Yet *you*, you being the first-class selfish cow that you are, seemed determined to make sure it wasn't going to be!'

Anne took a deep breath. *'Don't talk to me like that!'* This was, in the end, all the profound breath produced. Weak as it was, this hiss was all she could muster.

He was in full flow now and his anger had got the better of him. 'Hard fucking luck - I just have. There's an RPO just up the road, go and tell him what I've just said, and when he comes to arrest me, I'll agree with every charge you've brought. Do you want to know why? Don't bother to answer that, I'll tell you... because I would sooner spend ninety days *over-the-wall* in detention, than spend another fucking day on this boat with you, *you miserable bitch!* Now, if you know what's good for you, you'll piss off, and go and fetch him... I'll wait here.' He pointed to outside the saloon.

Sims stood to one side to let her past. As she reached the top of the ladder to the cockpit she turned round and looked down at him. 'What happened here just now will not be taken further - it would be an embarrassment to my father.'

'Oh bloody hell! How pathetic can you get... so true to form... as usual, hiding behind your dad again.'

Surprising herself, and him, she turned once more and said, 'Fuck off.'

On the jetty Anne came face to face with the duty RPO.

'Everything all right, ma'am?'

'Yes thank you,' and before she could stop herself, she added, 'just a lovers' tiff.'

Anne quickly turned away and walked up the jetty. *What did I say?*

Sims waited in *Alice's* cabin, any moment he expected the thud of heavy boots. Anne would not miss an opportunity like this to get rid of him - he'd laid it on a plate for her. He sat there convinced that his next three months over the wall were going to be very hard. Worse still, they wouldn't count towards the time he had left to serve - the two and a half years to his freedom had suddenly become two years and nine months. Sims almost shouted, 'Bollocks, why couldn't I keep my big mouth shut?'

After a tense half an hour's wait he realised she wasn't coming with the law, she'd kept her word. Sims smiled with both relief, and the recall of her last words to him; our chilly, well spoken and refined ma'am, had told him to *fuck off*. He had never entertained the slightest possibility that Anne might be attracted by him. Now, it seemed, the odds of that happening were quite a bit less in his favour.

He gave *Alice* a final check over, locked the cabin door and left. Cruising back to the Seamanship School, he thought, How can anything so lovely, be such an absolute cow? I'll give her a wide berth in future - next opportunity I have, I'll resign from Alice's crew.

*

Checking in at the Seamanship School a few mornings later, Sims was met by Maitland. 'Reeves, I've a couple of urgent deliveries for you... both top security, both to *Dolphin*. First to the commodore's office, and only to be handed to the commodore himself or, in his stead, Lieutenant Fox-Eastleigh. The second is to the classified supplies section, recipient, 2nd Officer Sherwood, also to be signed for... understood?'

'Roger, sir.'

'Do they say roger in the navy, Reeves?'

'I'm not sure, sir.'

'Quite,' said Maitland, who rarely looked quite sure himself.

Sims took the sealed packages into his office, checked over his Browning, slid in a magazine, cocked it and put the safety catch on. 'Made ready,' he said to himself. So much for giving her a wide berth. The prospect of meeting Anne face to face on her own territory was not one he looked forward to. After our little session, she might just be a bigger bitch than normal, if that were possible.

He moored his launch and decided to go to the commodore's office first. If he was lucky, he might get a chance to resign from *Alice's* crew today.

One hundred and fifty yards ahead, an RPO in the security office watched Sims approach. As he drew near he stepped out from the doorway; 'Security check. Let me see those packages, LM(e).' The RPO it seems did not possess a strategic grey matter: there were more sensible moves he could have made.

Sims stopped and faced him, 'These are top security documents. I am strictly forbidden to let them out of my control.'

'Don't play games with me... let me see what you're carrying.' The RPO, stepped forward and made a lunge for the packets. Sims, whose hand was already on the butt of his pistol, took two steps backwards and drew it out of its holster. The release of the safety catch made an ominous click. He levelled the gun straight between the eyes of a shocked and rapidly paling RPO. 'I am permitted to shoot any person who attempts to interfere with the classified mail I am carrying. For your information, I do not like RPOs... so, just give me a reason... I will not shoot to maim, Petty Officer, if you come one inch closer I will kill you - DO YOU UNDERSTAND? ... DO YOU UNDERSTAND, I SAID?' There are only a few people who are capable of retaining their composure and sense of authority when faced with a loaded 9mm Browning Hi-Power: this man was not among them. Although Sims was of a lower rank, the RPO replied weakly, 'Yes, sir.'

That bitch Anne is behind this, he thought. 'Who ordered you to check me out?' demanded Sims, who, taking advantage of the RPO's wobbly equilibrium kept the gun pointed at his head. The answer he got was not the one he expected. 'An intelligence officer.'

'Well, you tell him from me, to do his own dirty work

in future, and you, you make sure you don't bother me again - understood?'

'Yes.'

Lieutenant Fox-Eastleigh was in reception talking with the commodore's secretary when Sims arrived. From the expression on Christine Harper's face, he got the distinct impression he'd interrupted something she would have liked to remain private. 'Reeves, good morning.'

'Good morning, sir, good morning, ma'am. Sir, I have some documents to be signed for. Is there a secure office we can go through them?'

'Of course, in here, shut the door behind you. What's on your mind, Sims?'

'How long have intelligence officers been poking around *Dolphin*?'

'I'm not sure I follow you.'

'You'll hear about it shortly, I've just had cause to threaten an RPO with my hand gun... he tried to relieve me of these papers. It scared the shit out of him. So while he was still in shock, I got him to tell me who had put him up to it. He said it was somebody from intelligence. That's as much as I know... I'll inform Lieutenant-Commander Maitland of course.

'Are you sure he said intelligence?'

'Absolutely. He didn't say whether it was NID, MI5 or MI6. Frankly, I don't think he knew which... seemed a pretty thick bugger.'

Fox-Eastleigh thought for a moment. 'I was unaware they were around. Except for Maitland, of course, I'd like you to keep this under your hat for the moment,'

'Maitland will have to tell Billy, he can't not... and I

reckon our favourite admiral's going to be a bit pissed off if it wasn't one of his guys.'

'Hmmm.'

'James, I also need to have a quick word with the commodore... any chance?... about *Alice Alacrity*.'

'He's very busy, flat out in fact. Don't hold your breath... I'll ask him.'

'Come in, Reeves, you'll have to make it fast... what can I do for you... by the way, thanks for your regatta effort... first class... so pleased.'

'In that case, I'll be brief. Sir, I've got rather a lot on my plate at the moment, and as much as I love sailing *Alice*, I think I'm going to have to give it a miss in the future - I am really very sorry, sir.'

'Protocol now in force, lad... I'm not blind, nor am I deaf, I well understand the real reason you want to leave. Anne behaved abysmally, I have no idea what's got into her lately. Now, I'm not going to order you to, I'm going to ask you a favour. Promise me you'll stay your decision for a while... let me see if I can do something... get to the bottom of the problem.'

'As I said, sir, I very much like sailing in *Alice*, and without sounding like I'm grovelling, I also like sailing with yourself... it's good fun and I like being trusted with something so valuable... I appreciate it.'

'I don't think *Alice* would fetch that much.'

'Perhaps it's not a simple monetary value you place on her, is it, sir?'

'No it's not... will you stay then?... you can be First Lieutenant if you like,' he said, smiling.

'Okay, sir, with pleasure... I'll stay, as long as I think

my presence is not causing a rift between yourself and Anne. And sir, I'd appreciate it if you don't mention any of this to her. It wouldn't improve matters I think.'

'I will try to avoid doing so.'

Bugger, he didn't say, he wouldn't, thought Sims.

'On a slightly different matter, lad, I've promised to take *Alice* round to Hell Head sailing club, it's their open day on Saturday. Think you can make it for 0800?'

'It's not a problem for me... it might pay if you cleared it with Lieutenant-Commander Maitland.'

'Consider it done. Now off you go... and thanks once again.'

'De rien, sir,' he said moving to the door.

'Sims,' called the commodore, with a broad grin, 'You carried that off with the French girl, perfectly. It was so funny - just what Anne deserved.'

'I know... bye for now, sir.'

Sims left wondering how long it would be before the commodore heard about the RPO incident, and whether sailing *Alice Alacrity* would from now on be off limits.

Wren Pam Somerton smiled when he walked in - her day had just got brighter. 'I see you've still got your nice new gun. What did you have to do to get it?'

'Just a quick test, nothing much... had to make twenty wrens pregnant in under ten minutes... managed it with time for a fag between each one.'

'You're a dirty sod, and you still haven't officially told me your name's John Sims Reeves.'

'It's not, I told you, it's Roy Rogers.'

'Roy Rogers, the RPO killer - that's *very* sexy.'

'Christ! already?... when did you hear that?'

'About ten minutes before you walked in. Everybody hates that bugger, thinks he's God's gift to women... you're quite a hero... you've come closest to doing what most here would love to do... I could probably rustle up another twenty wrens in the next half hour if you've got the time and energy.'

'Nice offer... stacks of energy, but I like to do the choosing myself. Anyway, you'd probably charge an entrance fee: know what I mean? As attractive as your offer is, Pam darling, I'm actually here on business. I've a package for 2nd Officer Sherwood. I must deliver it to her hand and have it signed for.'

'She's out of the office... be back in about ten minutes, I guess.'

'She's back now,' said Anne, who had been listening to the entire conversation from the doorway. She turned and went into the office shared with Joss.

'I'd better do it officially... let her know you're here.' Pam whispered, 'She doesn't look very happy does she?'

Joss was transfixed; mesmerised by the tableau before her. Anne stood by her desk in her immaculate dark blue uniform, beautiful, severe. Sims stood facing her a couple of yards away, both were looking into each other's intensely defiant eyes, just looking - not a word uttered. For Joss, time had ceased all operations, she felt as if she was floating. Good God! she thought, so this is what it's all about... why she's been so ratty lately - she's in love, and either doesn't know it, or can't admit it.

Time slowly recovered its composure and direction: Sims moved forward, handed Anne the package and the receipt form, and pointed to where she should sign. She signed. They resumed looking at each other, hardly blinking. He broke the stalemate. 'Thank you, and good morning, ma'am.' She did not reply. Passing Joss, he said, 'Good morning, ma'am.' Both heard him say; *Bye, sexy*, to Wren Pam Somerton as he left the building.

'Gosh! E... LEC... TRIC,' said Joss, for a moment I thought you two were going to fuse the lights.'

The spell was broken by Pam coming in to the office, going to the window, and watching Sims walk away down the road to the docks. As he passed the security office, she said, 'I wonder if he'll shoot him properly this time?'

'Shoot who?' asked Joss.

'Haven't you heard, ma'am, he threatened to shoot an RPO this morning - isn't he lovely... *so* sexy.'

'Thank you, Wren Somerton,' said Anne.

With Pam Somerton safely out of earshot, Joss said, 'What on earth was *that* all about?'

'I don't know what you mean, what was *what* all about?' Anne left the room.

For Joss, the remainder of the day was an anti-climax. The static that those two people had generated just looking at each other had left her emotionally numbed. What's going to happen if they ever touch? she thought. They'll probably ignite!... She could see the headlines: immolation of wren officer and stoker after accidental touching... weeping friend of consumed wren, said; all he did was to hand her a pen, their fingers briefly met, and... bang... all the lights went out.

Part Frog.

*

Commodore Sherwood, away from Hell Head House for three days, returned looking haggard. Anne waited for him in his study, 'Big problems?' she asked.

'Yes, but not with work - they're resolved, in the short term at least. Anne, we need to talk,' he pointed to an armchair. 'Sit down.' He waited until she was seated, 'Anne, at no time I can recall, have you made me feel uncomfortable in company before. Do you mind telling me... spelling out for me... what it is you've got against Sims?'

She had not expected this and put the absence of his usual greeting kiss down to tiredness: his question threw her off balance.

She blustered, 'He's a show-off. He risked our boat just to impress that... that French hermaphrodite.'

'I didn't let him risk anything. You must get this straight, there's a huge gap between being a show-off and being competent and confident. Over the years I've had hundreds of men under my command... I know the difference.'

'That's just *it*, under your command,' she exclaimed, 'I don't agree with the *Alice Protocol*, I can't stand the idea of him calling you by your first name. Ever since he towed us back to *Dolphin* he seems to think he's in command of *you*. I think he lacks respect.'

'Rubbish, he dropped the protocol as soon as we were entering the dock, and even when the protocol's in force, Sims never takes liberties with me. Anne, get used to the idea, I respect the man, and the more I know him, the more I like him. That day, for the first time in my life,

I was ashamed of you, and, I hate to say this, I think your mother would have been too. Has it never crossed your mind that I might not want to be the perpetual commander, that I might want to relax now and again, to go sailing with people who genuinely like the past-time... people who aren't simply looking for a quick leg-up the promotion ladder?... and just for the record, Anne, the day he towed us in, he *was* in charge... the launch was his responsibility, we were adrift... he did a damn good job... through him we avoided not a little embarrassment... commodores should not be seen to be adrift.'

Her father had never spoken to her like this before, and she knew he would not have done so unless he believed it needed to be said. It was however, the echo of her own situation that hit Anne as hard as anything: "looking for a quick leg up the promotion ladder", he'd said. She felt ashamed and turned away. Sims had spotted it: she hadn't noticed. Her father had been enjoying himself, he *had* been relaxed. Perhaps Sims was right, maybe she was an unremitting bitch and a selfish cow.

Although she made no noise, Commodore Sherwood knew she was crying. He stood up and gave her a long hug. 'Something's not altogether right, is it?'

'What would you like me to do about the other day?'

'Look to your conscience, you must decide that for yourself. Now go and get yourself ready. Fox-Eastleigh will take dinner with us tonight.'

'Can I invite Joss too?'

'Of course. James and myself will have to talk a little business at some time... good idea... give her a call... he might be able to give her a lift.'

She phoned, 'Joss, I've never needed to see you more

than I do now... can you come to dinner tonight?... Father will get Lieutenant Fox-Eastleigh to give you a lift. What do you say? Please come.'

'With *James Fox-Eastleigh in his car* - wild horses Anne, wild horses... but what on earth's the matter?'

'Later.'

She entered Hell Head House on the arm of Lieutenant James Fox-Eastleigh. How do you do it? Anne thought, does he not realise his entire future is already mapped out for him?... how *do* you do it, Joss?

As she walked past, she slightly raised her eyebrows and gave Anne a smile that conveyed all; see? it's easy... look what I've hooked myself.

After supper the commodore and James took their leave, and themselves into the library. Anne laid the facts down, clearly and fully. She told of the regatta, how badly she'd behaved, the argument, and what her father had said to her earlier that evening. Joss listened closely, she knew what the problem was. She had known Anne long enough to know that it would have to be Anne who found the answer. Nevertheless, a little nudging may be necessary, she thought.

'Anne, I saw what happened the other day... I think you're going to have to ask yourself some serious questions... you're going to have to be honest with yourself. I think you feel more for him than you admit... and I'm *not* talking about anger. When you go to bed tonight, you'll be on your own... it will be quiet. Use the time... the moment, to think seriously about his demeanour and his behaviour since you've known him. See if your criticisms hold water... because frankly, I don't think they do. I accept you've had more contact with him than I have, but, from what I've seen of him, he seems lovely, intelligent, and he's funny... if he called you what you say he did, you certainly can't accuse him of wanting to use you as a career springboard... and as Wren Somerton says; he's *so* sexy.' Joss studied her; she thought of their confrontation. It sent a shiver down her spine. 'Tell me what you felt when you first saw him.'

'*No!*'

'Okay, then do this; when you're on your own tonight, ask yourself how you would feel if at that moment he walked into your room. And, Anne, answer the question, *honestly.*'

She could not sleep. She got up, sat in the cushioned window seat and looked out over the moonlit Solent. To the south, the lights of Ryde and Fishbourne were ebbing and flowing in the light mist. She thought of Joss's words; "I think you're going to have to ask yourself some serious questions... you're going to have to be honest with yourself. I think you feel more for him than you admit... and I'm not talking about anger". She was right of course. If Joss had not been present in the office that morning, Anne doubted that she could have maintained her silence when he stood opposite her. It had been a last ditch attempt to persuade herself and Sims that there would never be a meeting place for them.

Anne knew that nature had defeated her. It was time for her to accept what she had known for a long time. What she felt for him was far more than strong attraction. She was now in no doubt that she was in love with him; deeply and had been from the first time she'd seen him. She was no longer prepared to pretend otherwise to anyone: least of all to him.

She asked herself, how could he ever think well of her after the awful things she had said and done? Her only hope was that he was as good as Joss and her father thought. She would try to make amends: *how*, was going to be the problem. Anne sat with her feet on the cushions, her head resting on her knees, 'I wish he were here right now.'

***

Chapter Twelve
The Hairy Cupid.

'Come in Reeves.'

'Good morning, sir. I was wondering if Admiral Jessop shed any light on *Dolphin's* snooping intelligence officer?'

Maitland cautious, 'Afraid not... at least, nothing certain. He suggested it was probably MI5... some investigation necessary he said.' His navigation always suspect, Maitland wandered off course, 'You know, Reeves, while we were talking, he referred to you as a pikelet in a carp pond.'

'Is that good or bad, sir?'

'For sluggish carp, no... ...for NID, yes.'

Sims had grown into the job, summer was close, and with it a decreased desire to return to the Far East and its flesh pots. 'So he didn't threaten to sack me, then.'

'Why on earth should you think that?'

'I wasn't sure how he meant me being a pikelet... not a saying I've come across.'

'It was the monks, you know. They put a young pike in the pond to keep the carp on the move... it would nibble their fins. It stopped them resting on the bottom. If carp did that, it tended to make their flesh taste muddy.'

Good God, where's he off to now? thought Sims. 'I shouldn't think there's anything worse than muddy carp... there would have been hell to pay if they were dished up earthy fish on Fridays... monks knew how to look after themselves, didn't they, sir?.. good thing they never tasted British Rail coffee.'

'Quite, quite. Beetroot can taste earthy too,' Maitland said, absent mindedly.

He often veered off track like this. Sims was getting used to it - he enjoyed these odd diversions that seemed to creep into conversations with his boss. He steered him back on course. 'Is there anything *we* can do, sir?'

'Yes... no... ...where were we?... Ah yes, Reeves, I'm not sure there is at the moment... best wait for Admiral Jessop.'

Our man was in an impatient mood. He had been doing exactly what Billy had asked; keeping his eyes open. He felt unannounced security agents on NID's patch warranted a faster response and, as nice as he was, he was not sure that Maitland was always up-to-speed. Fuck this, he thought, I'm going to do a bit of carp nibbling.

'Anything for *Dolphin* today, sir?'

'No, not today, Reeves.'

'Can I go anyway?'

'I suppose so... would you have a particular reason?'

'Me being a young pike, I thought I'd go and stir up a few carp.'

'Quite, Quite.'

Sims turned for the door.

'Reeves!'

'Sir?'

'Perhaps it's best not to shoot anyone today.'

'Roger... I only threatened him, sir.'

'Quite,' Maitland said, thoughtfully. He had still not resolved whether one said *roger* in the navy. 'Quite.'

The Hairy Cupid.

Sims stalked into *Dolphin's* security office, he was in an awkward mood. Hackles rose. He stood coolly looking at those RPOs present. Like air round a high tension cable on a misty morning, the atmosphere crackled. Hostility quickly reached critical mass. They knew who he was; he had form - they suspected he was more than a stoker courier. He thought; Oh my, this is fun... boot on the other foot... come and get it you bastards, this is wind-up time. He moved his hand and rested it close to his holster. His message was clear: one move, and you're all dead meat... oh fuck, this is such fun. 'Where's the RPO who was stupid enough to challenge me the other day?'

'He's been drafted off the base.'

Bugger, he thought. Sims slowly surveyed them, and in a clear voice, and as though he was the instigator of the removal, said, 'That was quick. So, he's gone already... *listen*! *Dolphin*'s a cushy number for you lot. If you want to stay here, toe-the-line, or I'll have you transferred like your dick-head mate. So, don't fuck me about. Now, I want answers to three questions I have about the intelligence bloke. One; what intelligence service was he from? Two; what was his name? Three; what did he look like? We'll start with you,' Sims said, pointing at the RPO who'd just answered him.

'MI5... didn't get his name... medium build, moustache... ginger... posh accent,' he answered, stiffly.

'Was he armed?'

'Yes. Don't know what make or model.'

'Anybody got anything else to add to that?'

They shook their heads.

'Remember what I said about toeing-the-line.' He left

the office.

Sims was happy, it was a lovely day. A peach of a posting... giving RPOs the shits was a perk Billy never mentioned... what a good job this is... RPOs, fuck 'em. He hummed to himself as he walked down to his launch. What a lovely job this is...

Maitland removed his glasses, 'How were the carp, Reeves?'
'Muddy and forthcoming, sir. Our man was from MI5. But I dare say Admiral Jessop knows that already.'
'Oh, well done, Reeves. Even so, you'd better go and give him your report face to face.'

At Tunworth House they were waiting, 'Come in, Reeves,' said Billy. 'Hungry, Reeves?'
'I'm a stoker, sir.'
Billy smiled, 'Yes, of course. You're hungry, then.'
He gave his report, Billy asked him to wait in the hall while he conferred with Stinton. Called back in, Billy asked if he had seen this agent before. He replied he hadn't ever seen him, he was merely repeating what he had been told. Billy asked whether he thought the RPO was genuine, whether he could have been another MI5 agent, and what did the RPO look like. Sims said, 'Pale, sir.' Billy laughed. He was told he had done well. He saluted and drove back to Portsmouth.

'Pale, Stinton, pale,' Billy laughed again. 'Hanging him out as bait might just be wasting his talents.'
'It's possible, sir. Do you think it was Throagh?'
'I certainly do. MI5 on our patch again. We'll get that

bastard, Stinton. Mark my words. We'll draw him out into the open and *gut* him.'

*

It was a fine morning and the windows were wide open. Anne listened to every voice that came anywhere near her office. If Sims came in, she would make any excuse to speak to him. She had given Joss a kiss when she arrived and thanked her. She, Joss, asked, 'Did you come to a conclusion?'

'Yes.'

At around 1030 they heard Sims' voice down the road. 'No deal, girls,' he said.

'Oh come on, Roy. We'll even supply the ciggies.' The two wrens nudged each other, laughed, and walked on their way. They looked back at him, waved, called something carried away on the breeze, and laughed again.

He strolled into reception: dumped a package on the counter. 'Hi gorgeous... ordinary post, Ben's busy, no signing necessary.'

'I've got a question for you, Roy.'

'Okay, as long as it's not about my inside leg measurement, which for security reasons I have to keep under wraps, fire away.'

'I've said it before... you're a dirty bugger, Roy. Anyway, your oppo Ben... what's he like?'

'Good guy... I like him... why?'

'Married?'

'No.'

'Girlfriend?'

'No... not permanent. Out with it, Pam, do you want to get to know him better?... if you like, I'll perform the introductions... I'll be really diplomatic... leave it to me'

'He doesn't come here that often... he seems nice.'

'I just told you... he's a really good guy.'

'I haven't got anyone permanent either... he doesn't carry a side arm... I guess I can fantasize about the gun though, can't I?'

'Leave it to me... I'm good at this sort of thing. I'll try and bring him over this afternoon.' He left before Anne had a chance to speak to him.

'Got anything on this afternoon?'

'No. Why?'

'Fancy a trip?... I'll clear it with Maitland.'

'Yeh... okay... where we going?'

'Dolphin.'

'Why?'

'Special mission... need to know basis only.'

Anne saw him in deep conversation with Ben walking up to her office. What Sims was explaining required his arms to flail rapidly: Ben's response similar.

'Hi, Pam... this is Ben Whitley... Ben, this is Pam Somerton, she keeps asking deeply personal questions about you... on the quiet, you lucky thing you, I think she's after your body... ask her for a date... I'll wait outside.'

Sims left the office, leaving the couple at a loss and staring dumbly at each other for a moment.

Pam broke the apparent impasse, 'Nice and diplomatically done, Roy,' she called after him.

'He can be a bit brutal,' said Ben.

'You hear about the RPO?'

'Who hasn't?' This was Ben's break, 'If he's that violent, I'd hate to upset him... would you like a date?'

'Yes.'

'I'll check my roster, and be in touch then... might have to use the hairy cupid outside.'

'Good.'

Anne watched Sims through the window while he waited. She was about to call him when the phone on her desk rang. By the time she'd rid herself of the person on the other end, he and Ben, conversation resumed, arms flailing, walked back to the launch.

'Smooth git... I heard what you said.'

'I owe you half a tot... I've fancied her for yonks.'

'She's only worth half, then? I'll tell her.'

'You drive a hard bargain mate... better be worth it... Want to buy my fanny boat card?... advertising may no longer be necessary,' he said, rubbing his hands together. 'She's bloody gorgeous. Did you see the way she looked at me?'

'Latent astigmatism... I feel sorry for her.'

'Fuck off... *me;* catch of the century.'

*

Sims was at work preparing *Alice* for sea when the commodore, Anne, Joss and James Fox-Eastleigh arrived. He had already hoisted the jibs - they flapped loosely in the light early morning air that seemed still only half awake and unsure of which way it should blow.

Anne looked down at him from the jetty, she felt nervous. Commodore Sherwood, first on board, took Sims to one side, 'That RPO has been removed from the base, it's not the first time he'd overstepped the mark. I've given instructions that his replacement, or indeed any of the regulatory branch, are not to bother you again.'

'I heard that he'd gone, sir.'

'I have another problem: I'm not able to get away until this afternoon - you're in charge... skipper once more. Anne knows the way to Hell Head and into the harbour like the back of her hand - she'll be your navigator.' Then he turned to the others. 'Sims is to be skipper... Anne you're navigator. One more thing; on board *Alice* we have a protocol - first name terms only. I'll try and catch up with you all this afternoon.' The commodore turned back to Sims, and the two men shook hands. 'Okay, she's all yours - enjoy yourself, and the rest of you too.'

'We'll take her out under steam - the air's too uncertain... it'll improve further out. There's a bit of sea mist - the sun will burn that off fairly soon.' He started the engine. 'Let go for'ard, let go aft, fenders in.' Throttles opened gently; the thump of *Alice's* engine throbbed and echoed off the dock-side walls as she moved smoothly into the estuary.

Commodore Sherwood walked to the top of the sea wall feeling guilty that he'd lied about being not being able to get away. He thought it worth the risk putting Anne to work alongside Sims. With Joss and Fox-Eastleigh on board, she might be better behaved. He'd been hard on her the other night - she'd taken it badly - he didn't want to do it again... it *had to be* worth the risk.

He heard the engine stop, saw the main sail being hoisted, then the mizzen. He clearly heard Sims call for adjustments to the set of the sails. Gradually the sails filled and *Alice, his Alice,* was on the move again. Watching her gently sliding through the water, he, uncertain of his feelings. He'd never seen her under full sail from a distance before and was caught by an uneasy feeling both *Alice* and Anne were leaving home.

He did not expect a reply. 'Okay, Anne, which way?' he asked.

'That buoy ahead marks *Gilkicker Point.* When we reach it, follow the coast up past Lee on Solent - it's not far... I'll let you know when to turn onto the harbour tack... anyone fancy coffee?'

She spoke! he thought, and, as if to compound his surprise, she added, 'How do you take yours, Sims?'

'Black... just black, thank you.'

'I'll give you a hand,' said Joss, following her down into the galley.

'He doesn't seem the sort to blow an RPO's head off, does he?'

'Perhaps we don't know him well enough, *you* didn't see him bash those two men in Cowes. *God*, it was impressive.'

They took the coffee up to the cockpit, Anne handed Sims his first; a moment when they exchanged the briefest of glances. Sims thought he saw a softer look in her eyes. Perhaps a trick of the light; no, most likely just a trick, he thought.

The four of them sat quietly. Most of the light patches of mist had been stirred by the breeze and burned off by the strengthening sun. It was soon warm enough for Sims to strip off his jersey and Tee shirt. Anne, leaning back, sat with her eyes closed, her face into the sun, the light airs ruffling the curls around her ears. Watching her, he thought, she is so bloody gorgeous. Joss was looking at Sims and thinking, Anne Sherwood, if only you understood your feelings as well as he does his, you might both get on with it - perhaps you need a good shove. The arrival of a slow swell from a distant tanker broke *Alice's* equilibrium. She rolled lightly enough to rouse Anne and make her sit up. He quickly looked away.

James Fox-Eastleigh, oblivious to the tension felt by Anne, Sims and Joss, had already fallen in love with this old boat and went forward to the bows inspecting the ropes, rigging, and bronze fittings worn smooth from years of use - it was the first time he had sailed in *Alice* - *Mabel* had a rival for his affection.

Anne collected the cups and went below. Joss took the opportunity of being alone with Sims to lean over and whisper a shove, 'Anne... she's very beautiful isn't she?'

He nodded. 'Yeah, really gorgeous.'

Back into the cockpit Anne sat close to him. Joss stretched and said, 'Sims, I have a question. You're always doing things to this sail, or that rope, tweaking... adjusting this or that, and sometimes only by a small amount, how do you know if you're making a difference?'

'Have you sailed much before?'

'Only small stuff... dinghies and the like.'

'Doesn't matter really, same principles rule.'

He was silent for a while. Anne wondered if he was going to answer. Then, suddenly, he pushed the tiller hard over, brought *Alice* into wind - her sails gently flapping. 'Joss, put one hand on the tiller and the other on the gunwale. Shut your eyes and concentrate on what you feel when I get her moving again. Feel *Alice* through your hands, your feet and, if I may be so indelicate, through the seat of your knickers.'

Anne smiled, Joss laughed.

Sims steered away from the wind and *Alice* was under way once more. 'What do you feel as she speeds up?'

She concentrated; she felt the rigging tauten. 'It's just as though she's waking up... stretching,' she said, smiling.

'Exactly... stretching, I like that, a good way of putting it. We'll do it again,' he leaned towards her and quietly said, 'This time, put both your hands in your lap, keep your eyes closed and listen carefully. Listen to the sound of the water under *Alice* - listen to her feelings. See if you can hear her chuckle, then as we speed up; giggle - if there were more wind she'd laugh. Make any change, and she'll talk to you sweetly; she'll tell you how she feels.'

Joss, completely enmeshed by the quiet intensity of Sims' explanation, his understanding and by the magic of what her senses were telling her, exclaimed, 'Oh yes... I know now... I can hear exactly what you mean... *listen!* She really can talk... do you think she's alive?'

'Well, I guess so... I suppose she must be if she can laugh,' he replied, amused that she had got so carried away.

Anne had moved closer to listen to him talking to Joss. A shiver ran down her back, it had been such a beautiful and sensitive way of getting the point over. She had been watching them closely and did not want to break the spell they had been under. They needed to change course. She leaned towards him and put her hand on his arm. 'Sims, it's a moment I hate to break, that was so lovely, but it's time we headed for Hell Head Harbour.'

Chance given, he took the opportunity to look directly at her. 'How about you taking her in?'

She smiled at him. 'Do you trust me?'

Sims nodded. 'Yeah, of course I do. I saw how you handled her on the regatta... you won't have any problems'... God, she gets even more gorgeous when she smiles... and not for the first time, he thought, I'm not sure I can handle this.

Her behaviour during the race was the last thing she wanted to be reminded of. She would like nothing better than to wrap it up and jettison it overboard with a large weight attached. 'Thank you... I think you're just being kind.'

'No way... really, I'm not. I told you then, and I meant it... you did such an impressive lap... much better than mine, or your dad's. Come on, it was one of those days, we didn't exactly see eye to eye... if it had been rubbish, I think I might have told you so,' he said, smiling.

'I can believe *that!*' she said, lightly slap-pushing his shoulder.

Joss saw and heard the exchange. That's it. That's definitely it. They're going to get a damn good shove.

Anne frowned. 'Sims, if I take her in, then you must stay close in case I get into trouble, it might be a bit busy in there. Father usually does this bit.'

'Yes, ma'am, of course, ma'am.'

The memory surfaced, Anne looked horrified. She

took hold of his hand. 'Sims, please don't call me ma'am... ...my name is Anne. Please, *always* call me Anne.'

How much preparation does one need for a moment like this? - never enough it seemed. She had floored him, he floundered then recovered, 'Okay, I'll do that, I'll stay right where I am... but you won't need me, you'll do fine.'

She caught hold of his arm again. 'Nevertheless, I want you to stay close by.'

Joss thought; all these messages: trust me; stay close: close by - they're not even coded. For God's sake, Anne, why don't you just jump on him?

He needed somewhere with firmer footing, 'Best I do a safety check on the engine.'

'Yes please - when do you think we ought to drop the sails?'

'The breeze will get lighter as we get closer, you could almost sail straight in, and drop them at the last moment... it would be impressive... what do you think?'

'Now he's saying "drop them at the last moment" - do they know what they both sound like?'

'If we do, promise you won't call *me* a show off,' Anne said, smiling.

'No way, not if it's crawling with Frenchies... just to get my own back you understand.'

'In that case I think we do it. God forbid that Marie-Claude is there.'

"I think we do it!" When is this going to end?

'James, get ready to drop the main and jibs. Sims, will you see to the mizzen?'

Commodore Sherwood peered through his binoculars as

The Hairy Cupid.

Alice approached - they're bringing her in under sail. He saw Anne at the helm and Sims alongside her - it was obvious from their gestures they were working together; looks like it was worth the risk. To side step making her more nervous than necessary, he moved to the rear of the other watchers.

'There will be a space reserved for us at the quay side,' Anne said. A few yards outside the harbour mouth she called for the engine to be started and the sails dropped. *Alice* slid inside the harbour. 'God! they haven't left us much room.'

'Easy, Anne, we'll do it together. Remember, her stern will kick to starboard when we throw the engine astern, so go in very slowly at a shallow angle to the quay - bows first... when we're a few feet off, throw the tiller to port... her bows will swing out and her stern in. Then, stuff the engine full astern and we'll stop square on.'

'Okay, I've got that... only tell me if I'm getting it wrong... Joss, out fenders and ready with the bow rope.'

Alice slowly moved towards the harbour wall, he could feel the tension in Anne.

'Keep going as you are, you're doing fine, my love,' he said, not really paying attention to what he was uttering.

Anne heard, but did not mind at all.

She pushed the tiller hard over to port. 'Full astern,' she ordered, then called, 'Stop.'

Alice had been brought alongside just so, not a bump or a scrape. Her father leapt aboard and threw his arms round her. 'Anne darling, that was masterful, I'm so proud of you. Sims could not have done better.'

'Sims couldn't have done it at all... that's why I conned

her into doing it.'

Turning to Sims, she said, smiling, 'He deserves a little bit of the credit - but only a tiny little bit.'

Joss came up to them and gave Anne a kiss. 'Well done, well done. You two work *so* well together.'

And so started Joss's campaign of unification.

'Did she behave herself?

'Impeccable, *Alice* always behaves herself, sir.'

'You know very well to whom I'm referring, young man.'

'Ah, top form, she's a damn good sailor, there's nothing she lacks in open water... perhaps a bit more confidence coming alongside... but that's all, sir... damn fine sailor.'

'You didn't think it a risk letting her bring *Alice* in?'

'Not one bit, sir. You saw how well she managed.'

'Sims, why are you calling me, sir?'

'I often do... it's a bit of a habit... difficult one to shed. In this case though, there are a couple of officers over there in civvies. I recognise them from *Dolphin,* sir.'

'Thank you for letting her do it, lad.'

'Hands on experience... I haven't forgotten Cowes the other week... it's the best way to learn... sometimes the only way, sir.'

Anne used any excuse to be near him. She introduced all the people she knew, and then people she didn't know. She got him to answer questions she was quite capable of answering herself. When she was running short of excuses, she reintroduced the people he'd already met. Sims was puzzled by her behaviour; pleased, though puzzled. She took hold of his arm and led him away from three teenage girls who had cornered him. 'Excuse me,' she had fibbed, 'Sims, that group over there are particularly interested in the best way for coming alongside in a crowded harbour. I'm sorry,' she said to the girls, 'he's in short supply today.'

'What about tomorrow?' the eldest of them asked.

'He's busy,' Anne replied, dragging him off to the fictitious group. This is how Joss would handle him, she thought to herself.

Bemused and happy, Sims looked at Anne. During introductions and reintroductions she held onto his arm longer than was strictly necessary - he was happy about that too.

Joss had laughingly called her shameless. Anne did not care a jot. If being shameless was what it was going to take, then so be it - shameless she would be.

She constantly watched him, took in his every detail. He was at ease talking with complete strangers, and they it seemed were at ease with him - "there's a huge gap between being a show-off and being competent and confident", her father had said. He was so right, she acknowledged. Sims was confident, relaxed, and this had an enviable way of putting people at their ease.

The day wore on and the visitors thinned. Commodore Sherwood gave orders to prepare to return to *Dolphin*. Anne who, that day, had repeated bouts of the stomach pain she'd suffered on and off for the past week, reluctantly decided to return home. Joss gave James a kiss, and went with her.

Another shove needed. The question needed to be broached and this was the time to raise it. In the lane to Hell Head House, Joss stopped Anne and asked her, 'Do you love Sims?... are you in love with him? Now, if you say no, or don't answer, I'll tell him you don't... do you want me to tell him no?'

'That's unfair... that's blackmail.'

'No it's not, I'm not demanding money.'

'That's beside the point.'

'I mean what I say - do you or don't you?'

Anne knew she meant it.

'Yes... I do... very much.' She turned away.

'Thank God for that. Now, what are you going to do about it? Oh, for Christ's sake don't look so miserable, this bit's supposed to be enjoyable.'

'I've every right to feel miserable... I haven't a clue what to do...'

'*Rubbish*, you were doing pretty well today, a natural. You know what to do alright... just get on and do more of it.'

'I was so awful to him at the regatta, he'd have every right to feel nothing but contempt for me. You have no idea how mean I must have appeared.'

'That is such a lot of tosh. I not only saw the way you looked at him when he had his shirt off, but I also saw the way he looked at you... you can't tell me you didn't notice!'

'I think he's just being friendly, that's all.'

'Listen to an expert... trust me, he was being much more than friendly. Put yourself in my hands. This is what you do; the next opportunity you have... *no!*... not have; *make!* say you're sorry. That's all you need to do, men can't handle apologetic women... he'll take all the blame... simple.'

'Oh that it was.'

'What on earth do you mean.'

'What will my father say?'

'I know you love your father dearly, but he's not your future, Anne. Sims is... isn't he?'

'Hope so.'

*

'Are you taking her back, sir?'

'Certainly not. I've got myself a first class skipper now, I'm going to relax, enjoy the ride... nice evening, might even have a scotch. Fancy one?'

'Normally, yes, sir... not when I'm driving - skippers should set an example.'

'Penalty of responsibility,' said the commodore, laughing, 'You'll join me, James, I know?'

'Certainly, sir... Can you manage everything on your own, Sims?' said James Fox-Eastleigh: a parody of shallow concern.

'No bother.'

The sun was getting lower in the sky, the wind freshened and the three men gave every impression they could talk about sailing for ever. 'Did you know Sims had sailed a brigantine in Hong Kong, James?'

'Too well. An american and his wife used to pick him up from the *Alacrity* in an open topped Cadillac. No one else got a look in. Come on, Sims, you never let on... how did you do it? What was your secret?'

'No secret... just charm... it's inbuilt.'

'So you're not going to give us the low-down, then?' said the commodore.

'Well, it's a long story and I'm not sure it's suitable for sensitive ears... especially when *they've* been drinking and I haven't. I shall not be pushed further.'

'What if I were to order you to?'

'I should remind you of the *Alice Alacrity Protocol*. The person on the tiller, is skipper.'

'I'll get that story out of you one day, lad,' he laughed.

'Perhaps, sir.'

It was the end of a glorious day, *Alice* with rigging singing rode the wave crests: climbed out of troughs. She made it easy for the three men to get lost in their thoughts. To different people, contentment comes in different forms. At its finest, it must be neatly tailored to fit the shape of the moment.

With James it came from discovering the delights of an old wooden boat and having been tipped helplessly upside down by someone called Joss.

To the commodore, contentment was letting someone he trusted take the strain, a glass of scotch, and his daughter behaving and looking happy once again.

For Sims, it was sailing a beautiful ketch, a fresh wind, a following sea, and a smile from a girl who hated him.

They moored *Alice* and tidied her up. The commodore more relaxed than after the regatta.

'Sir, can I sleep on board tonight? There are a couple of jobs I'd like to do on the jib sheets in the morning.'

'By all means... James, make sure Sims is victualled in *Dolphin*... on the other hand we can always put you up at Hell Head.'

'That's very kind, sir, I have to get away fairly smartly in the morning... they've given me a spot of leave, so I'm going to clear up some outstanding business I have in London.'

Later that evening He entered the noisy dining hall crowded with *Dolphin's* own staff and the crews of several submarines tied up alongside down in the docks. Pam Somerton saw him join the food queue and pointed him out to the dozen or so people at her table. After some nudging from those near her, she got up and climbed onto the stage at the end of the room. 'Can I have your attention please,' she shouted. She waited until everyone was listening. Pointing at Sims, she said, 'Ladies and gentlemen, I give you, Roy Rogers, RPO Killer, otherwise known as, LM(e) John Sims Reeves.' It seemed everybody there had heard about the incident. The uproar was instantaneous and deafening... cheering... clapping and thumping on the tables.

Pam returned to her place, Sims gave a polite bow and as the din died down there rose from her table the first lines of *'Home on the Range',* this was immediately taken up by the entire dining hall, followed quickly by *speech... speech... speech.* He loped to the front, vaulted onto the stage and raised his hand for silence. 'Thank you... thank you... friends, fellow mariners and Wren... Pam... Somerton... what can I say... other than I was simply doing my duty... I'm sure that if any of you had been placed in my position, you'd have done the same... in fact, many of you would probably have gone further, and pulled the trigger.' He waited while the whistles and shouts of approval had abated. *More... more,* they shouted. He raised his hand once again and said, 'Thank you fans... an RPO killer's lot is a busy one... you can all get knotted, I'm hungry and I want my supper.' During the applause he strode up to Pam's table. He made her stand up and gave her an immense kiss. A wren sat next to her asked, 'Sims, is it true you had time for a fag between each one?'

*

The halyards, agitated by the fresh breeze, rattled against the mast. The harbour water choppy adding more movement to *Alice Alacrity*. Though she had been along-side for only one night, Sims knew she was jittery, impatient, already fed up with being in harbour. *Alice* wanted to get out into The Solent and feel alive again. 'I know just how you feel,' he said out loud.

He sat on the foredeck concentrating on whipping a rope's end. The rattling and *Alice's* jittery movement masked Anne's footsteps.

'Hello. What are you doing there?' she said, just a little nervously.

He turned round with a start and then standing up, said, 'Oh, you know, just tidying up some bits and pieces.'

Her nerves got the better of her. 'Reeves...' Then with her hand to her mouth, correcting herself. '*God*, what am I saying... I'm so sorry, I mean, Sims.'

She looked at him for what seemed to him an age

before taking a deep breath. 'Sims, I'm really sorry for how I behaved at the regatta, and for what I said to you... ...and, and the omelette was really delicious, it really was.'

'*Oh God*... I *did* ask your father not to say anything.'

'My father is a good man. He's become a commodore because he's not scared to make decisions; very good ones. Look, he's been the skipper of many subs, he knows the value of a top crew. He's of the opinion we'll make a good one, and we should stick together. I agree with him.'

They stood facing each other. After a considerable and tense pause, she said, 'If you must know, he was very angry with me. He said, I should have more respect... he said, I should respect a person's character; his talent; his use of that talent; not his class. And, for the record, he didn't ask me to come and apologise to you. He would always leave that sort of decision to me. I came of my own desire, Sims.' She looked straight into his eyes. 'I am *truly* sorry for how I behaved and for what I said, and I hope you will forgive me. I *mean* it. I wanted to tell you that yesterday, but I couldn't get you alone.'

If previously Sims had floundered, he was now totally out of his depth; drowning. Anne had completely wrong-footed him. What he did next, he did without thinking. It was a spontaneous reaction that took them both a little by surprise. He stepped forward, took hold of her two hands, squeezed them and gave her a kiss on each cheek. 'That's how they do it in France... it's really nice of you to say that. Thank you.' He smiled at her. 'Want to know something? For one nasty moment the other evening I thought you might grab a knife and stab me... the look on your face... memorable.'

Anne slapped him on the forearm. 'And, do *you* want to know something? Looks don't deceive, you don't know how close I came.'

'I guess I shouldn't have spoken to you the way I did, either... couldn't stop myself. Thanks for not fetching the law.'

'You don't think I would have done that, do you?'

He shrugged. 'You looked pretty wild... perhaps better to say, savage.'

She giggled, 'Well, I couldn't have ever done so, and that's that.'

'Why?'

She tinted up a couple of notches and looked away.

The watershed had been made, both relieved they could now talk as two normal friends ought to be able: except that they weren't ordinary friends. Elation immediately followed relief, they both knew what they felt for the other, though neither of them had a clue as to how and when it would be told.

'Fancy a cuppa?' was the sum total Sims' love fuddled brain could think of producing.

'Just in case we'd still be on speaking terms, I asked Mrs Calver to make some sandwiches. I think a cuppa would be the perfect thing to go with them.'

'Who's Mrs Calver?' Sims asked, thinking she might run a cafe nearby.

'She's our cook and housekeeper. She's been with us for ages; just about as long as I can remember. I told her you were a stoker, and she said; "In that case, I'll make them two inches thick and fill them with fried eggs and crispy bacon." As you can see, she was true to her word.' Anne hauled out what looked like two cottage loaves that had been sliced down the middle and filled with a dozen eggs and a small pig.

'Look at them,' Sims exclaimed. 'That woman is no cook come housekeeper - she is a mind reader of enormous ability... she is, let me tell you: clairvoyant. The woman must be given an immediate pay rise. See to it immediately you get home. You might also tell her I'm deeply in love with her.'

Anne laughed. Sims: the first boy friend to make her do so.

Happy and relaxing in each other's company they sat sheltering from the breeze in the stern cockpit with their sandwiches - proper crispy bacon sarnies cannot be eaten delicately; they require munching. Anne matched Sims' gusto.

'I heard about your speech last night. Seems it almost caused a riot. I also heard you gave Pam a kiss... not allowed you know.'

'What, causing a riot or the kiss?'

'I'll let you off the riot... the kiss, out of bounds.'

'I just gave you two. You never said a word.'

'That's different.'

'Anyway... she set me up, she deserved it.'

'From what I hear, she certainly *enjoyed* it.'

'I like to keep my hand in....' he leaned over, ...do you mind if I turn the radio on for a moment... there's something I want to hear.' He turned on his *Roberts* portable radio; a beautiful contralto was singing.

'Oh, that's Kathleen Ferrier, my mother loved her.'

They sat silent, and listened until the very end.

'What a voice... Jesus, what a voice... where does something like that spring from? She came from a working class family, yet worked with the world's best. She not only had an incredible talent, but had the necessary drive, confidence to express it and perform it as well... where the hell *does* that spring from?'

Her mind took a quick pace backward. It was the first time she had come face to face with this aspect of Sims and his love of music.' It stopped her dead. Surprised, she could only ask, 'What was she singing? I'm sure we've got it at home.'

'Brahms; Alto Rhapsody... I'll buy that recording one day... do you like classical?'

'Yes, very much. We've still got my mother's collection.'

'Do you miss her?'

'Yes... every day.'

The subject needed changing. 'I think we would have been better placed if I had done what you asked, and as soon as you asked me to,' she said, looking directly at him.

'No, I don't think so, the wind backed and I went too far - it wasn't your fault. Look Anne, let's dump all that behind us... how about it?'

'Oh God yes, I wish it were chalk on blackboard... I'd like to wipe it clean forever. Sims, I'm going to have to go soon. Next time we're on board will you show me a few knots and splices and things? You're not the only one that wants *Alice* to be the most beautiful boat on The Solent.'

'Sure, absolutely no problem, I'll bring my father's old seamanship manual for you to look at. It's a 1926 version, completely unfathomable - it has these wonderful, and completely, bonkers sayings like: "worm and parcel with the lay, and serve the rope the other way". I never did discover what they meant by that. I bet there are hundreds of retired matelots still scratching their heads over that one. And, did you know, apparently, a *marline spike hitch* is preferable to a *catspaw* because it never jams... talk about saying the bleedin' obvious... well, I mean, everybody knows that don't they? It goes on: "it is formed," and I remember this because it was the answer to an exam question; "it is formed by the standing part picked through a loop laid over it, so that the spike lays under the standing part and over the sides of the loop." Jesus Christ, Anne, what can *anyone* make of that? Anyway, I'll bring it; have a good read, and when you start to feel faint, I'll interpret some of the instructions. My gran who did a lot of knitting gave me the complete low-down. She said she couldn't see what the problem was - it was a piece of gateau... thank God we've got an army.'

James had told her and her father about Sims' story telling, and how often he was more than guilty of embellishing the facts. Good things and even Sims' stories must come to an end; she had to leave. She was also feeling a little unwell.

'I was told you don't always tell the whole truth.'

'A malicious rumour... probably spread by the pope again, tsk, tsk... never lets up does he? Beat the bloke at three card brag... will he forgive me? Not on your life.

I even went to confession. You know what that bugger said? He reckoned absolution's not possible for stokers and card cheats.'

'Is that true?'

'Every word.'

She laughed again and slapped him. 'I must go, I'm already late.'

'Do you mind giving Mrs Calver a message from me?'

'Of course not. What is it?'

'First thank her... and then ask her if she'll marry me.'

'She's sixty three you know, and you've *not* been introduced.'

'Age doesn't come into it: just remember to tell her I love her, and her sarnies, deeply.'

He watched her as she stepped on to the jetty and started to walk away. Lovely legs, he thought. During the next few yards she turned round and waved to him several times. He smiled at her and nodded. She had gone about one hundred yards: he noticed her hesitate. After a few moments, holding her side, she moved on.

He cleared the deck of the work he'd been doing, locked the cabin and checked *Alice Alacrity's* mooring ropes. He walked the few yards along the pontoon to his launch, untied her, jumped in, started the engines, cruised out of *Dolphin's* harbour and headed back to the Seamanship School. She's just being friendly, he thought, though I reckon the odds of an improved outcome, may have shifted a bit in my favour.

Feeling quite queasy, Anne walked on. She dismissed the idea the cause was the sandwiches. Although they were a bit greasy, she wasn't a fussy eater, nor did she habitually suffer from an upset stomach. Forgotten while with Sims, the occasional stabbing pain she'd had in the left side of her abdomen had returned and was now moving to the right side and intensifying second by second. She felt less in control, more ill by the moment. Overcome, she sat down by the side of the road, groaned and passed out.

***

Chapter Thirteen
A Fresh Identity for Bear Bait.

It was a busy few days. When time and circumstance allowed, Sims visited his two properties - he visited both the agents that managed them, and his tenants. He kept a very small apartment in one, and a large room in the other in which he stored all his treasured possessions. There were a few pieces of antique French and English furniture from his parent's and grand parent's houses. He had carefully packed away old porcelain - which included a pair of beautiful Sevres vases his grandmother had inherited, a very old Worcester Sparrow Beak Jug, and a superb, complete Caughley tea service that his mother and father had collected during the early years of their marriage. There were boxes full of books. Sims had catalogued the lot - he could lay his hands on any he wished. Among all these things he treasured, he valued most the things they had touched and played - their violins.

After his duties as landlord complete, culture took over. In the day time, every available opportunity was given over to visiting as many art galleries and museums as could be fitted in. In the evenings: concerts his indulgence; especially opera. It was always a tiring, satisfying time.

A Fresh Identity for Bear Bait.

On Thursday, he found his father's seamanship manual he'd promised to show Anne. He bought a ticket for a Saturday evening performance at Covent Garden, and returned to Pompey; there were things he needed to clear up there as well. Friday or Saturday, he would return.

*

Sims took an early train back to London. He left his carriage and walking down the platform, behind him, he heard the opening lines to *Home on the Range.* He turned round to see Pam and Ben walking towards him, arm in arm.

'Dirty week-end?'

'I should be so lucky,' said Ben.

'Actually, we're going to visit my parents,' said Pam, glaring at both of them.

'Fancy a coffee, or are you in a rush?'

'Plenty of time,' Ben replied.

Pam was away from the table, Sims said, 'Visiting mum and dad already?... things going a pace, then.'

'Yeh... she's a cracking girl... well worth the tot... her mum's birthday.'

Pam sat down and took a sip of coffee. 'It's so good to get away.'

'Would you like a bite of something?' Ben asked her.

'No thanks, love... what a week,' she sighed.

'She's been flat-out... her boss's in Haslar hospital... really bad... peritonitis.'

'Which boss?' asked Sims, standing up. 'Who?'

'Sherwood - 2nd Officer Sherwood,' said Pam.

'Peritonitis; Christ! No! I've got to go,' He slapped Ben

on the shoulder, gave Pam a kiss, and hurried out of the cafe.

'What's got into him?' asked Ben.

'Can't be Sherwood, *can* it?... she hates him.'

*

'I've come to visit 2nd Officer Anne Sherwood, can you tell me where I might find her?' Sims asked the nurse at the reception desk of Haslar Naval Hospital.

'Just a minute, I'll check for you - Sherwood... Sherwood.' The nurse muttered as she ran her fingers down the register of patients. 'Here we are. We have over 400 in at the moment... only one Sherwood. Are you a relative?'

'A sailing friend.'

'And your name, sir?'

'John Sims Reeves,' he replied deciding it better not to reveal his stokerdom.

'I'll have to clear it with the ward sister first. Would you care to sit over there?'

A brief talk on the phone, she called to Sims, 'Yes. That's okay, report to Sister Freeman on ward A3. Go to the end of this corridor and then follow the signs.'

'Would you be Sister Freeman?'

'Yes, that's me,' she said, surveying him; giving him more than a quick once-over. 'Hmm, and I bet you're the gentleman looking for 2nd Officer Sherwood?'

'Yes,' he said, smiling, never having thought of himself as a gentleman. 'Tell me, is it all right if she eats Belgian chocolates?' Sims showed her a Harrods bag and the package within.

'Yes of course, if she doesn't fancy them, I'll have the nurses form a line to help her out. I'll pull rank and be at the head of the queue... I'm afraid I can only allow you an hour's visit... she's been very ill... recovering well now... out of intensive care and in a private room. I'll just make sure she's decent. Follow me please.'

At the end of the ward she gently tapped on a door, without waiting, opened it and looked in. 'There's a gentleman to see you, ma'am. Shall I show him in?'

'Yes of course,' said a soft voice.

'You can go in now.'

'Anne, how are you?... I've been in London, I didn't know you were ill until this morning - I came straight away.'

'Sims!' she said, her face beginning to glow, 'How nice of you... you look so smart.'

'Thanks,' he said, trying and failing to appear coy, 'it's just a little something I knitted while on watch.'

She giggled. 'You mustn't make me laugh... I'll split my stitches... a bit knocked about... but okay.'

'Are we on *Alice Protocol* or not?'

'What would you like?'

'Well, if I'm to give you these,' he said, handing her the chocolates, 'I guess we'd better use the protocol.'

'*Sims!* How on earth did you know I love Belgian chocolates?' she said, looking at him with astonishment.

'Oh, just a lucky guess really... I wasn't sure if these were the sort of things women went for,' he said, raising his eyebrows. 'Difficult decision... these or a pork pie, so I went for both... I ate the pork pie before I got to the station, so you ended up with second best.'

'They'll *just* have to do,' she sighed.

Anne, no longer giving him her full attention, had taken the beautifully printed tin box out of the Harrods carrier bag; opened it, and was sniffing the contents making, *oh my*, and *mmmming* noises. Then, 'I think I'll try this one... no, this one. Oh my God that's *divine*.'

Neither of them had noticed a small square card that had fallen to the floor.

'Shall I come back another day, or go for a walk for half an hour until they're all gone?'

'I couldn't possibly eat them all in that time - better make it the full hour,' she said. 'Sims, I was about to say, you shouldn't have done, but thinking about it, that would have been completely stupid. Gifts of this kind should be made much more frequently.'

'I'll bear that in mind. Perhaps when you stop to take a breath, you can fill me in with the gory details of your op.'

She closed the tin. 'I'm going to ration myself to three a day.'

'And the rest: tomorrow, when you've forgotten your resolution, comfort yourself with the notion that you need to build yourself up.'

'What were you doing in Harrod's?'

'Looking for something for a girl friend.'

'Is she nice?' asked Anne, worried. She had not considered that he might have one.

'*I* think you are, yes.'

She flushed with pleasure. Deep inside her things were stirring - things that had absolutely nothing to do with appendectomies.

They talked happily. It was lover's chat; footsie played with looks and words. He tried winding her up, seeking out her soft spots, with Anne giving as good as she got. Neither noticed the time slipping away. Towards the end of his hour, she asked, 'Would you really have shot that RPO?'

Sims leaned towards her, and without blinking, replied, 'My grand-dad told me to respect all human life. Now, the get out clause here, is that, quite apart from deserving it, RPO's are sub-human, and therefore they're an okay target... with them, it's *always* open season. So, to answer your question, too right I would have done.'

'I don't believe you,' she said, slapping him on the forearm.

'Listen, think of it as an act of kindness. Can you imagine being trapped in a semi-human form, and having only a conker sized brain like theirs?... just a few phrases circulating like a looped tape... "come here lad - get your 'air cut lad - admiralty regs this... admiralty regs that - where am I? - who am I? - get your 'air cut lad - it's gorn dark, oh no, everything's okay, my hat's slipped over my eyes - someone's cut me legs orf, oh silly me, I'm sat down... get your 'air cut lad."'

It was a brilliantly funny impression and Anne, desperately trying not to laugh, clutched his arm and said, 'Stop it now, Sims Reeves.'

He didn't. 'That's all they know, love. They must be desperately unhappy. Imagine every day seeing first hand what it must be like to be intelligent, free spirits like stokers, cream of the Royal Navy. I'd have seen it as a mercy killing.'

Sister Freeman came in. 'Another five minutes, and no more, Mr Reeves.'

'Anne,' he said, standing up and looking at his watch, 'I'd better be off, I've a train to catch.'

'Thanks so much for coming to see me, and for the chocs as well. They're not just special, they're out of this world.'

'That's okay, I'm glad you're in a fit state to eat them. If you hadn't been, I'd have had to suggest to your dad we need a new crew member.'

'Don't let that thought see the light of day,' she said, with a little more passion than intended. 'I'm a part of *Alice's* crew, and I'm going to be fit to do my bit during the next regatta... don't you forget that, John Sims Reeves.'

'You'll be ready okay, I'll make sure of that... feed you up on bacon sarnies.'

He walked to the door, opened it, and was about to leave when Anne heard him mutter, 'Oh bugger... in for a penny in for a pound,' and with that, walked back to her bed, leant over her, and gently kissed her on the corner of her mouth. 'Take care of yourself,' he said, giving her hand a squeeze.

'Will you come to see me again?'

'Sure. I'm away for the rest of the week-end... next time, *you* get the pork pie.'

He walked back to the door.

'Sims, come back here a moment, please.' When at her bedside, she said, 'Much closer than that.' Anne reached up with her arm, put it round his neck, pulled him towards her, and putting all she knew into it, kissed him. It was Sims' turn to flush up.

A Fresh Identity for Bear Bait.

'You really must hurry up and get better,' a smiling, happy, John Sims Reeves said, 'I wouldn't mind trying that standing up.'

He leant over her again. 'You know what this means, don't you?' Sims kissed her and then softly ran his finger tips down her face.

'I do hope so,' she said, smiling happily.

After he had gone, Anne reflected on the words he used, his humour, his gentleness. She reddened; squirmed to think how she had classed him beneath her and her family. He was Sims whether he was in civilian clothes or uniform... he is the same man, and this man is in a class of his own.

She recalled what Fox-Eastleigh had said about him at a recent dinner with her father. 'The person you think you are seeing, stands a very good chance of wearing some kind of camouflage. He's a social chameleon... he adapts his demeanour to whatever group he's with... he's damned good at it too. I think it's a survival tactic. Look at it this way, he has lived on stokers' mess decks for seven or eight years - it probably wouldn't have been wise to reveal his cultured side.'

'Cultured side?' Commodore Sherwood had said, surprised. 'I know him to be a damn fine sailor, and I confess I like the lad... I hadn't thought he might be cultured too.'

'Oh yes, classical music, opera in particular. He has very good knowledge and appreciation.'

She remembered with some discomfort her response to this. 'Are we talking about the same Reeves, if so, how do *you* know him so well?'

'We were on the same ship in the Far East, HMS *Alacrity*.'

'Yes, yes, but how did you find out about this dark secret of his; his love of classical music?' she had probed leaning forward.

'Telling that might take some time... you'd probably find it boring.'

'No, no, let's hear it all,' her father had said, rubbing his hands, 'a leading stoker with dark secrets, and a split personality. Come on, Fox-Eastleigh, out with it.'

'Not so much a split personality, sir, but a well hidden one,' James corrected his superior.

'The first time I became aware of *another* Reeves was when *Alacrity* was tied up alongside in Hong Kong harbour. Except for those on duty, all of the crew were ashore and I was Officer of the Watch. Well, that evening: it must have been about 2200, I took a turn around the upper deck. As I was climbing the ladder to the bridge, I could just make out music coming quietly from it. Hong Kong's social life being what it was, you could be certain the other officers were also ashore, so I couldn't imagine who it might be. Inside, I found Reeves sat close to his record player. He was so completely absorbed he didn't hear me. I asked him, is that Aida? He whipped the stylus arm off the record, realised who it was, and said; No, sir, it's Puccini's Tosca. I asked who the singers were. Callas, Di Stephano and Tito Gobbi, sir. There's probably no finer version. And there suddenly in front of me was Reeves the cultured. I should add, it was the first time of many he put me right about classical music.

He's got a super sense of humour too, I asked him

once if he liked music's modernism movement, his reply was classic Reeves; not much, nobody whistles bleedin' Schoenberg.'

'First time of many, eh? From that I gather you got to know him quite well,' her father had said.

'Yes, sir. How could I not be intrigued, I checked his records and discovered he was ex *Ganges*, a marksman with both pistol and rifle, and a qualified coxswain too. To tell the truth, there are an awful lot of seamen who would like his qualifications.'

'I can certainly vouch for his boat handling. He sounds too good to be just a leading stoker. Why isn't he further up the ladder?'

'I can't answer that... I have a feeling he won't stay in the service when his time's up.'

'Yes, but how did you get to know him so well?... that's the intriguing bit,' Anne had asked.

'Well, he assisted me on a few surveillance jobs. We developed a deep trust in each other. Later, I had cause to select a somewhat clandestine team to patrol the west Malayan coast. I put Reeves at the top of my list. I can't go into details, but I can say without hesitation, that I was very glad to have him alongside on more than one occasion during that trip, and on *one* occasion especially so. Reeves is tough... on *Alacrity* he managed to get special dispensation to train with the *Korean Tigers*... they're Korea's special forces. He learned a lot, he really knows how to look after himself.'

'We noticed,' said the commodore.

Anne would have liked to have known more, but knew better than to pry into areas of operational sensitivity. Instead she had asked, 'Just *where* did he get his knowledge of music from?'

'Both his mother, father, and his mother's parents had been professional musicians. I suppose it's in his blood.'

'Does he play himself?' Anne had probed again.

'I don't think so, he never mentioned playing to me.'

'His parents must be disappointed,' the commodore had said.

'Both his parents are dead, sir. Reeves was brought up by his grandparents; they're both dead too.'

Anne, who had lost her mother when she was twelve, felt uncomfortable with her treatment of Sims. She was only capable of uttering; 'How awful... the poor man.'

The illness had sapped much of her energy, she tired, and with these thoughts and the memory of Sims' company, fell asleep. She woke refreshed, and for one brief moment thought she had dreamt his visit. She smiled when she saw the tin of chocolates. 'Ummm, perhaps I ought to try just one more,' she said.

Before she could do so there was a knock on her door Hoping it was Sims returning, 'Come in,' she called.

In bustled Joss. 'Hello, how are you feeling, darling?'

'Oh, so much better thanks. It's so nice of you to come... I thought it was your free weekend?'

'Don't worry about that,' said Joss, not mentioning the extra duty she'd had to put in with Anne's absence. 'The important thing is, you're looking marvellous. You've got some colour back in your cheeks at last.' Glancing at the bedside table she spotted the tin of chocolates, 'What *have* you got there, Anne. Are you sure they're good for you?'

'Absolutely certain,' Anne replied, smiling at her

pathetic and transparent concern. 'You must try one.'

'Oh my God, *oh my God,* they're Belgian... I can't take these from you,' she said, dipping her hand into the tin, 'really, I can't,' now biting one in half, 'this is really too bad of me... isn't it?'

'Oh, really terrible, a sick person's only comfort too.'

'*Who* gave them to you... who do you know who shops at Harrods?... unforgivable, you've been keeping secrets from me.'

'Just a visitor.'

'This was not *just* a visitor. *Who* was it? I shall leave if you don't tell me... though perhaps I'll try another one of these before I go.'

Anne hesitated. 'It was Sims.' She quickly added, 'but don't read anything into it, he might only have been being friendly.'

'How long was he here?'

'As long as sister would allow... about an hour.'

Joss, now understanding the colour in Anne's cheeks, said, 'Anything else happen?'

She giggled. 'Well, yes... as he was leaving he did say, Oh bugger, in for a penny, in for a pound, and then came back to the bedside and gave me a kiss. But, as I said, I think he was only being friendly.'

'Where did he kiss you?'

'Just here,' said Anne, pointing to the corner of her mouth.

'And what did you do?'

'I was too surprised to do anything.'

'Oh, for God's *sake!* you didn't let an opportunity like that slip through your fingers, did you?'

'Not exactly; as he was leaving I called him back.'

'*AND!*'

'I made him come closer... I hope I gave him a kiss he won't forget in a hurry.'

'How do you mean *hope*, Anne?'

'Well, I've never actually kissed anyone I've *really* wanted to kiss so much before. So it was a bit experimental.'

'What did he do?'

'Hmm... well, he didn't struggle.'

'I'll bet he didn't.'

'And... and, he certainly looked quite pleased with himself.'

'Anne Sherwood, there's hope for you yet.'

'As I said, he might only have been being friendly.'

'For Christ's sake! He comes to see you after all you said to him; buys you Belgian chocolates and those must have cost him a week's wages, *and* he gives you a kiss. Are you daft or something - the man *loves* you... those Belgian chocolates equal desperation.'

'I do hope you're right.'

'Of course I'm right!'

A little pensively, Joss looked at her friend. 'So you're really smitten with him?'

'Completely. I admit I tried my best to resist falling for him, but it's such a strange thing, now I've given up trying, I can't imagine myself being with anyone else. *Joss,* at the risk of repeating myself, I'm the daughter of a naval commodore who shortly will be promoted to rear admiral, every suitor I've ever had has had their eyes more on their promotion prospects than they have had on me - that's not very flattering. Sims, apart from being the most gorgeous man I've ever met, is the first person to say what he really thought to me. And, amongst his many other virtues, he's accurate, he called me a first class bitch, and do you know what?... I was.'

'So, you find being called a first class bitch - *flattering*,' Joss said, laughing, 'Anne, you've got it really bad.'

Joss shifted her chair, looked down and noticed the dropped card. 'Is this your bookmark?'

'No. What is it?'

'It's a ticket for Covent Garden - it's for this evening,' Joss said, reading it.

Anne grabbed the ticket, 'Oh *no*, he must have dropped it! He'll never get there in time for the performance. He'll miss it. And even if he gets there in time for some of it, he won't have this... this is really too terrible.'

Joss leaned over and squeezed her hand. 'Sims won't mind. He's a man desperately in love with a girl who today has kissed him. He's going to be on cloud nine. Trust me.'

*

He, still glowing on Monday morning, walked in to the commodore's office. 'Has Lieutenant Fox-Eastleigh got anything for me?'

'You look happy today... it *is* Monday you know... not allowed,' said Christine. 'He's in his office, I'll find out for you.'

'Morning, Reeves, I haven't anything for you... I do need to speak to you though... come in to my office,' Fox-Eastleigh closed the door behind them. 'Take a seat.'

He would have needed to be blind to not notice the lieutenant was uncomfortable about something. 'Problem, sir?'

'James will do for the moment,' he paused. 'Sims, on Friday I went to a cabal meeting at Billy Ruffian's place... By the way, I heard about your meeting with Billy. He was pleased. I think he made a joke. He said he didn't want you visiting Tunworth too often, he couldn't afford the food. But that's not what I want to talk to you about... ...I owe you a hell of a lot... please keep your cool and don't breathe a word of this to anyone,' he paused again. 'I had been quite lucky in finding a garage in Alton; they specialise in old Sunbeams... I booked *Mabel* in there for a complete check over, then I took a taxi to Tunworth House. I was in plenty of time, so I paid the taxi off a mile or so away... I like walking. There was no one around when I arrived. The front door was open so I let myself into the library to see if coffee had been laid on... there was documentation on the table with your name on... it detailed your entire naval record as being a commissioned officer, and that at present, you are a lieutenant.'

'Hang about, James, did you say *lieutenant*?'

'Yes, but that's not the end of it. I thought it best to get out of the library as quickly as possible and waited in the hall... Admiral Jessop and Stinton must have been in the garden... they entered the library through the French windows. I heard Jessop say; better get those papers cleared away, Stinton. What was said then was a bit indistinct, but I'm sure they referred to you as *bear bait*... I could be wrong, but I can't take that chance... I then thought it best to go to the front door and ring the bell... to the best of my knowledge I don't think they suspected anything.'

'The slimy buggers, that doesn't sound very nice of

them does it?... by bear, do they mean Russians?'

'I have a horrible feeling... yes. Sims, at the moment I just don't know what to do.'

'I think you've done enough... you've risked a lot just telling me this... who the hell *is* the enemy, James?... who the fuck *can* you trust in this world?'

'Sims, I promise you, you *can* trust me... I regard you as more than a friend... I think friends are very important... I'll keep you informed of anything I hear.' For the first time since he'd known him, He heard James Fox-Eastleigh swear. 'Fuck the lot of them... they've no fucking right to do this to one of their own people... it's just not on.'

Both men sat for a while thinking. Sims trying to digest what he had just heard: James, how the hell he could assist.

'If you need any help, you must ask me... if I can't help as a naval officer, I might be able to with my family contacts... they're quite well-off you know... influential... have you any idea what you're going to do?'

'Keep my bleedin' eyes open for a kick-off,' he said, and then added, 'Look, I don't want to expose, Anne, Joss, the commodore or yourself, to any chance of getting caught in cross-fire... I haven't a clue what is going on or what to do about it... I shan't say anything to him, but do you think Maitland knows about all this?'

'No, I don't. He's an ex cryptanalyst... he's not a killer... decent sort... I don't think he's got a rotten bone in his body.'

'I think you're right.'

After more time thinking, James asked, 'At a time like this, it might seem an odd thing to bring up... but you listed Anne first.'

'And?'

'When we sailed *Alice* to Hell Head... I noticed her looking at you... quite a lot... anything going on?'

'I have reason to believe so, yes... so you'll understand I'd really like to have a bite at the bear *before* the bugger bites me... James, there is no way I'm going to put her in danger.'

'Absolutely right.'

'While we're on the more pleasant diversion of women; Joss seems a damn good sort. You and her seemed to be hitting it off quite well.'

'We are, yes,' he said. 'I have to tell you, previously, I could not decide whether I should leave the navy or not... this incident has unequivocally convinced me that I *should*... as I said earlier, fuck the navy, and all who sail in her.'

***

Chapter Fourteen
The Golden Mace.

'Hello,' said Anne, to the two women busy cleaning and restocking the shelves. 'I'm looking for a man called Sims Reeves, I believe he drinks here occasionally.'

Mo nodded, and Pearl said, 'Yes, we know Sims. Why do you want him?' As though they were going to need support for what was coming next, both women moved closer to each other.

'I have a message for him.'

Pearl thought, Sims, you've done it again haven't you?

Mo thought, Yes, now I can see why he's been a bit quiet lately, he's in love, and so's she by the look of it. He's picked a classy one this time, good for him... hope she's single.

Pearl moved a little closer to Anne. 'Are you feeling alright love, you look a little pale. Would you like a drink, or tea or coffee? Come and sit down.'

'Yes please. A tea would be perfect.'

Mo put on the kettle, 'What's happened to you?'

'Oh, appendix, I've just come out of hospital, I'm not sure it was a wise move coming here - I definitely feel a little wobbly.'

'You look washed out my love,' said Pearl, 'I'll put the fire on in the saloon and we can sit down there while we have a cuppa, and don't think you need to rush away.'

Pearl returned wiping coal dust from her hands, 'So, you're a friend of Sims are you?'

'In a way, yes.'

In a way! Mo thought.

'So we can tell him you called, what's your name?'

'Anne... he'll know where to find me. He said he had some leave owing and that he'd be away for a while. You wouldn't know where would you?'

'He said he was going to London, he's got a business there, do you know if he went, Mo?'

'It's not in London, it's just outside, somewhere in Surrey I think... but it was last week he was away, wasn't it.'

'He's got a *what*?' Anne asked.

'A business... don't know what it is though.'

'I had no idea.'

'He can be a bit of a closed book until you know him. Pearl and me, we've known him for years. There's a lot going on in that head of his.'

'I'm beginning to see that.'

The three of them sipped their teas, just their cups clinking in saucers and a little small talk. Anne felt comfortable in their company, 'Does he.... no, it doesn't matter.'

'Of course it matters,' said Pearl, 'or you wouldn't have begun. Come on, you haven't come all this way in your state, because it *doesn't* matter. What do you want to know?'

Anne put her cup down on the table, clasped her hands together in her lap, took a deep breath. 'Does he have a girlfriend?'

'Not at the moment... definitely not... no, not at the moment. Though, I'd put good money on it, he's got someone in mind, someone sat not a million miles from Pearl and me.'

Anne flushed and smiled.

'Mo, pass over those biscuits. Would you like a drop more?... a couple more biscuits won't do you any harm, neither.'

'Please, that's very nice of you.'

'Have you known him long?' asked Mo.

'No, not really. I must say, after talking to you both, I don't think I know him at all.'

'Well, don't worry... you won't hear a bad word said about him from us two.'

Anne finished her tea, Pearl said, 'You've got a bit more colour in your cheeks now, love.'

'Thank you so much, you've been so kind... I'm feeling much better now. May I use the phone for a taxi? I ought to be going.'

'I'll get one for you - where do you want to go?'

'Gosport ferry, please'

Pearl came back from making the call, 'He'll be about ten minutes. Look that's a nippy breeze out there, would you like a drop of something to keep you warm on the way back over the water? Come on, just a small one; a brandy,' she said, handing over a nip.

'Thanks, I think I need this.' Anne downed it in one.

'That's my girl - you'd better have another.'

'No, no, one more and I'll need a wheelchair. How

much do I owe you?'

'If you're a friend of Sims... nothing. Next time it'll be your round... you can buy us one.' Pearl said, smiling. 'You'd better give me your phone number in case I need to contact you... here's a Golden Bell card, call any time you like.'

The taxi arrived. Anne gave Pearl her number and got up to leave. She thanked them both again. As she reached the door, Mo called, 'Anne, he'll never work it out for himself, so when you see him next, make sure you tell him you love him.'

'That's what I came here to do.'

'What do you think to that then, Mo? She's classy, very nice mind you, but really *classy*.'

'I thought she was nice too. I'm really happy, she's dead right for him.'

'Is that *so*? What are all those tears about then?'

'I *am* happy. I would never leave Brian... she *is* right for him... me and my telly, him and his music, it wouldn't have lasted long: life's such a shit like that.'

'You thought about it then?'

'About what?'

'Leaving Brian.'

'Not really seriously... just day dreaming.'

'*Mo!* You and Sims haven't been at it again, *have you*?... ...you *have* haven't you? Oh Christ, I need a drink and a strong one at that. Mo, you silly bitch. You've got everything back together. A good husband who thinks the world of you, and you... you let that sod in again. How long has it been going on?'

'It isn't going on. It was just once, and it wasn't *his*

idea, it was *mine*.'

A gaggle of lunch-time customers came in and the two women turned their attention to them.

Pearl was angry; the two of them hardly spoke for the remainder of mid-day opening. Mo left at closing time. 'I'll see you tonight,' she said, giving Pearl a quick kiss.

'Okay, love, don't be late.

Mo had helped out in The Golden Bell since before leaving school: always busy. Pearl had watched her grow up. Overnight, so suddenly; a pretty girl, her wings filled and Mo emerged a beautiful woman. Pearl had been appalled at her first boy friends, later: men friends. She had worried about her; hoped she would get through life without making the same mistakes she herself had made. Pearl was deeply fond of her.

Mo walked in, smiled at Pearl, went over and gave her a hug. Pearl said, 'Sleep the night here. I want you to stay after closing time. I need to know what's going on... you've never told me much about you and that bugger... I'd like to know.'

Mo gave her another hug. 'I'd like that... it would be nice to tell *someone!*... he looks fixed up now, it's not something I want to keep to myself any longer.'

*

They wiped down the bar, washed the glasses, and swept the floor. The two of them went upstairs to the small apartment. Mo began to cry almost straight away. They sat on the old battered sofa, Pearl put her arm around her. 'Come on, my lovely, let hear it all... let's hear everything.' She poured two large gin and tonics, 'Let's make ourselves really miserable,' she said handing over a glass.

Mo sat hunched, leaning forward, her eyes distantly focused. She ran her finger round the inside of her glass then licked it. 'You know as well as I do what that bugger's like, into everything, so much fun. He was so wonderful to be with... you just can't imagine... he was never nasty like some of the others. He *could* be a sod though... sort of naughty, but never nasty. Every time we met... something different... something new he'd read about, wanted to try... I used to count every second until we met again... every time someone came in the bar I'd hope it was him, I knew it couldn't be... just hoped it was.

Oh, and his *music*, his opera and his classical... his mum and dad were professional musicians, they played violins. I know a bit of Tchaikovsky,' she rambled. 'He was never ashamed of me... he took me to a concert in London one weekend, a really famous violinist played a concerto - I can't remember which one. Sims used to whistle it. It was beautiful... I remember looking at him: his eyes were closed... oh Pearl, he looked *so* sad. It was like he was remembering something from when he was a kid... he looked *so* sad. I thought he might be in tears... he looked so *sad*... made me cry just looking at him.'

Pearl did not interrupt, she gave her a squeeze and let her carry on; Mo was grieving for someone still alive.

She took another sip from her glass, 'I bet you didn't know he could speak French... and Spanish.' The recall made her laugh a wet laugh. 'We went to a restaurant one night. The waiter sounded all Frenchified of course.

Sims spoke to him in French, completely buggered the waiter, Sims told him he was no more French than Winston Churchill,' Pearl laughed and Mo gave a wet snuffle. 'He said, cut the crap and go and get me a real Frenchman... Sims and the new waiter got on like a house on fire... we were given top treatment that night. He was brought up by his gran and gramp... she was French... lovely people... both dead now,' she said, drifting off into some remote niche; a place she hid her special memories.

Pearl poured them both another drink. Mo sat there quietly; still a million miles distant. 'There's something so different about him... told stories... he'd make 'em up on the spot, some were a bit bonkers. One was so beautiful... about my ancestors, I wrote it down when I got home... it was so lovely... I shall tell it to my children... I know it off by heart - every word.'

Pearl squeezed Mo again, and with her arm still around her, quietly said, 'That's new, it was always, *Sims this*; *Sims that*, you never mentioned anything about stories.' Pearl would sit there for as long as it took. 'I'm not just saying this, we've got all night, love. I'd love to hear it.'

'They weren't something I wanted to tell anyone else, they were like a very special present... didn't get many of those at home... they were very precious and private.'

Pearl topped up Mo's glass.

'On our first date he took me to Spice Island. I'll never forget it... do you know, in just a few minutes, that's all, just a few minutes, he completely changed the way I thought about myself. It was such a bright and lovely day, the sun was warm, mind you, there was ever such a chilly breeze, though. Anyway, we sat on a bench huddled together inside his overcoat. he always glowed... the inside of his coat smelled so nice too. I told him my family came from there way back. He asked what they were. Probably whores and rogues, I said. He didn't think so. I'll never forget what he said next... he said, there's a never ending line of people waiting to do us down... even stick the knife in. We don't have to join them. If you think whores and rogues, that's what you'll get. Do you know, then, right on the spot, he made up this lovely story. When I got home I called it The Golden Mace. Just like *that*, Pearl, just like that... I couldn't believe it. He just sat there cuddling me and out this beautiful story came.'

Mo drifted away into space once more.

'Come on, love.'

'Well, he pointed to an old building and said that it was once a spice warehouse and it had been owned by a nice and kind family. He said they loved their spices so much they could never be rich; only prosperous.'

'That's nice.'

'He said it was where my great, then ever-so-many greats, grandparents had lived. Well apparently, they had a beautiful daughter who had married a sailor, and that I looked just like her, and just as beauty can pop up generation after generation, so can goodness. He reckoned the aroma inside the warehouse was exotic and there was this enormous wooden counter that had been polished over the years by sacks of cloves, allspice, pepper, mace, ginger and coriander. And, they had this beautiful little girl; she had a favourite game that made her squeal with delight. When they wanted to put an extra shine on the counter they laid out an empty sack, and sat her on it and would slide her up and down as though they were playing shove half-penny. Pearl, as he was telling it, I swear I could smell the spices and hear the little girl squeal.' She started crying again. 'Oh, you can have no idea what it was like to be with him... ...he was magic.'

'Come on, love, keep going... tell me the rest.'

Mo sniffed. 'He said, of course, the beautiful young girl grew up to be a beautiful young lady and she learned the spice business inside out. She knew every spice and every country it came from. She knew the masters of ships that brought them from afar, and very importantly she knew the best price for every one. Just like you, he said, naturally she had many suitors. But there were none that impressed her enough to accept their offers... the spice trade had taught her *discretion*. One day though, a handsome young sailor came in and she was immediately attracted to him, and it should be added, him to her... a bit like the first time Sims came into The Golden Bell.'

Pearl stood up and went to the sideboard, 'Wait a sec... let me get some crisps and a top-up.' Tiredness and gins had their effect; she flopped heavily back onto the couch. 'Go on, love.'

'Well, the young sailor returned often, and soon it was plain to see they were in love. He asked her to marry him and even though she loved him dearly, she *had* learned discretion, she asked him the same question she had asked all the other suitors: What is it about me that is so special that it makes you want to marry me?

I don't know, he answered honestly, but I know this, I have a present for you. It's something so valuable to me, even so, if you refuse me you may keep it.

Then you would walk away with nothing.

Yes, but as I would never meet anyone else I would wish to give it to, it makes no difference.

Now just a little intrigued, the girl asked, Can I see what it is?

Sims said, the young sailor then took out a sandalwood box that had been so beautifully carved with the finest detail. In it was a silken purse of the most vibrant colours imaginable. From the purse he drew out a complete golden mace that looked like a comet flaming towards the sun. I mean, Pearl, how do you think up something like that? Listen to this bit. The sailor said, I kept a piece of mace with me for years as a good luck token and to ward off disease. When I was in India, I had it dipped in molten gold to strengthen it, but only a very thin covering so that the colour of the mace would ever so slightly shine through. After and over the years, I collected many seed pearls and had them threaded on a silken string and kept the necklace inside the golden mace to give to the girl I loved. He handed her the mace and she gently drew out the necklace.

It's so very beautiful, she said, but where did you get the large pear shaped pearl in the middle?'

It's not a pearl, he said, it's a mermaid's tear. I was given it when I rescued an old man from an island I'd stopped at to replenish the water tanks. He had two, they were given to him by a mermaid who had fallen deeply in love with him. Mermaids rarely cry, only when they lose the thing they love most. Then the queen of all mermaids told her to return to them or she would kill her human lover. The next morning the man woke up and found the mermaid gone and these two tear shaped pearls lying where her head used to rest on his chest.

The Golden Mace.

The young sailor then told her; Mace protects against illness; like true love, gold never tarnishes; seed pearls show us how wonderful nature can be, how it can take the smallest fragment of grit, put it into an oyster and turn it into something as pure as a baby's tooth and the mermaid's tear shows how sad we can be when we're separated from the ones we love most. Take it, it is yours.

Pearl, that is so beautiful, I promise you it came out just like that. Listen to this bit... Well anyway, the sailor thought for a moment. Thinking about it, there is something that makes you very special, he said. The years you have lived and worked here among the aromas of spices, liqueurs and brandy, have given you something so important: you possess the wonderful fragrance of Christmas pudding. And, I adore Christmas puddings.

There are worse things to smell of, the beautiful girl said, how could I marry anyone else? Let's set the date now.' Mo finished the story and sat sniffing.

'Christmas pudding,' said Pearl, dabbing her eyes, 'Sims... that bugger, what sort of bloke is he?'

'Special,' said Mo, 'very special. You know, I didn't recognise it that day, but later on when I knew him better, I noticed at times, especially when he was telling stories, he seemed a lot older than he really was... he didn't look older, it was in his mind... it was just the way he acted... then suddenly he would return, you know, come back, and he'd be the Sims I knew again, and sometimes a bit of a sod. I loved it when he came back.'

Pearl squeezed her. 'You still love him; don't you?'
'Yes,' she said, crying again.

'You said it was just once, and it was your idea... how *did* you let it happen?'

'Like I told you, I didn't let it happen; I *made* it happen... that night he asked me to leave Brian and marry him. I told him I would never do it... I did come close. I'd never seen Sims so upset... really upset... I almost gave in then.'

'But why did you do it?... you risked everything.'

'You remember that big accident in the dockyard... matelots and dockyard maties killed. When Sims stopped coming in, I was sure he'd been among them. I just believed that's what must have happened, and I thought of all the things I should have said to him... wanted to say. I felt *so* awful, and I'd left it too late... I couldn't wind the clock back... I was too late. I've always been a bit religious... I started going back to church regularly. And I know this sounds daft; I prayed every day that I could see him again... say goodbye properly, even if it was only once. Then I find out that he'd been drafted to the Far East.... that hurt so much; I couldn't leave Brian and do the same thing to him... he's such a nice bloke.'

As if someone might overhear, Pearl asked quietly; a whisper, 'Mo, is Sims the father of your baby?'

'No, honestly he isn't, honestly he isn't... though sometimes I wish he was,' she whispered back, 'then I'd own a bit of him forever.'

'Do you love Brian?'

'Quite a bit... he's very nice... ...Pearl, love, Sims taught *me* discretion... things *will* be different, and I know I will be happier when I've got two or three kids.'

***

Chapter Fifteen
To Bait the Bears.

'It couldn't have been organised better if we had done it ourselves. They really are doing most of the work for us. Would you believe our stoker-courier is based right alongside reception?' Throagh said.

'Do you think they suspect it's our post box?'

'No. No, they don't... not at all.'

'Is it time to inform the bears, you think?'

'He's based there now. If for some reason they were to move him we would lose a first rate opportunity perhaps.'

'Better see to it then.'

'Of course, my lord.'

'Buongiorno, Angelo. come va?'

'Non c'e male, signore.'

Throagh reverted to English before he got out of his depth. 'I'd like a quiet, spacious table for two. I have business to discuss.'

'Of course, certainly, signore.'

Throagh had been seated for some minutes before his contact entered the small restaurant in South Kensington. They shook hands, and then ordered. Throagh did all the talking. 'There could be a problem in Portsmouth. A naval intelligence officer is based there who may be getting very close to our people. At the moment this problem is contained.' The contact listened carefully, his face impassive. Throagh continued, 'This NID officer is masquerading as an ordinary naval rating; a leading stoker working as an armed courier, he drives a fast launch, and his base is the Seamanship School in Portsmouth dockyard. The school's premises are immediately alongside the wharf where the *Rihards Vāgners* docks. He has been making enquiries in HMS *Dolphin*, I am reliably informed that the courier is withholding his findings until his evidence is incontrovertible. He is going for glory. His objective is to secure a good position in the new organisation. I think it wise to remove him as soon as possible.'

*

Bows high, at a fair speed, Sims pushed his launch into the cul-de-sac that formed the space between the Latvian wood-boat and the Seamanship School pontoons. Another urgent trip scheduled, he needed to get quickly away. He spun his launch on its axis: at its narrowest, there would be no more than six inches to spare at either end. Concentrating on this, one of his favourite manoeuvres, he did not notice he was being photographed from the *Rihards Vāgners*.

*

She served Big Bertha and her companion. Papers on the table fell to the floor. Mo bent down to pick them up; photos of Sims slipped out of an envelope. She kept her head, gathered everything together and put them back on the table. 'Can I get you anything else?' she asked, smiling at Big Bertha.

'In a minute, my love.'

Remind me not to smile at her again, she's repulsive.

Bertha and her partner parted company.

*

That evening, Mo phoned Anne. 'Have you found Sims yet? I need to speak to him urgently.'

'No. I was hoping you might have done.'

'If he contacts you, tell him I must talk to him... how are you feeling now?'

'Much better, thanks so much for asking.' The two girls exchanged a few more pleasantries, then Mo said, 'Stick with him, Anne, he's worth it.' She then put the phone down.

A little later, Derek came into the bar. 'Am I glad to see you!' said Mo.

'What's wrong?'

'Where's Sims lately?... Have you seen him?'

'I'm here,' said Sims, who had walked in unnoticed while the two had been talking, 'What's the problem?'

'Where *have* you been lately? she scolded. 'Come down to the saloon this instant.'

'Should I come too?' asked Derek.

'Sure, you might learn something.'

'What's up, babe? Sims said, kissing her on both cheeks.

Derek watched them. 'Shall I come back later?'

'No, I might need protection.'

Mo stood with her hands on her hips. 'Stop it you two... this is serious. Big Bertha was in here again with the Latvian guy... they had photos of *you*, Sims.'

Sims took hold of her hands. 'Did you let on, Mo?'

She was pleased, 'No, I was really cool... my hands didn't even tremble.'

Stood holding her hands, he said nothing, simply stood looking at her.

Derek looked uncomfortable. 'I feel like I'm playing gooseberry... shall I go?'

'No. Listen both of you, I won't be in for a while... don't worry.' He looked at Mo. 'Apart from serving them, keep well clear... they mustn't connect you with me. That goes for you and Maggie too, Derek.'

He slipped his arms around Mo and kissed her. 'Look after yourself, darling,' he said, and left by the side door.

'What's he in to, Derek?'

Looking worried, he said, 'Best do as he says.'

'Go and fetch him, quick!'

Sims returned with Derek. 'I forgot something; Anne came over to see us... she's looking for you... she's very nice. *Talk* to her, she's in love with you.'

He walked to the door again and turned. 'She has your approval, does she?'

'Definitely... she's so right for you, my love.'

Derek stood there thinking, this is too complicated for me... I'm going home.

*

'James, I want you to drive me somewhere quiet, somewhere we won't be overheard or interrupted. We have something important to discuss... it can't wait... and don't talk while we're driving.'

Lieutenant James Fox-Eastleigh parked *Mabel*. 'Hood

up or down?'

'Leave it down; it's not too chilly.'

'Look, Joss, if you're going to have a baby... well... you should know I was going to ask you to marry me, anyway.'

'James, you're as clueless as Sims about women, even I wouldn't know by now.' She leaned over and with her arms round his neck, said, 'but since you ask, the answer's *yes!*'

He smiled. 'Even though I'm clueless?'

'You're not clueless about absolutely everything, are you?' she teased.

'Would you still want to marry me if I left the navy?'

'Yes of course... I'd prefer you to anyway. I'd like my man at home every night so I can get my hands on him... I'm all for it, why do you want to leave all of a sudden?'

'I don't believe in the navy any more... I feel like a vicar who has lost his faith. I used to think there was no finer or more honourable occupation. I was wrong. I'm ashamed of what it is capable of doing to its own.'

'I knew something wasn't right, that's why I wanted to come out this evening. You've not been your usual self lately... both you and Sims seem a little preoccupied. I thought you might be having second thoughts about me, that, or the commodore's secretary had got her teeth into you.'

'She's okay... not in the same league as you... I've never asked anyone to marry me before.'

'That's a relief.'

'What is?'

'That you're not already married... now, what's on your mind, James, tell me everything, and why is Sims avoiding Anne? I know he loves her... that's obvious, yet he won't even acknowledge her... why?... she's so desperately unhappy... she's my oldest and best friend, and I can't bear to see her like that.'

He closed his eyes: for a moment silence. Opening them again, he said, 'You mustn't breathe a word of what I'm about to tell you... I'm breaking all sorts of secrecy laws,' he took a deep breath. 'Sims and I are working for naval intelligence... NID has been tipped off there are spies working on our patch in Portsmouth.'

'Come again? You're a naval intelligence officer, and Sims isn't really a stoker?'

'Yes, to the first, but Sims really is a stoker... just a very talented one.'

'That explains the firearm.'

'There's more. I'm trying to get to the bottom of something that may be nasty... the other day I overheard a conversation... I can't be sure... I can't be certain, but I think he is being set up... I think he's going to be used as bait. He knows something's up and is avoiding Anne because he doesn't want to put her in danger. It may be he's found something out... he won't even talk to me. Maybe he just doesn't trust anyone... it might be he's protecting me again.'

'What do you mean? How do you mean, again?'

'When we were on *Alice*, Sims took his shirt off... you may not have noticed, but he has a scar just below his right shoulder blade. It's an old bullet wound... that bullet, my love, was meant for me, and would have got me if Sims hadn't shoved me out of the way and taken it instead.'

She didn't know what to think or say. Confused, she

opted for, 'Gosh, you two do know each other don't you... Anne and I both noticed, by the way.' Then, the impact of what he had just said hit her. She caught hold of his arm; gripped it hard, 'I don't like the idea of you not being here, James, darling,' she said, looking a little scared.

'Well, I am, and I'm afraid I'm responsible for him being in this mess.'

Still unsettled, 'Not a very nice way of saying thank you for saving your life, is it?'

'I had no idea this was on the cards. I thought it might help his career... a leg up the ladder... I didn't know then, he intends leaving the navy.'

'Leaving?'

'Yes, and I don't blame him, the navy doesn't have anything to offer a man like him. He's such an asset, but, there's no system for finding the right slot for him. Joss, somehow I have to find out if my fears have any substance.'

'Darling, we can't wait: we can't hang around, he could be killed while you're trying to get proof... we must tell the others.'

A phone call was made and a hastily arranged supper was laid on at Hell Head House. When they had finished, the commodore said, 'If we're all done, I'd like us all to retire to the library...'

'... James, I believe you're the only person to have seen Sims recently.'

'Not that recently, sir.'

'Well, before you tell us what's on your mind, I have to tell you all, I too have been concerned by his absence;

Alice is unused again. As I have said to you both before, Anne and James, he's good to sail with and a very likeable lad.'

Anne smiled; her father liked him. The commodore continued, 'I decided to get to the bottom of his absence,' he paused, considering the best approach for what he was to say next. He took a profound breath through his nose, then, 'Although it did not seem apparent on the open day at Hell Head harbour, I had previously been baffled by Anne's open hostility towards him, I was concerned the cessation of hostilities may have been a passing moment and had returned, that his absence was due to this.'

Anne closed her eyes. Her conduct during the regatta dogged her: erasure of the board impossible.

'Her attitude had been a complete mystery to me. Not being sure of my ground, there was only one course of action open; I consulted Mrs Calver. Her instant response was; Oh, it's fairly obvious, Robert, Anne's in love with him. She begged me to make sandwiches for him one morning, that's a sure sign.' He let that information sink in. Anne looked at her father, trying to gauge his reaction to Mrs Calver's very accurate assessment. 'The outcome of all this... the long and the short of it is, I've had a meeting with him.'

Anne's head snapped round, 'How is he?'

'In good time, Anne, all in good time. I put a very personal question to him, I asked him straight out; are you in love with Anne? Without hesitation he answered, yes.'

Relieved, but still worried, Anne said, 'I know he had a business in London, and that he had to attend to it, but why hasn't he spoken to me since?'

'I asked him if he was worried what I would think, he said, he wasn't, and that was something he was always prepared to have to deal with in due course.'

'Then what's the matter?' asked Anne.

'I'm coming to that. Can you then tell me what the problem is, Sims? I asked. He said, No. I then, said; Reeves, I'm ordering you to tell me what this is all about. He looked me straight in the eye, and simply said; With respect, sir, it's a very private matter, and none of your business.'

Joss snorted and put her hand to her mouth.

'I've no need to tell you, this was a difficult situation... in all my career as a naval officer I've never been told a naval matter is none of my business... I could have had him court-martialled, but then, Anne would never speak to me again. And, as I have said, he is a young man I have a lot of respect for. I know he's prepared to stand by his own judgement. I could see pursuing the subject was pointless.' He turned to Anne. 'If you are in love with him, you should know I think he's a damn fine choice.'

'Thank you. I think so too,' she said, getting up and putting her arms round him.

'Did you say some, or *a* business?'

'A business, Father.'

'Do you know what?'

'No, no I don't.'

Joss nodded to James who was leaning on the mantle piece, he stood up straight. 'Sir,... Anne,... I think I can shed a little light on things. I must ask that what I am going to tell you, is never mentioned outside these walls. I'll keep it as brief as I can,' he paused for a few seconds. 'You know my true role at *Dolphin*, sir... what you may not know is that Sims also works for naval intelligence. He may have discovered something... he may be on to something extremely dangerous... I am as certain as I can be, he's not been in contact because he doesn't want us to be associated with him... he's protecting Anne, and the rest of us, he's put himself into quarantine.'

'Are you sure? How sure of that can you be?' asked the commodore.

'It is very possible, that I am alive, or at the very least able to be here today, because of his bravery... in the Far East, he shielded me and took a bullet on my behalf... he's done it before you see... I know the man, sir.'

Anne gasped, the news that Sims was working for intelligence had already left her without words. following the news of his shooting in the Far East, all she could do was put her hand to her mouth and sit down.

Commodore Sherwood also sat down. 'Anything else I should know?'

'It might be more correct to say, shouldn't know, sir, or at least, I shouldn't tell you. I overheard part of a conversation I wasn't meant to... Anne, I'm sorry that you should hear this,' he looked to Joss. Knowing what was coming she got up in readiness to comfort her.

'I'm pretty sure Sims is being set up... is going to be used as bait... I've seen a document that completely rewrites his naval record. According to this document he is a commissioned naval lieutenant... exactly why they've seen fit to do this I cannot say... perhaps a stand-by in case a cover-up is needed.'

'*Where is he!... how long have you known?*' Anne angrily demanded.

'I don't know... and not very long... I spoke to Joss earlier... I'm sure about what I read, I'm still not certain about what I heard... I don't want to take any chances.'

'Bait for whom?' asked the commodore.

'As you know, sir, the CIA has let it be known there are Russian agents operating in this area. NID may be using Sims to draw them into the open.'

'Bear bait.'

'Exactly, sir, but that's not the only problem. There's always a threat of enemy espionage, we live with that fact. Now, however, we are subject to another complication: there is an almost internecine battle going on between the various British intelligence agencies. They are to be brought together under one roof and one supremo. I fear NID will be no more in just a few years at most. These are dangerous people and times, sir. NID is trying to restore its lost reputation after Buster Crabb and Portland... for their part, MI5 and MI6 will go to any lengths to make sure NID doesn't achieve their aim, and anything MI5 or MI6 do, will probably be backed by the government.'

'What are we going to do?' asked an ashen faced Anne.

James continued, 'I went to see his CO, Lieutenant-Commander Maitland, he told me that Sims had specifically asked not to do *Dolphin* runs for a while... this was okay with Maitland. It appears that he didn't always carry classified documents. He never knew whether they were genuine or unclassified, the idea was to get him seen... the incident with the RPO gave him more than enough publicity for the immediate future. His operations now seem to centre on the Isle of Wight... he has been doing quite a few trips there lately.'

'Is Maitland in this too?'

'Yes, sir, he doesn't mind Sims spending time over there, it widens their surveillance net. I think whatever Sims is caught up in must involve The Island. I have a suggestion to make... I have decided to leave the service... I have no career in the navy to risk. In my opinion, there is no point in confronting Sims at the Seamanship School. I suggest, sir, I am unofficially relieved of my duties as your aide. I will track Sims, see what I can discover, and make myself ready to assist him if necessary... none of you need to risk anything. He is my friend... I owe him my life.'

'If you think for one moment, I'm going to let my fiancé try to do this on his own, think again James Fox-Eastleigh... I am going with you.' Turning to the commodore, Joss said, 'I would like to take all leave due to me immediately.'

'And that goes for me too Father... did you say *fiancé?*'

'Yes, James proposed earlier today... I haven't had time... this was the first opportunity.'

Anne looked at her in amazement, she's pulled it off, just as she said she would, she thought. 'Oh well done,' she said, though her mind still firmly fixed on Sims.

The commodore stood up. 'Well, congratulations to both of you - we will definitely celebrate this wonderful news at a later date. We must now get back to work... as you rightfully put it, James, confronting Sims in Portsmouth will serve no purpose. There again, nor will dashing over to The Island without a plan... it could even be harmful. I agree that we must look for him, but, there are things we need to put in place first. We need communications, we need a base on The Island, and one here in *Dolphin*, we need rapid transport... a helicopter at our disposal. Do any of you know if Sims has friends that might know where on The Island he is likely to hole up?'

'I can do that... I know some... I'll go first thing in the morning,' said Anne.

'For this operation to be successful, we must know where each of us are at all times... where are you going?'

'To Pompey, The Golden Bell in Charlotte Street... he is well liked there.'

'I will man the base here, if I'm busy and it's urgent and you need to contact me, the code will be *Alice*. I will arrange with Lee-on-Solent the availability of a chopper... the CO is a personal friend.' He looked at Anne, 'I will also arrange a medical team to be at the ready... with Lee-on-Solent's air sea rescue duties, this shouldn't be a problem. We'll wait until we've heard your report. I suggest we meet in my office as soon as you return.'

James took Anne's hand. 'Try not to worry, Sims is not stupid... he's aware something's up... he'll keep his eyes open... he's tough... he knows how to look after himself.'

***

Chapter Sixteen
The Nineteenth Variation Bombshell.

The freighter docked two days before. In the evenings, Sims took to sitting in his darkened office watching it; noting who came and went - he needed to recognise them if he saw them again. Its throbbing engine and top deck activity suggested it would leave that night at high tide.

Lights from the dockyard reflecting off the water sent shimmering flames across the ceiling of his office. It was a quiet place at this time of night, he was unlikely to be disturbed. It was a place he could listen to his music in peace.

Surrounded by the sound coming through his head phones, he sat closely watching the ship. An old recording; unique - Sergey Rachmaninov playing his own work, Rhapsody on a theme of Paganini.

He had heard many different versions, recent ones recorded using much superior equipment. In his opinion, as scratchy as it was, none matched the brilliance of this performance.

The record had belonged to his grandparents, they'd actually met Rachmaninov. His grandmother had said, he had such big hands yet they were so quick across the keyboard. His grandfather thought he would have made a great test cricketer, slips fielder perhaps... pity Russians didn't play cricket.

Sims' favourite variation, especially on this recording which never failed to make shivers run down his spine, was the nineteenth. He considered it the most intense thirty-six seconds in classical music. As a child it had reminded him of a scared animal alone in a forest at night. It hears a sound, becomes alert... uncertain, listening, then certain, then fleeing.

As if choreographed by some almighty puppeteer, just as the nineteenth variation began, he saw a figure emerge from a hatchway and lower a rope ladder down the side of the *Rihards Vāgners*. He thought this was both interesting *and* unusual. Seconds later another figure climbed down the ladder and into the water. Dragging a thin rope, it swam across to the Seamanship School's pontoon where their launches were moored. The person climbed out of the water and stayed crouched holding on to the rope.

Sims resisted the temptation to grab his Browning and confront the intruder. He thought of Hennerbury's words: draw them on, Reeves... wait until you can see the whites of their eyes, Reeves. Okay, let's find out what you're up to first... I'll have you later.

The person on the freighter attached a large package to the rope and lowered it while the crouching figure on the pontoon hauled it in, he then lifted it to his side. It was rapidly unwrapped. Immediately this had been done, the empty package was dragged back to the ship. The man on the pontoon scuttled down to Sims' launch. He opened the engine compartment hatches, climbed inside and shut them behind him.

Ten minutes later the hatches opened, the figure reappeared, dived into the water and quickly swam to the rope ladder. No sooner aboard, the ladder was hauled in, the freighter let go its mooring ropes. Going astern, it left the dockside.

He needed to think fast. First, he would have to find out what the parcel was; birthday and early Christmas presents were out, he thought. Inspection impossible until the freighter was out of sight. He would also need to be sure there were no dockyard personnel lingering around.

The dockside cleared twenty minutes after the ship had slipped its moorings. He took a torch and ran to his launch. In the engine compartment he could see a taped package strapped to the fuel tank. Running his fingers along it, he followed an electrical wire from the package to behind the port engine. Tracing the cable Sims could see it was fastened to the exhaust pipe. Heat sensitive thermal fuse, he thought, pretty crude but effective... clothes peg... contact plates... *Woods Metal* holding it open. 'Those bastards are trying to blow me up... why?' he said out loud.

Back in the office, Sims formed his plan. If someone was trying to get rid of him, he was going to let them think they'd been successful. He wrapped up the Browning, its four full magazines and money he had drawn out of his account. He put everything into two plastic bags and sealed them. Grabbing a life-jacket he tied the sealed pack to it.

The spring tide was beginning to ebb. He couldn't wait too long - in some places near the harbour mouth tidal currents could reach three or four yards a second. Fog had been forecast - wisps had already started forming. He decided to wait no more than forty minutes to let it fully develop. Whatever he was going to do would be done under as much cover as possible. This, he decided, is a good opportunity to disappear.

Sims fired up the starboard engine only, let go the mooring ropes and headed out into open water. Uncertain if heat in the engine compartment or vibration would be enough to set the bomb off, he kept the launch as far away as he dare from the ships tied up to the dockyard wall. Clearing the northern part of the docks, he turned south and headed for the harbour mouth and Spice Island. When this lot goes up I want it to be seen and heard but not write anyone else off.

His guts in knots, he was soon drenched in cold sweat: any adjective describing his tension during the voyage, rendered weak. Further ahead he could see the fog had formed a dense bank hovering a few feet above the surface of the water. While he could still see landmarks on both shores, Sims checked his position and noted the compass heading he should steer when engulfed by the fog. At any instant he expected the launch to disintegrate under his feet.

*

Anne, worried for Sims' safety, did not sleep well. She got up around half past five, turned on the radio, made herself a cup of tea and listened to the news.

"There's been a massive explosion in Portsmouth harbour. A Royal Naval fast motor launch with one man on board was travelling at high speed in thick fog, a naval spokesman has indicated that the prevailing conditions were unlikely to be the cause of the accident. Naval authorities assisted by Portsmouth Harbour Police are conducting an on the spot investigation. It is thought the pilot of the launch is unlikely to have survived the explosion. Having no next of kin to inform of his death, he has been named as LM(e) John Sims Reeves."

Commodore Sherwood was woken by a stomach chilling keening from below. Racing downstairs to the kitchen he found her sitting on the floor rocking backwards and forwards. 'Anne, Anne,' he said, shaking her, 'whatever's the matter?' He lifted her up and sat her on a chair.

'Sims is dead, he's dead... he's been blown up... it was on the news,' she screamed.

'Oh my god... I'll phone James immediately... I'll get him and Joss over straight away... stay where you are.'

Anne, in deep shock, stayed motionless on the sofa, James sat with his head in his hands, Joss beside him gently sobbing. Commodore Sherwood had left to see what he could discover about the accident.

'I want to be there when they find him,' whispered Anne, to herself.

Commodore Sherwood returned, his years of experience told him to get bad news over with quickly. He took a deep draught of air, prepared himself, and entered the library. 'There is little or nothing left of the launch... they have not recovered his body... I'm afraid there is little hope. I am very sorry, Anne.'

*

Sims had resisted the urge to get the hell out of the launch, he stayed at the wheel until he was well inside the clammy cover of sea fog. This is it, he thought, putting on and inflating the life-jacket. He then checked the pack was still firmly attached and started the port engine. He immediately stuffed both engines full ahead, and jumped clear. As soon as he rose to the surface he back-stroked towards where he thought the shore ought to be.

The launch was about four hundred yards away when it erupted. The blinding glare from the explosion bounced off the underside of the fog and back on to the water - Sims was briefly aware of the shock wave approaching: a torque of turbulent mist - it hit him hard.

The cold water revived him. Sims had no idea how long he had been unconscious or whether it had been caused by the percussion of the explosion or from the debris of the launch that had been flung in every direction. He felt his forehead and guessed he'd taken a hit, he could taste blood - glad there aren't sharks in Pompey harbour, he thought.

Swimming as best as he could, he made his groggy way to the shore. It was a very tired and much relieved John Sims Reeves that dragged himself out of the water and onto the road that dips into the harbour at Spice Island. He could hear the noise of approaching vehicles coming down Broad Street. Quickly he removed the life-jacket, deflated it and rolled it up with the package. Relieved he still had his Browning, he dodged into Bath Square and cautiously made his way parallel to Broad Street via West Street and Tower Street. He found a telephone box and called Derek.

'Who's there?' grumbled Derek, 'Who is it?'

'It's me, Sims... I need picking up *now!*... I'm wet and cold... the bastards tried to blow me up... with a bit of luck they'll think they've been successful... bring something to mop up the blood.'

'Where are you?' said Derek, wide awake.

'Spice Island... I'll lie low in Tower Alley... try not and use Broad Street it's crawling... don't hang about, I don't feel too good.'

'I'm on my way... stay put.' Getting dressed, he said to Maggie, 'Our lad's in trouble... sounds like he'll need a bit of cleaning and patching.'

At the top of Broad Street Derek turned his car round and parked ready to make a quick getaway. It was a short walk to Tower Alley. 'Sims,' he whispered. Sims stumbled out of the shadows.

'Thank Christ you've come... let's get the fuck out of here.'

'Get in the back seat and lie low, we'll be home in ten minutes if we're lucky... you smell like you've swam through a sewer outfall... worse than sickey... I heard the bang... went back to sleep, what happened, lad?'

'I'll tell you when we get home.'

Maggie was waiting. 'Get in the bathroom straightaway... get those wet clothes off... get in the bath... Derek, get him a tot of neaters.'

'That's a lot of gets, Maggie,' said Sims.

'Do as you're told... we need to get you warmed up.'

'Maggie, I think I can manage this bit on my own.'

'Silly sod... I'll turn my back... get in the bath now!'

He lowered himself into the hot water. 'Oh God,

that's so good.' Derek came in with a beer and a large glass of Pusser's rum. Sims took a large gulp of the beer and emptied half the glass of rum. 'Oh God, that's even better.'

She fussed over him, dabbing at the dried blood and cleaning his cuts. 'You look a real mess, my love... who did this to you?'

'You might find this hard to believe... I don't exactly know who, or why.'

Maggie, ever practical, 'I'll get your clothes washed and dried, in the meantime you'd better wear these of Derek's... they'll be a bit baggy, but at least you'll be warm... when did you last eat?'

'About three years ago.'

She fried up a pan of bacon and eggs. They sat quietly watching while he cleared the plate.

'I need to ask you another favour,' Sims said, looking at Derek. 'Please go to Hell Head House and tell Anne Sherwood I'm okay... tell her I'll be going undercover... It's important... if I get through whatever's going on, I shall probably marry her... oh, and tell her I love her as well, if you don't mind.'

'I thought your girlfriend was called Mo,' said Maggie.

'I kept telling you, *ex*, but you wouldn't listen!'

Derek, who was not the slightest bit interested in romance small talk, said, '*Sims!* WHAT THE FUCK HAPPENED?'

'*Derek Hill!* mind your language, normally, you *never* swear.'

'This isn't normal.'

Sims told them the entire episode, blow by blow. He

then said, 'As soon as my clothes are dry I'm leaving... I've already put you at risk... where's the pack I put in the car?'

'Still in it.'

'I need it,' he said, standing up. Whether from the effects of his concussion, beer and rum, or both, was a little unsteady on his feet.

'Sit yourself down... I'll fetch it.'

Derek came back and put the life-jacket and pack on the table.

Sims opened it carefully and pulled out the Browning and magazines. 'Good... they're nice and dry... this stays loaded from now on.'

'That looks dangerous,' said Maggie.

'So's this situation, that's why I'm leaving as soon as I can.'

'You're doing no such thing, young man. You're going to stay here until I know you're fit enough to travel, then, and only then, I might let you leave. When you're okay, you can remain here or stay on The Island at the cottage... you're our friend... Island people know who to make their friends... when we do, we don't let them down, Sims Reeves... understood?'

She looked so fierce that Sims thought the best thing to do was to agree - there are times, even if you have a loaded, made ready, Browning, it's a good idea just to back off a bit.

'If you decide on The Island, I have nephews there, they're completely trustworthy... they'll do as I ask.'

'I can believe that.'

'You'd better get some kip now... you look all in... I'll get on my way to Hell Head,' said Derek.

The Nineteenth Variation Bombshell.

Sims took out the roll of money and peeled off twenty pounds and handed it, diplomatically, to Maggie.

'And what's *that* for?' she said.

'All this is bound to cost you money... call it a float.'

'Put it away NOW! you might need it later.'

Before Derek left, Sims shook him by the hand and gave Maggie a kiss. 'Thanks very much both of you.'

As soon as Derek left for Hell Head House, Maggie pushed him, 'Right, Sonny Jim, up to bed.' She guided him upstairs; got him into bed, and tucked him in. 'Get some sleep, my dear; you need it. If you like, I'll cook you another breakfast when you get up.'

'Thanks, ma.'

'You can call me Maggie, or you can call me mum; but not ma,' and with that, she kissed him good night.

'Thanks mum, sounds good to me,' he mumbled. Feeling safe and comfortable he fell into a deep Pusser's rum and fatigue induced, sleep.

She reached the door and looked back at him. She thought, mum's a bit worried about you, my love.

*

The front door bell rang - Mrs Calver went to see who it was. 'Can I help you?'

'I must talk to Miss Anne Sherwood... it's urgent.'

'We have had some very bad news... we have lost a family friend... I'm sure you'll understand, they won't wish to see anyone at the moment.'

'Please tell Miss Sherwood I have a message... from Sims.'

'Oh my... wait here a minute.' Mrs Calver called the commodore into the hall. 'Robert, there's a man at the door who says he has a message from Sims for Anne,' she whispered.

We'll see about this,' he said, stalking to the front door. 'I'm Anne's father... are you the press?'

'No sir,' Derek paused, Sims had said the commodore was a good man. He took the decision to tell him the news, 'Sir, Sims is not dead... he's alive, a bit bloodied and battered, but alive.'

'No!.. ...Oh thank God... come inside,' he said, pushing Derek ahead of himself into the library. 'Listen, Anne... everybody; good news, Sims is alive, a few injuries, but relatively unscathed.'

Anne stood up slowly. She went; almost staggered, to Derek, 'Tell me how you know?' she said, looking dazed.

Derek looked at James and Joss. 'He trusts few people at the moment... he said I was only to tell you.'

'These are his friends.' She frowned, 'How do I know you're telling the truth?' she demanded.

'Sims thought you might not believe me... he told me to tell you this.' Poor Derek, who according to his wife, normally, never swore, looked acutely embarrassed and whispered in her ear, 'Well... it looks like... well, well... you once told him to fuck off.'

'I did indeed,' she said, crying and laughing at the same time.

'I'm a friend of Sims... this morning he phoned me and asked me to pick him up at Spice Island. He'd been in the water for some time concussed by the explosion... he made it to the shore. He is still a bit dazed and has a few cuts and bruises... but he's okay.'

Derek told them everything Sims had told him and

Maggie. The reality that he was alive and BBC news had got it wrong, sunk in. Anne who was still in shock from the bad news, was now in shock from the good. All attempts to stay calm were impossible, she simply broke down, sank to the floor and sobbed with relief: her man was alive. Helped her to her feet by her father she went to Derek. 'Thank you so much... if Sims trusts you, you must be a good friend.'

'Sims doesn't have too many people around him... perhaps he felt he had no option but to trust us... I have to go now... I fetched Sims from Chatham in a staff car... it wouldn't take much adding up to see there might be a connection if I don't turn up for work normally.'

'First class thinking,' said the commodore, 'I didn't get your name?'

'Derek Hill, if you need me, ask for Derek the driver,' looking at Anne, he said, 'He apologises for not letting you know this was going to happen... he hadn't the time... he had to act immediately.'

'Where is he? I must see him.'

'Sims was insistent that you should not know... he doesn't want any of you involved... any of you put at risk.'

The commodore looked at James and raised his eyebrows. 'Just as you said.'

Derek's moments of embarrassment were not yet over, once more he whispered into Anne's ear, 'He also told me to tell you that... well... he loves you.'

'He's told both you *and* my father that he loves me... I want to hear him say it to me... please tell me where he is,' she pleaded.

Derek moved to the door. 'I'm so very sorry... I must

go.' Anne followed him to the waiting taxi. 'I beg you to tell me where Sims... *my Sims*, is... you must understand this... I must be with him... trust me please... live or die, I want to be with him... please understand what I'm trying to tell you.' She was still in shock. What she had pleaded came from a deep and primitive part of her: a part as old as humanity.

He shook his head, 'I'm sorry.'

In desperation, she tried a different approach. 'We think that whatever he's doing involves The Island, are we right?'

He nodded,

'Is he safe?'

'He won't be safe until it, whatever *it* is, is over... he's a brave lad... he'll want to get back to you... he won't take unnecessary risks.'

'I'm most worried about the necessary ones he'll take... I've seen him operate.'

Derek got into the taxi and wound down the window. Looking out, he said, 'He's a lovely lad, and he's a survivor... he'll be alright.'

'I know... thank you so much for coming... tell him I love him too.'

'He also said, that when this is all over, he might like to marry you... I can't say I blame him.'

'If that was a proposal he sent you with, tell him I'm all for it... don't forget.'

She watched the taxi drive away and thought, who are all these good people? I know so little of them. She returned to the library. Joss came over and they hugged each other for some time, words not being possible. A little later, Anne said, 'Joss, are you completely certain being in love is enjoyable?'

'I was, but now I'm not as sure of myself, you've been through hell, darling... I hope it's worth it in the end.'

'It will be... but it's not over yet. Last night I said I would go to The Golden Bell... I shall go as soon as I've cleaned myself up.'

Commodore Sherwood called for their attention. 'We will, for the moment, stick to the original plan and wait for Anne's report... Joss you'd better hold fort down at the office... I shall start the process of having you and Anne backed up... remember, we have a navy to run as well.'

*

Pearl answered the door, she looked terrible. 'Anne, my poor girl... I'm so sorry.'

'He's okay. I must speak to Mo, where does she live?'

'She's here, upstairs, come on up.'

Mo, red eyed, sat on the old sofa. When she saw Anne she rushed over to her. 'Oh, you poor thing, I'm so sorry for you, it's not fair, my love.'

'Mo, It's all right. I came to tell you that he's alive... if you both want him to remain that way, you mustn't let anyone know... anyone at all... I think you and Sims were very close to each other once... I thought you ought to know.'

Pearl put the kettle on.

Through cascading tears: 'Oh, that's really nice of you... just like him to come back from the dead... that man *is* a sod isn't he?' Mo said, putting her arms around Anne.

'If you ask me, I couldn't imagine Sims being dead...

he's not the sort of person to give up so early... here, take this my loves,' Pearl said, handing both mugs of steaming strong sweet coffee. 'I think we need this and a little something to splash in it.'

'If I remember correctly this is my round... he *is* a sod isn't he'

The three women sat quietly drinking, the occasional snuffle, the occasional hug, they were friends now - even explosions can have an upside.

'Mo, there are certain things I must know about Sims.'

She looked a little uncomfortable, just a touch concerned Anne was going to pry perhaps too far into her past with him.

Anne sensed the worry. 'This is about what Sims has been doing recently... he's involved in something... something he's trying to work out on his own... Mo, it's too big for him... he's going to need help. Do you know of anything... something he may have said for instance?'

She hesitated. 'Yes, he asked us not to breathe a word... that's not possible now, is it?'

'I don't think so... we're all having to break confidences... I hope he'll forgive us.'

Pearl had made more coffee with a splash, and the three of them sat in a conspiratorial huddle. Mo and Pearl related everything they knew about *Big Bertha*, the men from the freighter and the photos they had of Sims. Mo then said, 'Sims said it wasn't just these people he didn't trust, but those he was working for as well... he's not been in for some time.'

'He wouldn't want to involve you, he's like that.'

'You remember what I told when you were leaving last time... did you do it?' Mo asked.

'Not in so many words, I still haven't seen him to do so.'

'Please tell him as soon as you can... he's very lonely you know... he's still not got over his gran and grampy dying. When things settle down, make him tell you stories... he does it so beautifully... he ought to write you know.'

'I know I said this to you before; I think I hardly know him at all.'

'How can you... you haven't even told him how you feel... you still have a long way to go yet, and then some,' she said, squeezing Anne's hand.

*

Sub-Lieutenant Hennerbury walked in to Les Goodwin's workshop. 'Heard the news, Les?'

'Yeah, while I was having breakfast... what was the poor bugger into?'

'God knows... we did our best, Les... I've got a course waiting,' Hennerbury said, and looking as severe as Les had ever seen him, walked out.

And I wouldn't want to be in that lot's shoes, Les thought.

*

Ben took the mail to *Dolphin* and called in to see Pam. Her reddened eyes gave her away. 'You've heard about Sims then?'

Ignoring all fraternisation rules, Pam came round the counter and put her arms round him. 'He could be a bit brutal with it, but he *was* our hairy cupid, wasn't he?' she said, sadly.

*

Lieutenant-Commander Maitland sat in his warm, small, comfortable office in the Seamanship School. He knew he would have to go and see Billy Ruffian and give him the details as far as he knew them. It was not a meeting he was looking forward to. He must have overlooked something, something obvious.

***

Chapter Seventeen
Quarr Abbey.

Leaning on the guardrail of the Gosport ferry, Anne looked back at Spice Island and thought of the drama that took place there just a few hours ago. She went over the meeting she'd just had with Pearl and Mo - both had been deeply affected by the news of the explosion. Pearl behaved as any good friend would have done on hearing the news that someone close had been killed. Mo's reaction wasn't as straight forward. It seemed she had been as distraught as Anne had been. While they had been talking, Mo had taken her hands, and said with such intense sincerity how happy she was that Sims had found her. If previously Anne had only suspected Mo and Sims had been together in the past, she was now certain of it. She could also see that Mo was still deeply attached to him.

She wondered what had happened between them. If their separation wasn't formed by a natural drifting apart, or mutual hatred, why weren't they still together? Sims still used The Golden Bell and had obviously remained on good terms with her. What had happened?

Anne was not jealous. He was hers - she knew that. She

liked Mo, there was nothing disingenuous about her. Anne could not imagine any man not liking her. Be that as it may, the uncertainty of everything in her life at that moment hardened her resolve to find him and to be with him.

She went straight to her father's office and told him what she had found out.

'We don't need to panic. He's safe while everyone who was after him thinks he's dead,' said the commodore. 'We'll all meet this evening, 1900. I'll arrange with Mrs Calver for dinner to be ready for 2000. Now go and tell Joss and then go home... you look exhausted.' He got up from his desk and took hold of his daughter's hands, 'Remember, stay calm - we'll get him back... I'll do everything I possibly can, I promise.'

She gave her father a hug. 'I know you will.'

*

It was gone mid-day when he sat up in bed. Just for a waking moment, he couldn't think where the hell he was. Maggie heard him moving around in the bedroom and went to see if he was in shape enough to come down stairs on his own. 'How are you feeling now, my precious?'

'Head's thumping a bit... slept well though... the cut on my forehead started bleeding again... made a bit of a mess of the pillow case.'

'That might need a stitch or two,' said Maggie, inspecting the wound.

'I can't afford to go to hospital, they'll ask awkward questions. We'll treat it ourselves... pull it together with

Quarr Abbey.

some plaster strips.'

'Sims Reeves, I was a nurse for ten years, I *know* what to do!'

'Sorry mum... didn't know that.'

'Now, do you fancy something to eat?'

'That breakfast you promised sounds good.'

While Maggie was cooking, Sims sat at the table, 'Bacon smells good... Maggie... I'm going to need some clothes: jeans, shirts, pants, you know the sort of thing... I shall also need a knapsack. I'm not short of money, I'm *going* to pay for them - so please don't argue.'

She went shopping; Sims had time to think. He hadn't a lot to go on, only a handful of people knew he was alive. He reasoned if NID were using him as bait, it was a strategic non-starter to go to them for help - nope, he would have to do whatever was necessary on his own.

The one positive link I have, he thought, is between Big Bertha Glass and the Latvian blokes. He settled on laying low on The Island until the *'Rihards Vāgners'* returned to Portsmouth. If his assumption that Glass acted as a collector and postman for the Russians was correct, she wouldn't appear in Cowes until just before the boat had docked in Pompey. If she did so, he would make sure she saw him, and if he was lucky, someone would come looking for him. If he was even luckier, it would be the ones that tried to blow him up. Sims decided he would take no prisoners - he *would* kill them.

*

That evening the commodore addressed the small, serious group gathered in Hell Head House. 'You've heard from Anne what took place this morning at The Golden Bell. There are many questions we would like to ask *and* their answers known. High on the list must be why they had taken photo's of Sims. The only explanation I can offer for that, is someone from our lot must have leaked his true role at the Seamanship School. If that is not the case, there was no reason that I can see why they should fear him. Our task is to find Sims and support him... any ideas?'

'I think Derek knows where he is, he has more or less admitted it. It has something to do with The Island for sure,' Anne said, 'I'm also pretty sure that Derek will be able to contact him. The problem is getting him to help us.'

'Anne, I want you to give Derek and Maggie, and Pearl and Mo, the direct connect number for my office at *Dolphin* and our contact code: *Alice.* Get their numbers as well. We may need their assistance. Today, I spoke to the CO of our air base in Lee-on-Solent, unless there is an exceptional emergency, he can have a helicopter in the air and on its way in under five minutes. Something you wish to say, James?'

'Yes, sir. Whatever Sims *is* doing, he is definitely not hiding, you can be absolutely sure of that. It's not in his nature. In essence, that is why we need to find him, he will seek them, he will try to take them on by himself.'

Anne did not wish to hear this. She remembered his fearlessness when confronting the three men at the regatta. Unpalatable as it was, she knew it was the truth. 'I think we ought to go to The Island as soon as possible... it's our only chance of finding him isn't it?' she said, desperately.

'As I told you this morning Anne, he is safe, as long as those that were after him think he is dead... you have a point, Joss?'

'Well maybe... perhaps we're not looking at this the right way. We're all thinking of ways to find Sims. The possibility of finding him by chance, or bumping into him, is a bit remote... The Island's a big place. So, why don't we get Sims to find us?'

The other three looked blank. 'If NID is using him as bait, why don't we play a similar game?... bait him,' she said.

'Best to explain that, darling,' said James.

'It's so easy,' she said, impatiently, 'look, if we took *Alice* to Cowes and tied her up in your usual mooring place and Anne lived on board, there is no way he could stay away. He would have to make sure she was okay... we would have set a honey trap. If, then, we were to watch from a distance, soon enough he would turn up, and we would spot him... follow him even.'

'That, Joss, is a superb idea,' said the commodore. 'How do you like the idea of being used as bait, Anne?'

'I think I like it very much,' she said, with a delighted smile.

For the benefit of Joss and James, the commodore said, 'We cannot make a move immediately. *Alice's* engine is being modified to take electric start. This will take several more days to complete, it will give us time to plan and prepare.'

There was now something positive they could get their teeth into - it was a much happier group that sat eating dinner that evening.

Quarr Abbey.

It had been weeks since Sims had visited her in hospital, though to her it seemed like months... years. She could hardly contain her excitement. 'I'll take my Mini over, leave it there, and come back as a foot passenger. I'll get enough provisions for *Alice* to last at least two weeks.'

'Anne, before you do anything, wait until we know for sure when *Alice* will be ready,' said the commodore, quite aware that she would leave that instant if he were to suggest it.

*

'Mum,' Sims said, giving Maggie a cuddle, 'I want to get going; I can't stay here forever - there are things I've got to settle.'

'You're going nowhere until I'm sure you're over the concussion and that cut has started to knit... so forget it for now, and rest... I've seen you wobble a couple of times, and you've looked a little queasy now and again... you'll go to The Island when I think you're fit to... I'll not have you driving around in the condition you're in at the moment.'

'How long is this concussion going to last?'

'How long is a bit of string, my love... you don't look too bad, a few days perhaps... by rights you should have seen a doctor. I'm not taking any risks, you need to rest... and, you're not doing yourself any favours prowling around all the time.'

The telephone rang. 'Yes... yes it is... I understand, love... no... I am sorry... no... the last time I saw him, he was doing fine... yes of course I will... I promise... try not to worry, love... I know... okay then... yes, I'll tell him if

I see him... and you... goodbye.' Maggie came back into the room. 'She sounds nice, Sims.'

'She is. What did she say?'

'She wanted to know how you were, where you were, and sends her love. She said something though I didn't understand, I may have got it wrong, she said, "if you'll meet her, she'll buy the pork pie".'

'Must be pretty bleedin' desperate then.'

'Don't you think you ought to meet her somewhere safe?... put her mind at rest.'

'No, definitely not, no!'

Sims took Maggie's advice and rested. He had taken a bigger battering than he'd initially reckoned and was surprised just how much he slept. By the day after *his killing*, the effects of bruising made themselves known; he felt incredibly stiff all over.

Maggie took his temperature. 'That's okay,' she said, checking the thermometer. 'You've taken a bit of a beating, my love, you'll be all right in a couple of days... you're a young man, you'll get over it soon enough.'

The following day, the stiffness easing, and he, restless. 'I must get going... I need to get to The Island before the *Rihards Vāgners* returns to Pompey.'

'If you look well enough tomorrow, I'll take you over to the cottage. Today, you rest up some more, Sims Reeves... are you absolutely sure you don't want to meet Anne before you go?'

'I'm sure.'

'How about just giving her a call?... she'd love to hear your voice... I know it.'

'Look, Mum, of all the people in this world I'd like to see and talk to right now, it's Anne... you have no idea... but it's not the right thing to do at the moment... it wouldn't be fair.'

Maggie loved him calling her *mum*; she took him over to The Island the next day.

'These are two of my nephews; this is the eldest, Edward Albert, and this is Alfred Ernest... they're always known as Ed and Al... they look after the cottage while Derek and myself are away on the other side of the water,' Sims shook hands with the two men. 'They know every inch of The Island - you can trust them with your life.'

Ed looked Sims over, 'If you need anything, you come and see us. One of us, or both, will come in each day to see if you're okay. Aunt Maggie says you're to use the old Austin A40 Devon they keep here... it starts a treat, and it's full of juice... here's the key.'

'I told them you were coming,' said Maggie, 'so that everything would be ready for you. I've only told them that you're a very special friend of ours, how much you decide to tell them is up to you. As I said, you can trust them with your life.'

She stayed long enough to show Sims around the cottage. 'I'm off now, got to catch the next ferry back to Pompey... can't keep Derek waiting for his dinner.' She said goodbye to Ed and Al. 'Now boys, mind you look after him.' She gave Sims a kiss, told him not to take any risks, patted his arm, and went to her car. Sims followed her outside. 'Can you get Derek to call in to The Golden Bell and ask Mo or Pearl to let him know as soon as the

Quarr Abbey.

Latvian boat is in... then, can you phone one of the lads, and get them to let me know?... take care, and give my best to Derek.' He watched her drive away, and returned inside the cottage.

Speaking for the first time, Al asked, 'What happened to your head?'

'Somebody tried to blow me and my launch up in Pompey harbour.'

'Bloody hell, that was you, was it? The radio said you were dead.'

'Well, as you can see, I'm not... BBC news got it wrong. There are only a few people who know I'm still alive. I'd like to keep it that way.'

'Seems like you've been mixing with some pretty dangerous buggers, if you ask me,' said Ed. 'Are they here on The Island?'

'Not yet, but I hope they will be soon.'

'What you going to do if you catch up with them?' asked Al.

'Get my own back... it's open season on Russian agents. If they don't get me first, I shall shoot them, and I won't be aiming just to do a little bit of damage... I shall probably do them quite a lot of harm.'

'*Russians!*... spies are they?' asked Ed.

'I guess they must be. Now listen, I don't want to involve you two, or Derek and Maggie, if things go wrong. So here's what I'm going to do; I'm going to hot wire the A40, and break the lock on the back door: I'll pay for the damage. Put the A40's keys where you normally keep them... it'll look like I broke in. We'll keep all visits until after dark, and then, to an absolute minimum.'

'You're to eat with us tonight,' said Ed, 'and with him tomorrow.'

'Thanks for the offer, but for the same reason, I can't be seen with your families either.'

The two men went home. Al nudged Ed, 'I'll tag him in the morning... you in the afternoon. Okay?'

Ed nodded.

Sims was on his own, just himself and the quiet cottage: a light breeze rustled the leaves in the trees outside the open window. He sat down in an armchair, 'What the hell do I do now?' he said. His mind wandered from his immediate problem: his thoughts turned to Anne and the message she sent with Derek. He wished she was here with him, yet at the same time, he was glad she was elsewhere; safe. Love and logic, it seemed, were never meant to share the same bed.

Come to think of it, it's bloody obvious, he thought, after having sat resting for some time. He decided he would go to where he first saw her down by the Cowes, East Cowes ferry. He would go there every day just before the *Rihards Vāgners* was due in port and wait until Big Bertha showed up again. If she was going to contact her man from Samuel White's, she was most likely to do it when he could get time off without being noticed, as before, lunchtime a good bet.

The next morning Sims drove to Cowes, he bought an ordnance survey map and a few essentials. He walked along the quayside; he was hungry. He spotted the *Sea View Cafe*, there's original thinking. Must have taken one hell of a marketing team to come up with that one.

Quarr Abbey.

He ordered breakfast and coffee, and studied the map. Hennerbury's voice reached over The Solent - draw them on, Reeves; draw them on. He was beginning to appreciate the soundness of this advice, he needed a place to lead the heavies to. It had to be away from people. Somewhere he could limit their options; somewhere his back would be protected - a wall, or the sea. Intimately knowing the roads on The Island might give him some advantage over whatever car the heavies might drive, but Maggie's old A40 was not the quickest vehicle he had ever driven. Wherever he was going to choose, better not be too far away.

Looking at the map he was suddenly hit by an intense wave of loneliness and doubt. It came not from what he was planning to do, he had already accepted that he might not come out of this alive. The sponsor of this action crippling thought, was the awful possibility that he may never see Anne again. The perversity of it all hit him hard. Fuck Billy Ruffian, fuck the Russians, he thought. Both had it in mind to set him up as a target, and yet without them he would never have met her. Life was, without doubt, perverse.

He took a deep breath and reminded himself that this bunch of bastards had tried to blow him up. The thought made him angry again. He did not intend staying in hiding all his life; he was not going to give in. No! In his mind, there was only one way out of this: maybe he couldn't wipe every Russian agent out, but one way or another, he would send them a message: a simple one, easy to understand. It will cost you your lives if you fuck with me.

He finished his breakfast and ordered another coffee. Perhaps I can concentrate better back at the cottage, he thought. He paid his bill, collected his things together, walked back along the quayside and took the ferry back across the Medina to East Cowes.

He side-stepped quickly into an alley leading off the street where he'd parked the A40. 'You following me?' he asked, as Al drew level.
 'No,' lied Al, 'had to come into Cowes... wasn't sure if it was you or not.'
 'Nice try, but that's a load of bollocks and you know it.'
 Al looked at Sims helplessly. 'Look, Sims, we know what you said about not getting involved, but for Christ's sake, me and Ed would sooner face the Russians than Aunt Maggie in one of her rages... you've no idea.'
 'I had a feeling she could be a bit forceful,' said Sims, smiling.
 'Forceful!, if you want to know what forceful means, just get on the wrong side of one of her slaps. My arse is still smarting from when I was fourteen... said the wrong thing... I've been bloody careful ever since.'
 'Okay, now we've just *accidentally* bumped into each other, maybe you can give me a bit of lowdown on the area.'
 'Right... sure... no problem with that,' said Al, relieved to be of use and less likely to incur a pasting from Aunt Maggie, 'What d'yer want to know?'
 'I'm looking for a place on the coast... away from too

many people... at the top of a cliff to protect my back... not too far away. A building or something like that... a bit of protection... shelter for me... not for them... any ideas?'

Al pondered a moment. 'Got a map?'

'Sure... we can't stand here looking at it... fancy a pint?'

'There's two things I fancy, and a pint's definitely one of them.'

'What's the other?'

'The reason I've got five kids.'

Sims laughed. 'Where we going?' It felt good to have company again.

'Marsh Road... good pub and good beer,' said Al, rubbing his hands, 'Not a bad lark this, is it?... fighting Russians.'

They sat at a table and spread out the map. 'I reckon this is as good as anywhere,' Al said, pointing to a small field between Fishbourne and Ryde. 'No more than four miles from Aunt Maggie's cottage, or six from here. Ed and me used to go on our bikes and play there when we were kids, it's got an old gun emplacement left over from the war... cliff right behind it, woods either side of the field... I can take you there when we've finished, if you like.'

'It looks perfect... I'll go on my own, and don't follow me... fancy another?'

'My round.' Al picked up their two empty glasses.

'No it's not... my push, or I'll tell Aunt Maggie you've been drinking on duty.'

'You bugger... that's unfair pressure, that is.'

Sims drove out of Cowes and headed for the field. At

Wootton Bridge he crossed over into Fishbourne, made his way to a lane over-looking the Portsmouth ferry terminal and parked. He reckoned it about half a mile to the old gun emplacement and started walking along the shore. The map had shown two copses either side of the field. Ahead he could see the trees came to an end, then further along they continued. He guessed what he was looking for was where the gap was. Climbing up the shallow incline from the beach, he made his way through the trees until he came to the edge of a small field.

'This has to be it,' he muttered, 'and *this* has to be about perfect.' About twenty five yards away, butted right up against the eroded cliff edge, the gun emplacement sat surrounded on three sides by an earthen bank. Sims walked past the mound with the intention of going to the other side of the field. He was stopped short by a long pond, the ground beyond which was a dense marsh. Foiled, he walked back to the bunker.

Facing the woods he had come through, and cut into the earth mound, was a long incline that ran down to a rusty steel door. On it he could just make out the words *'Ammunition Store'*. Below that in a more modern hand was scribbled, *Vera Costin drops her nicks,* and underneath that, in yet another hand, was added, *for monks - cash only.* He smiled and creaked the door open. Inside there was a faint light from a window let into the wall that overlooked the cliff. In the centre of the room, the ceiling was supported by a large central pillar, must have been a big gun above once, he thought. Around the walls, and around the pillar were deep alcoves once used for storing artillery shells. He added a torch to the list of things he needed to buy.

He walked back to the woods he had come through. There was a track leading away from the cliff, he followed it until he came to a group of old buildings. His map read, 'Quarr Abbey'. Returning along the track to the cliff top, he thought, I must come here as often as possible. I must know every inch like the back of my hand. Content that this was the perfect place, he walked back along the beach to the car.

Quarr Abbey was less than a mile's drive from where he had parked. From there, Quarr Lane gave on to Quarr Road, and then to the entrance to Quarr Abbey. It doesn't get much easier than that. Navigation made simple... just as I like it, he thought, pulling up alongside the entrance. On the assumption that monks are a reasonably peaceful bunch, he decided to stroll through the monastery's grounds and make his way back up to the field using the track he'd walked down earlier. There was more good news - he would be able to drive, with or without permission, all the way to the cliff's edge. Walking back through the monastery, he wished a passing monk good day. The monk nodded but did not reply. Miserable bugger, thought Sims, who knew little about the daily routine of Benedictine monks and their observance of 'hours of strict silence'.

Back in Cowes, he found a chandlery, bought a large coil of rope, a ball of tough twine and a usefully sized sheath knife. It is a fact of life that no true sailor ever feels completely happy unless he has these three items readily to hand. What they do not usually regard as essential, are signal guns and flares. Sims noticed these displayed in a cabinet and immediately decided to buy them, might create a nice diversion, he thought. In an ironmongers, he bought a spade, a lighter and fuel, a torch and spare batteries.

Over the next few days he visited the field at least twice a day. He approached it from the west, the south and the east. He memorised his way through the woods above the monastery, and he could find his way round the inside of the ammo store with his eyes shut.

Half a mile to the east near Ryde, there was a small jetty. He drove there and walked along the beach to what had become *his* field. He reconnoitred the woods to the east of the pond then made his way to the bunker.

'I thought I'd find you here,' said Ed, 'haven't been here a while myself... how're you doing?'

'Fine,' said Sims, cheered by having company again, 'how are you doing yourself?'

'Okay... Aunt Maggie's been on the phone... wants to know how you are,' Ed hesitated, 'Derek says there's a girl asking for you... apparently, you'll know who she is. Also, somebody called Joss, asked somebody called Ben, what you'd been doing before you were killed, and he said that you'd been doing lots of trips here to The Island... Aunt Maggie thinks the girl - her name's, Anne...'

'I know,' said Sims, interrupting.

'...this Anne, has put one and one together and thinks you're over here.'

'Bugger, she's far too smart for her own good... bugger.'

'Anything *I* can do?'

'Know anyone with a shotgun?'

'Why, is this Anne dangerous?'

'No, she's going to be my missus.'

'So what?... my missus is dangerous... always has been.'

Sims chuckled - Ed was okay.

'I've got a couple of 12 bores, so's Al... why?'

'Might want to create a diversion... an old one will do.'

'When you've got four kids, *old* is all there is,' said Ed philosophically.

He didn't find it a good notion being a financial burden: he was costing Ed and Al money. The problem was, how could he sub them without offending them? He decided the direct approach was best, or, more crudely put, if in doubt, jump in feet first. 'I know you're both shit scared of Aunt Maggie, and frankly, I don't blame you... you both follow me around - don't think I haven't seen you... I appreciate it... really... I mean, if Aunt Maggie told me to follow Dracula, I'd do it until I ran out of blood... but, Ed, *I'm* not a vampire, I don't want to bleed you two dry. Let's come to a truce. You can follow me all you like, as long as you let me pay my way... I'm not broke.'

Ed looked doubtful. 'I don't know about that, it doesn't seem right to take money from someone in trouble.'

There were possibly more subtle approaches he could have made, feet first still best, he thought. 'I'll put it as straight as I can,' Sims drew out his Browning, 'You let me pay my way, or I'll shoot both of you.'

'What the fuck's that?'

'That, my man, is a Browning 9mm Hi-Power... in my hands it's deadly. Do we have a deal?'

'Come on, Sims, give us a break.'

'No,' said Sims, bluntly, 'every day you follow me, means you're not working, and on top of that, it's costing you juice as well... the break I'll give you is this: I'll say nothing to Aunt Maggie, and you'll take a weekly float... you split it between you... no arguments, right?' Sims pulled some notes out of his wallet and handed them to Ed. '*Right?*'

'*Right*, very much appreciated.'

'When this is all over, I'll take you and Al on the biggest piss-up imaginable.'

'I'll hold you to that... only, don't bring that Browny thing with you.'

Ed walleted the notes and got up to go. 'After dark, I'll put the 12 bore and some cartridges in the car... right, I'm off down the pub, then... see you mate,' he said, grinning and waving his wallet. 'One other thing, Al and me think you'd be better off waiting for whoever, down at the Fishbourne ferry terminal. If they're coming from Pompey, they've more or less got to arrive there.'

Sims sat on the grass bank for a while after Ed had left. They were right, Fishbourne made a lot more sense. He was annoyed he hadn't thought of it. He wondered what Anne was up to, got to his feet, went and stood at the cliff edge and looked north. Somewhere over there, not many

Quarr Abbey.

miles away, was his girl. He had known her long enough to know she would not remain a spectator while this saga played itself out. He pictured her obstinate frown; No, she's bound to try something, he thought. 'Bugger,' he said, going down into the ammo store to check his rope and things were still safely stored. 'Bugger,' he said again, and walked back to the car.

He drove straight to the Fishbourne terminal. He needed to find a spot where he could get a good view of the cars and their passengers alighting from the ferry.

On the slope down to the dock he parked on a small grassy pull-in. It was no more than one hundred yards from the ferry itself - he would get a perfect view from there. The cars would be passing within feet of him, and having just left the ferry would be travelling slowly. I'll park the car facing uphill, he thought, this way, I'll be on their tails as soon as they've passed.

He hung around for some time - nobody told him to move on. Maybe it was the effects of the concussion - he had difficulty working out just how many days it had been since his launch had been blown up. It has to be at least ten days he reasoned, the *Rihards Vāgners* could be in dock any time in the next two days. Sims felt a moment's panic. What if Big Bertha had already been to The Island? There's no point in worrying about that now, if she's been and gone, so be it. he thought. And, if she hasn't, I'll get her tomorrow or the next day. Right! nine o'clock on the dot I'll be here waiting.

'Shit, that's hot,' he spluttered, after taking a sip of near scalding coffee straight from the Thermos. Sims sat watching the cars slowly disembark, he wished he'd asked James what make of car Big Bertha drove. The thought was discounted - how could *anyone* miss her?

His plan, if it indeed was a plan at all, was to follow her to Cowes; he would park his car close to hers. The rest, he would play by ear. Whatever happened, she would see him, and she *would* recognise him - even if it meant him standing in front of her and saying: I'm a stoker, we're a tough breed, my name's John Sims Reeves, and your lot failed to kill me, you bitch.

At 1145 Sims could see a ferry approaching. It docked, lowered its ramp, cars began to roll off. He started the engine and waited, ready to pull out the moment he saw her. The seventh car off was Bertha's. He could tell it was her from fifty yards, an unmistakeable nightmare upholstered in tweed. She passed, and he pulled out to follow. Seeing her again so close, he thought, if being ugly was an Olympic event, she'd 'ugly' for Great Britain.

Bertha took her time and drove carefully to East Cowes and parked in Link Road, a short walk from the chain ferry to Cowes. Sims drew up right behind her and waited for her to get out of the car. He was going to follow her to see who she met this time. She made her way directly to the ferry - he stayed no more than twenty yards behind. Reaching the other side, she walked down the quayside and stopped at the cafe where he had been regularly taking his breakfast. She took a table outside in the sunshine. Sims chose one inside, and watched her through the window. The manager came over. 'Didn't see you this morning, sir.'

'I couldn't make it... too much on... I'll take my breakfast now if that's possible... though I might have to dash... better take the money just in case,' he said, handing him a ten shilling note, 'There's something else... can you do me a favour?'

'I'll certainly try, sir.'

'Can you reserve that table for me, the one next to the *beast in tweed*? and if I go and sit there, please bring my breakfast over, and say, Will we see you the same time tomorrow, Mr Reeves? That's all you need to do. Can you do that?'

'I don't see any harm in that; as long as you keep your part of the deal and come tomorrow,' he said with a grin.

'The deal's on,' said Sims, shaking his hand.

Big Bertha sat reading a paper and sipping from her cup. Occasionally, she would look down the road that led back to the ferry. No doubt about it, she's waiting for someone all right, he thought. The 1300 siren sounded at Samuel White's shipyard and ten minutes later, the electronics designer appeared. He went straight to Bertha's table and sat down. Sims waited until he saw a package handed under the table to her. Bertha slipped the package into her folded newspaper. He caught the manager's eye, and gave him the thumbs up.

Making plenty of commotion, Sims sat down, and true to his word the manager brought his breakfast over, and asked, 'Will we see you the same time tomorrow, Mr Reeves?'

'Of course, us sailors are men of strict routine... you

should know that.'

Bertha looked over, recognised him and nearly fell out of her chair. Sims acted as though completely unaware of her presence. Leaving her contact to pay the bill, she hurriedly got up and left. He watched her almost trot back to the ferry, no point in following her, she got the message okay. He went back inside. 'If that's alright with you,' he said to the manager, 'I'd like another breakfast and a pot of coffee to go with it... what do you reckon?... and well done, that was spot on... perfect.'

'Always like to please our regulars, sir. Who was she?'

'I'll tell you one day, I promise.'

***

Chapter Eighteen
All Flares Fired.

They met for supper at Hell Head House. 'The work on *Alice's* engine is now complete, everything has been tested and she's ready to go. I must say, it's going to make life a lot easier. Anne, weather permitting, you can take *Alice* when you like... I'll show you the starting routine tomorrow when you return from the Isle of Wight.'

'I can go tomorrow?' she said, standing up and hugging Joss.

'Yes, but get back in plenty of time for your instruction... we might even have a couple of practice coming along-sides.'

'I can go tomorrow, Joss. We can start looking for him,' said Anne, flushed, elated.

Sims woke up with a start - Al was calling, 'Sims, the boat's here... came in last night.'

He dragged on his jeans, ran down stairs, by the time he reached the kitchen he was heart thumping awake. 'What do you know?'

'Aunt Maggie called to say Mo had told them, that the *Rihards Vāgners* docked late yesterday evening. Mo says, the bloke you saw with Big Bertha came in on his own just before closing time.'

'And that's all Maggie said?'

'Yep, I took the call myself.'

'Okay, thanks... don't hang around.'

Sims took the Browning out of its holster, gave it a thorough check over and slid the magazine back into position. He gave it a quick kiss and said, 'Whatever you do, my love, don't let me down... this won't be any soft trip down the combat range, this will be for *real*.'

Again he could hear Sub-Lieutenant Hennerbury's words: Draw them on, Reeves... draw them on... wait till you can see the whites of their eyes, Reeves.

Another wave of loneliness washed over him, and for the first time he admitted to himself he felt scared of what might happen to him in the next few hours. He took a deep breath, and recalled what they'd tried to do to him. This was exactly the right thing to have done - he was angry again and with the coming of anger his fear left him. Keep pissed off, he thought, it's the perfect panacea for fear.

He sat and thought over the options. They are most likely to meet at The Golden Bell this morning. Big Bertha will tell them about seeing me yesterday. There were two of them working together to plant the bomb... it's reasonable to assume there will be two involved today... *Rihards Vāgners* does a quick turn round, they won't want to hang about, they'll be over here later on today for sure.

*

She left Hell Head House not as early as she would have

liked. Joss had called from *Dolphin* - Anne was needed to countersign urgent supply documents. It was nearly 1100 before she could get away. She cursed the day the old floating bridge ferry from Gosport to Portsmouth had gone out of service - she now had a fifteen mile drive round the harbour to get to Portsmouth and the Fishbourne ferry terminal. It had been too long - she was impatient to get to The Island and find her man. This is how she now thought of Sims; *her man*.

Her father had arranged with an old colleague that she could leave her Mini among the Saunders-Roe buildings in East Cowes. Anne parked, and rather than wait for a bus, she took a taxi from East Cowes to Fishbourne. She paid the driver in advance in case the ferry was about to leave on their arrival. Travelling down the sloping road to the ferry she came to the conclusion that by the time she got back to Hell Head House, it would be too late to leave that night.

'Stop!' she yelled. He was leaning against an old grey car. Anne almost threw herself out of the taxi. 'Sims!, Sims!' she called racing across the road. He looked up just as she launched herself, flung her arms round him and held onto him very tightly. 'I thought I'd never see you again, darling,' she said, kissing him all over his face. 'What happened, how did you get that?' she said, frowning at the plaster on his forehead.
'When the launch blew up.'

He stood taking in every detail of her beautiful face. With the back of his fingers he stroked her cheek. He then ran his fingers through the dark curls around her ears. 'Anne, you must believe me when I tell you, there's nobody in this world I want to see more than you. You are in my mind all the time; but you must go... things are hotting up.' He looked out into The Solent, about a mile away a ferry was approaching. 'The people who tried to blow me up could be on this next ferry... you have to go; *now*!.. it's too dangerous, love.'

'*No!*' Anne did a good line in frowns. 'I'm going nowhere. Live or die, I'm going to be with you.' she paused and smiled at him. 'Sims, for weeks I have lived with the words you spoke to me the last time I saw you. You said: "you really must hurry up and get better, I wouldn't mind trying that standing up". Well I'm better now, we're both standing up, so come on, give it a go.'

John Sims Reeves; male; stoker; normal; healthy; young and very much in love with the girl holding him - not a lot else could he do, was there?

He, his hands grasping her shoulders, 'If these guys see you, you become a target too... they aren't coming for a chat... it's kill or be killed... they can't afford to fail a second time, or, at the very best, it'll be the salt mines for them.'

She frowned at him again.

'I've seen that look before, please back-off and *go!*'

'*No!*'

Sims stroked her face again; kissed her. 'What the hell am I going to do with you?' Although a strictly rhetorical question, she replied, 'Take me with you... as with two heads, two sets of eyes must be better.'

'Get in the car,' he said, 'if they do come, they'll probably use Elizabeth Glass aka Big Bertha's car. If I spot them, duck down so they don't see you.'

'What does she drive?'

'A truly horrible powder blue Ford Cortina.'

Sims watched all the cars drive by. There was no Cortina, no Big Bertha, and no men that looked at all like Russian agents. 'We'll wait for the next one,' he said.

'Tell me your plan,' she asked, holding his hands.

He told her of the gun emplacement, and what he'd hoped to be able to do if they followed him there. Anne unzipped his jacket and exposed the Browning. 'I thought I felt that... it will be so nice to kiss one day without a loaded pistol coming between us.'

'Fat chance at the moment... there's a shot gun under the blanket on the back seat... reckon you could handle it?'

'I've fired Father's plenty of times,'

'I bought some signal flares and their pistol as well...'

'I know how to use those too,'

Sims looked steadily at her for some moments. 'What are you thinking?' she asked.

'I'm thinking how just looking at you makes me so determined to come out of this alive.'

She leaned over and kissed him. 'Pam Somerton said you were only a kid when you won at Bisley, she said you were as cool as a cucumber and that you upset a lot of pro's... keep cool Sims and upset *these* pro's for *me*.'

'Hmm, your father's shot gun, did it have hammers?'

'Yes.'

'Do you know how to load it?'

'Of *course!*'

'We ought to phone him... he'll be worried sick... I know I would be.'

Leaving the car where it was, they walked hand in hand to a phone box at the top of the road.

'Daddy, it's me, Anne.'

Now what? the commodore thought, Anne normally, unless she was apologetic, called him *Father*... *Daddy*, rang alarm bells. 'Where are you?'

'I'm with Sims,' she answered, and before he could reply, said, 'I'm staying with him, Father.'

Now, there were also many inflections Anne could apply to the word father, this particular one said; I won't be argued with. Although he knew this of old, he tried regardless, 'Anne, I'm ordering you to come home at once!'

She simply replied, 'Do you remember ordering Sims to do something he wasn't prepared to do, and what he told you?'

Her father sighed. 'Let me speak to Sims then.'

'Hello, sir.'

'You must send her home immediately.'

'Ordering her, is the easy part, sir, trying to get her to take any notice is where it gets a little more difficult... I have tried, sir... really.'

'I believe you, lad.'

'Sir, is James at hand? If he is, I'd like to speak to him.'

'Sims, how are you? Were you hurt bad?'

'No, listen, I'm fine. I saw Glass yesterday in Cowes. She was handed a package from one of the top designers at Samuel White's shipyard. Can you believe they did it right in the open? If any heavies do come looking for me, she's likely to be with them, if not, pick her up. She was as scared as hell when she saw me, get her before she does a runner. This is your big chance, don't miss it.' Anne whispered in Sims's ear. 'Anne says to tell Joss, I've got him... hand me back to the commodore please.'

'Sims, my friend, take care; I want to go to your wedding, not your funeral... I know Joss would say the same, I'm sure she would also send her love.'

'Sir, there's another ferry coming in. If you don't hear from us shortly, you'll know they're on board. I was going to try and do this on my own... I can't risk that with Anne here... I might need some assistance. She tells me you've got a chopper on stand-by at Lee-on-Solent, is that correct?'

'Yes, lad.'

'If everything goes to plan, we'll be in an old gun emplacement overlooking a cliff... it's in a clear field half a mile along the coast from Fishbourne towards Ryde. You can't miss it, the rest of the cliff is wooded. I reckon it's not six miles from Lee, just slightly east of due south. If things look bad, we'll fire some flares. If you see them, it would be nice if you could come as rapidly as possible, sir.'

'Message received, Sims - half a mile from Fishbourne towards Ryde, and just east of due south,' he repeated.

'That's correct, sir.'

'Sims, this might seem like a stupid thing to say, but take care of my daughter as well as you're able.'

'The ferry's getting close, sir... we're off.'

It had almost docked as Sims and Anne hurried back

to the car.

*

'George, it's Bob Sherwood, there's every chance I'm going to need the Wessex... I suggest myself and my aide are picked up at *Dolphin* as soon as you can, and then we head back to Lee to wait... full Medic crew, George.'

'We're on our way.'

*

'You explained what you are going to do if you get them to the field, but *how are* you going to get them there in the first place?' Anne asked.

'Well, that part has always been more what I would like to happen than a plan. In the USA, to get a stray steer back home, cowboys tied a donkey to it. The thing is, the donkey wanted to get back to the ranch where its food was. So, every time the steer moved in that direction the donkey went with it. If the steer tried to go any other way than back to the ranch and grub, the donkey dug its heels in... didn't budge. Eventually, the donkey and steer would arrive home... I know it may sound crude... that's what I was going to try. I've had it in mind just to react to what they did, and draw them closer and closer to the field. So much depends on what they decide to do, though.'

'And you were going to try and do this all on your own,' she said, 'just to protect us.' Sims didn't respond to this.

'What will we do if they're on this one?'

'Follow them to Cowes... they'll probably start looking for me at the cafe I use. I'll make sure they see me, then I'll try and draw them to the field.'

The ferry now docked began to lower its ramp. 'There's still time for you to get out and go... please.'

That frown again. 'No, John Sims Reeves! And that's final.'

'They're here,' he said, he leaned over and kissed her, 'second car off... stand by.'

She felt a wave of fear and excitement.

'It's her all right... plus two heavies,' he said, pulling out into the traffic.

A white Lancia Flaminia, two cars behind them, honked furiously. Sims, who had more pressing matters on his mind than obeying the rule of the road, ignored it and the Lancia.

Bertha drove as carefully to East Cowes as she had done the day before. She parked at almost the same spot in Link Road. This time, Sims parked further away. He and Anne watched them get out of their car and move off towards the ferry. He turned the car round facing the way they'd come. 'This is what we do, we'll let them get to the cafe and settle in, then we walk past as though we are a courting couple...'

Anne indignant, 'Not as *though!* we *are!*'

'...as I was saying, we walk past, go a few yards further on and then return. You will *never* look at them... you will *always* stay on the river side of me, and you will *always* keep me between you and them... is that understood?'

She nodded, 'Yes.'

'Right, let me see you load the shot gun; then put it back under the blanket... don't cock it until you need to...

the trigger's quite touchy.'

She took two cartridges out of the box, snapped the breech open, and inserted one into each barrel and closed the breech. Then she took another six out of the box and put them in her pockets.

'Done like an expert,' he said, smiling at her. He took the Browning out of its holster, undid the safety catch and slipped it into his right hand jacket pocket. 'I will keep my hand on it at all times...'

By the time they reached the ferry, Big Bertha and her shadows had already crossed.

'I think we ought to behave a bit like courting couples are supposed,' Anne said, and held him close.

'When we're walking I must have complete freedom of movement... no holding hands, love... I doubt if they'd be stupid enough to try anything in a crowded street... but we don't know that for sure.'

He needn't have worried whether Big Bertha would see him, walking past the cafe the manager spotted him, he waved and called, 'Shall I reserve a table for you, Mr Reeves?'

'A bit later... I'm going to show my girl friend around The Island first... see you this evening,' he said, loudly. The manager waved his approval.

'We might as well turn round now,' he said, pretending to point to some item of interest on the cafe building. They sauntered away back to the ferry. Sims occasionally turned round and pointed out some other non-existent architectural feature. 'Take your time, darling, don't rush... the two heavies are cool... Bertha almost wet herself... they're staying well back... we'll get on the ferry just as it's leaving... we don't want them for company on the trip.'

On reaching East Cowes they continued their *sightseeing walk* - Sims making sure Big Bertha and her escorts could keep them in sight. They loitered arm in arm on the side of Bridge Road, just as any couple might do watching the river traffic pass by.

The ferry was coming back over to their side of the water. 'Okay, let's walk slowly up Castle Road back to the car... nice and easy,' He stopped and kissed her, 'Might not get another chance for a little while,' he said, looking over her shoulder back towards the ferry. 'They're coming... let's get back to the car.'

Ignition wires hooked up, Maggie's old A40 started straight away. 'Get the shot gun and keep it on your lap with the blanket over it until we're out of town,' he said, pulling out on to the busy street. 'We follow this road as far as Alverstone Cross; then head for Wootton Bridge and Fishbourne. Instead of going down to the ferry terminal, we carry on a few yards and then turn right into Quarr Lane and on to Quarr Abbey.' Sims said this as much for his own benefit as Anne's.

In the rear view mirror, he could see Bertha's car following in the distance. 'Don't look back at them. We don't want to let-on we know we're being followed.'

Not many minutes later he could see they were catching him. 'Time to put my foot down,' he said. Sims knew putting one's foot down in the A40 was a term best thought of as the distance travelled by one's foot and pedal - it did not promise the driver any hope of adrenaline pumping acceleration.

At Alverstone Cross they turned for Wootton Bridge. He looked back to check they were still with him, and for the first time he noticed they were a three car convoy - the white Lancia was behind Bertha. Nothing was said to Anne about this, it could be coincidental.

The Lancia was still there when they were on the road to Quarr Abbey, perhaps no coincidence, he thought. 'In a minute I'm going to turn into the abbey, I hope they think we're just going to have a look round... we're going to take a track through the woods... I'll stop the car about a hundred yards from the cliff... ready?'

He turned into the Abbey and followed the route he had walked several times in the previous days. At the narrowest part of the track where two trees constricted its width, Sims drew to a halt. 'Get out and keep the shot gun with you, but under the blanket... let's look as if we're still on tour.'

There was no sign of their pursuers. 'It might take them a few minutes to work out where we've gone,' Sims said, as they reached the cliff edge. 'There's the gun emplacement... keep cool... keep on my left... walk normally.'

'I don't know if my legs will let me,' said Anne. Now worried that Sims, as well as looking after himself, might lose concentration thinking about her.

'Your legs are fine... trust me, I spent enough time looking at them on *Alice*.'

She managed a smile. 'I definitely would have stabbed you if I'd known you'd been ogling me.'

'Not ogling - slavering.'

'There's a difference?' she queried, keeping up the

game.

'Yep... ogling's just heavy duty looking - slavering involves quite a bit of drooling.'

'I didn't notice you drooling.'

'Doesn't have to come from the mouth.'

'Sims, that's *disgusting!*'

'I know... I'm famous for it.'

This way they reached the bunker. In that short and apparently casual stroll, she realised that life with Sims might have angles attached to it, details of which she'd not previously considered.

'Listen, immediately in front of that door, there's a support pillar; it has alcoves in it. I have stored some equipment under a tarpaulin in the topmost one... there are iron rungs set into the concrete so that you can reach it. Go down there now and quickly fetch the signal gun, some extra flares and a torch I've put there... *hurry.*'

Anne came back. 'I've got them... what now?'

Sims checked the flares and their gun. 'They look fine... now, on the left of the bunker there's a small window overlooking the cliff and the sea. I want you to put the gun and spare flares on the window ledge. When I tell you, aim as high as you can and fire one every 30 seconds until you run out. Before that, put the shot gun in the alcove you got the flares from... better get going, I can see some movement.'

Anne came back to the door. 'I've done that, darling.'

'Keep calm, love... two of them coming across... I saw some other movement lower down the track... might be Big Bertha... might be someone else... I need them to get most of the way here before we use the signal gun, or they might turn back... once they're here they're stuck... they may well think I'm unarmed... they've taken out their guns... they're almost here. Count to ten and then start firing flares... go to it, love.'

Sims walked down into the bunker.

*

'Flare! sir, there's a flare!... exactly at target location,' called the chopper pilot who had already opened his throttles wide. They were hardly airborne when they saw the second flare.

'How fast will this go?' asked the commodore.

'This one, just over 130 mph flat out, cruise, just over 120 mph... we'll be going at max, sir,' the pilot added before the commodore asked him to go flat out. 'ETA less than five minutes, sir.'

They watched the flares continue being fired, while they're being let off, one or both of them is still alive, the commodore thought. Hardly had he done so, than he realised there were no more being fired. He held his breath and watched the drifting smoke trails.

Sims could hear the throb of the approaching helicopter. Anne whispered, 'All flares fired, darling.'

'You've done fine, love, I'm really proud of you... can you hear the chopper?... your dad's coming. This is what you must do now... climb into the alcove, lay flat, tuck yourself tight into the corner... pull back the hammers on the shot gun and point it at the door... and shoot anyone who comes in carrying a gun or looking...' he smiled. 'looking like a Russian... just shoot, ask questions later.

It might pay for you to remember I'm not, nor do I look like a Russian. I thought there might have been three of them... I'm not so sure now... we do know there are at least two. They've positioned themselves either side of the alley. I'm going to let the chopper get closer... so I'll wait a few moments just inside the door to get accustomed to the light out there, then, I'm going out at a run.'

Anne looked scared and doubtful. He gently squeezed her arm. 'It's the best I can think of. I don't want to wait and let them come down to the entrance. At the distance they are now, it's a smaller arc for my arm to traverse; the closer they get, the wider... whatever, it will be down to accuracy - theirs and mine. Don't worry, love.'

He gave her a quick kiss. 'Anne, just so you know, you should understand I love you very much and, if I get the go-ahead, I might even marry you.'

Before she could say anything in reply, he went to the doorway and crouched down. Eighteen seconds later, still crouching, he ran out and towards the two men.

What happened next took less than two seconds. The impact of a bullet spun Sims to his right. He felt his right leg buckle, but even as he turned, his eyes and head stayed fixed on his targets. All that showed of the Russian agents were their upper bodies. Sims flung his gun arm out and snapped off two shots. He was dimly aware of a heavy thump on his left arm. The last thing he saw before his forehead smashed into the concrete wall was the Russians' heads recoiling... draw them on Reeves, draw them on... wait till you see the whites of their eyes. A million miles away he heard Anne scream his name.....

Anne had heard five shots in quick succession; then silence, nothing moved. She stayed where she was for only a few moments. 'What am I doing? What am I thinking of?' she said, and climbed down carrying the 12 bore with her. For less than a second she stood looking at the awful scene in front of her, then screamed, 'Sims! Sims!' and dropping the shot gun, rushed to him. He was covered in blood. His right leg was bent at a grotesque angle, and she could see his left arm was also very badly broken. Falling, he had hit his head and reopened the wound on his forehead. Anne dropped to her knees and with one hand she tried to stem the flow of blood pouring from his thigh. With the other she looked for more wounds; she was oblivious to the rush of people around her. 'Sims, oh Sims, please don't die... please don't die,' she pleaded.

Her father took hold of her shoulders and lifted her to her feet. 'Let the medics do their job now, darling,' he said. A young medical lieutenant caught the commodore's eye, and when he was sure that Anne could not see, slightly shrugged his shoulders.

The medics had Sims stretchered and were rushing him to the helicopter. 'I'm going with him,' said Anne, racing after them. Looking back at James, she shouted, 'Big Bertha was with them... she's in a light blue Cortina.'

The commodore said to James, 'I'm going with Anne to Haslar, I'll send the chopper back for you and these two,' he said, pointing at the two dead Russians.

James had also seen the medical lieutenant's gesture. He sat on the grass bank for a moment and put his head in his hands. Then, without showing any emotion, he got up, went over to the two bodies and retrieved their weapons. 'I'll take care of these just in case anyone tries a cover-up,' he said out loud, looking at the bodies. He went through their pockets, they were empty, there was nothing to identify them. A pretty quick death - one through the eye, and one through the neck. God let Sims live so I can tell him, he thought.

Two men approached, James shouted for them to stay back, 'Don't come any closer.'

'We heard the helicopter, is Sims all right?' asked Ed.

'You know Sims?'

'Who are you?' Al asked.

'Lieutenant James Fox-Eastleigh. Sims and I work together. I'm also a friend of his.'

'Is he all right?' asked Ed again.

'Come on over... don't look at the bodies, they're not a pretty sight.'

'Sims,' Al said, ' how is he?'

'Not good... might not live.'

'Christ, Aunt Maggie and Derek are going to be really upset,' said Al, 'they thought the world of him.'

'You know Derek?'

'Yes of course... he's our uncle,' said Ed.

'Can you get a message to them and tell them that Sims is in a bad way. There's a chance he won't make it... they'd better get to Haslar hospital as soon as they can.'

'What about his girlfriend Anne?' Al asked.

'She already knows... she was here with him... she's okay.'

'Poor lass,' Ed said, looking down towards the bunker door. 'That's my 12 bore down there, can I get it?... we'll take Aunt Maggie's car too if that's all right?'

'Sure... go ahead.'

James heard the helicopter returning. 'You two better be off before that lot get here,' he said, pointing towards the advancing chopper.

***

Chapter Nineteen
Where a Gentle Grebe Waits.

The surgeon told the four of them that Sims was in an extremely critical condition but out of immediate danger, he would be under heavy sedation for some time... days, and there really was no point in remaining unless they wished to.

Pearl said, 'Perhaps we'd best all go back to The Golden Bell and drink to his recovery... come on.'

They sat in the worn armchairs and sofa in her apartment above the bar. The worst of the shock was over - glasses of brandy loosened their tongues.

Mo, she fiddled with her rosary, 'He was always a bit of a worry.'

'Are you religious?' asked Maggie.

'Yes, always have been. I'm not good though... just religious.'

'What about Sims?... him too?'

'Good God no!'

'That was a bit definite,' said Maggie.

'I should think so! He went to church with me a couple of times. He didn't say prayers or do mass. He just wandered around looking at things. He said he didn't believe in God... wasn't religious, but he liked old buildings... two times was plenty enough though... I had to stop him coming.'

'Why was that?' asked Pearl.

'*Christ!*, Pearl, you know him as well as I do; he was a complete sod... the first time we went, he asked me what confession was... I was such a fool... should have been suspicious straight away. The second time, I'd finished my devotions and lit a candle... I couldn't see him anywhere. The next thing I knew, a young priest came rushing out of one of the confessionals... all in a sweat, and crossing himself like he'd been in there with Dracula or someone... seconds later, that bugger Sims appeared looking all innocent... he said he thought he'd try it out, and as he couldn't think of anything he'd ever done wrong, he made a few things up.'

Derek laughed: Maggie gave him a hard stare.

'Well, I got him out of that church as quick as I could. When we got home, I was really angry, and I made him tell me what he'd said. Anyway, apparently, he'd told the priest he'd tried his hand at *begatting*, and the priest said it wasn't a sin if one was married in the eyes of the lord. Do you know what that sod then said? He said, he was glad to have had this conversation, because he'd never realised it was possible to commit half a sin. It was so embarrassing, that innocent young priest then asked him; How do you mean my son? Sims said, well, about what you just said about being married... I wasn't; she was - so were the other two.'

Derek, now holding his sides.

'That arse... that *complete* arse, then told him, there would have been four, but the bed wasn't big enough...

to cap it all he started telling him what they'd got up to... well I won't repeat what he told him, angry as I was, even I started to get over-heated. Honestly, he was the loveliest bloke I ever knew, so gentle... but he could be *such* a sod.'

Derek still holding his sides and making quite an odd wheezing noise in his failing attempt not to laugh. Maggie said, 'It's not funny, Derek Hill. I'll have a few words to say to him when he gets better.'

'And I'll ask him for a few tips,' muttered Derek, under his breath.

'Was he really that bad?' asked Maggie.

'Not always... sometimes the sod was worse,' Mo said, laughing, 'I could never stay angry at him for long though... about two minutes usually.'

'You must know him better than anybody.'

'Used to,' Mo corrected her. 'You mustn't think he's bad, he was so lovely to be with... 'cept in church.'

Pearl poured out more drinks - Mo sat cuddling hers. 'He told some lovely stories... someone's got to persuade him to write... get him to tell you 'Felicity', I almost wet myself... and 'The Hoopoe's Message'. I didn't really understand what he was getting at with that one... but it was still nice. My favourite is the one he told me on our first date; 'The Golden Mace'... made me feel like a little girl again... gave me determination.'

Derek and Maggie eventually made their way home. 'Do you remember what you said after that first night Sims came to supper? You said something about an absent husband coming home, and finding he hadn't got a wife any more. I think you were right, love. When you hear how Mo talks about him, I think it was a very close run thing.'

*

'Our courier... he survived the explosion. The two dead Russian GRU agents on the Isle of Wight were his doing. Badly injured in the process... chances are he won't survive this time.'

'Issue the new identity; immediately,' said Billy Ruffian.

*

Sims was floating on a small lake. He lay on what appeared to be a soft bed of reeds - a nest. Mists rolled in and with them came the grebe. She stroked his arm with her soft neck. He was comfortable here. The mists receded a little and he could just make out the shore. Figures appeared that seemed to form themselves from the very mistiness of the place. Some were almost recognisable. Now and again they would wave to him, their arms nebulous, made of dampness and vapour.

The further the mist rolled back to the shore, the more agitated the grebe's rubbing became. When the scene before him was at its clearest, the grebe stopped stroking his arm and gave him a sharp peck on the back of his hand. The mists rolled quickly back in and Sims could hear voices, soft footsteps, clinking of metal, the rustle of clothing, the sound of machinery: wheels turning. He thought, there's a cart coming past on the shore.

The mist now completely engulfed him. As it cleared, he could make out Anne sitting beside his bed holding his hand, stroking his arm. She had not noticed he had regained consciousness. 'You're okay then?' he rasped. He was tired and in much pain, and before she could reply, he decided to go back to where it was comfortable, where the mists were thicker, no sounds came, and a gentle grebe waited.

The nurse had been out of the room for only a few seconds when Sims had seemed to be fading. Anne had called for her, his breathing was getting too shallow for her to bear, she had slapped his wrist hard. He gasped, took in a huge gulp of air, his breathing then became steadier. She was looking towards the door for the nurse when Sims had woken. By the time she had turned her head he had gone.

The nurse came in. 'He spoke to me.'

'That's good... he'll probably dip in and out of consciousness for a while.'

She was shaken and shaking. 'He almost stopped breathing... I slapped him on the wrist... he started again.'

'Hmm... I'll get the duty medical officer to take a look at him.'

'He looks as good as can be expected,' said the young doctor. When wheeled in, he had not rated Sims's chances of survival as being above fifty-fifty. 'When he spoke was he coherent?'

'Yes, he said; "You're okay, then", then lost consciousness again.'

'That sounds promising. You look all-in... ought to get some rest.'

'I'm not going anywhere until I know it's safe to.'

Hours later She looked up and saw that he was watching her. 'Hello, darling... are you with us again?'

Sims gave a slight nod and managed to curl a finger around one of hers before drifting off to sleep once more.

Over the next few days, his brief periods of waking were more frequent, relatively longer in duration, and he became more coherent. Exhausted both physically and emotionally, Anne, who had only dozed at his bedside was finally persuaded to get some sleep. A strong sleeping draught was prescribed, she slept for nearly ten hours straight. When she woke, she washed, dressed, and without eating, rushed straight to find Sims being fussed over by two young nurses. 'Are you sure it needs two of you to wash him?' she asked.

'Yes ma'am, we have to be very careful.'

'They have to be very careful,' Sims said, sleepily. He had been quite enjoying the attention.

'I can see you're feeling better.'

'Who wouldn't be,' he said, smiling at Anne's tetchiness.

'Excuse me a moment,' she said to the nurses, and to demonstrate she had full possession of this man, gave him a long and quite intimate kiss. 'There, you can finish him off now.'

A day later, he had been washed again, tidied and now all remaining traces of dried blood removed, felt much improved. 'I've taken on board some water, but had sod all to eat... I'm bloody starving.'

'Never mind food,' Anne said, leaning closer to him,

'Tell me again what you said to me in the bunker.'

'I can't remember much... it happened so quickly... all a bit of a blur.' Sims had recovered sufficiently, to resume being a sod.

'Then I'll remind you - you said, you loved me... and ..' she hesitated, 'and, something else.'

'You sure?... must have been delirious... loss of blood.'

'Darling, you said it before you were shot.'

'What's all this darling business? There must be some Admiralty Standing Order that forbids terms of endearment between wren officers and hoicks... irrespective of how desirable that sexy hoick might be.'

'If you don't answer, I'll bash you... despite your injuries. And don't try to change the subject. Tell me what you *said!*'

'Now's not a good time, sir.'

'Why not?... and don't call me, SIR!'

'Because Commodore Sherwood, that's your father by the way, is standing right behind you.'

'Young man, if you hadn't brought it upon yourself, I'd almost feel sorry for you. If you know what's good for you, you'll tell her what she wants to hear. She'll never give you any peace until you do. Might as well get it over with once and for all.' To Anne he said, 'I haven't got long. Sims and myself are going to have a chat about all sorts of matters.'

'There's nothing you can have to discuss that I can't be party to.'

'2nd Officer Sherwood, if I have to pull rank I will.'

Apologetically, he said, 'She's always been a bit of a handful.'

Anne looking extremely indignant, left the room.

*

James was waiting to see Sims.

'They took three bullets out of him - the surgeon picked up the fact that he had a healed bullet wound in his back.'

'I know - that was the one I told you about,' said James, lack of sleep leaving him completely washed-out.

'Joss knows you meant well, but she still thinks dragging him into this, wasn't the best way of saying thank you.'

'Please don't think I'm happy about it either. I really thought it might help him up the ladder.'

'Perhaps it's best to look at it this way, if you hadn't done so, I would never have met him, and for that, I thank you from the very bottom of my heart,' she said, kissing him on the cheek.

*

Before arriving at his purpose the commodore asked, 'Are you going to marry her, lad?'

'If she'll have me, sir.'

'There's not much doubting that, is there? Go to it, Sims, you won't find me objecting... be glad to have you on board.'

He sat down beside the bed: seemed hesitant. 'I'm finding it difficult to know where to start.' He paused. 'In the ten years since her mother's accident, I've only seen her cry a small handful of times - most of those times have been in the last few weeks.' In a desperate effort to control his emotions, he paused again. 'She is the only link I have left with my wife, Alice. Every day

I'm reminded of how much they act and look alike... she means so much to me... I owe so much to you... trying to protect her... us... was incredibly brave... you must have known you stood a good chance of being killed... what she would have done if you had been, I dread to think.' As he said this, he reached over and grasped Sims' hand, 'I will be very proud to have you as my son: *so* proud.'

It didn't escape Sims' notice the commodore had said son and not son-in-law. He tried to ease the sharp tension. 'Maybe you're forgetting I'm from the lower deck, sir... perhaps you'd like to rephrase what you've just said.'

'I wouldn't want to rephrase it, even if you were a stoker,' he said, quite firmly. 'It so happens, you're not.'

'Sir?'

'James told us about the document he saw at a cabal meeting. It seems that someone thought you were not going to make it... overnight they had your history changed. It's even on the name card on your door and at the foot of your bed - not that Anne has noticed yet. I have checked... your old naval life is no longer on record. Your room at *Victory* has been cleared out... as far as I can see, you are a lieutenant in her majesty's Royal Navy. Lieutenant John Sims Reeves, may I be the first to congratulate you?'

'Does this mean a pay rise?... how much does a lieutenant get?'

The commodore laughed, 'Is that all you've got to say, lad? Aren't you surprised even?'

'I've said it quite a few times recently, nothing, nothing at all, would surprise me at the moment... and to tell the truth, the only immediate benefit I can see, is the extra disability pension I get when they throw me out of the service.'

'On that matter, lad, don't do, or say, anything in haste. You have around two and a half years left to do, correct?'

'Unless they kick me out first.'

'I have an idea, Sims. You're going to have to trust me that it's a good one. As I just said, don't act in haste.'

'Sir, doing things in a rush is not on the cards at the moment.'

'On another point, I've spoken with the surgeon commander... when your wounds have healed properly, they want to move you to a convalescence home in Surrey... I know Anne wouldn't want that... frankly, nor would I... how would you like to live at Hell Head House... there's plenty of room.' And, as if it was necessary to further convince him, he added, 'There's always Mrs Calver's cooking to consider.'

'Now, that's the clincher, sir... bit doubtful at first... wall to wall bacon sarnies... I'm completely sold on the idea... I think I'd like that very much, thank you.'

'I think it's me that should be doing the thanking... and another thing, perhaps in future we always invoke the *Alice protocol* when we can.'

'I'll give it a go... it will take some getting used to... perhaps you'll forgive any slip-ups.'

Anne knocked on the door and looked in. 'Haven't you finished *yet*, Father?' she said, scowling at him.

'You can come back in a minute.' Again he grasped Sims' hand, 'Thanks once again, lad. Remember, don't act, or say anything, in haste... promise?'

'I promise... one thing before you go, did you get their

guns and mine?'

'James did.'

'Will you keep them for me? And will you keep guard over these three bullets the surgeon gave me? he said, handing him a small glass jar. Perhaps the best thing to do is to give everything to James to look after.'

'Why do you want them kept?'

'Curiosity's sake... now you're going to have to trust me,' he said. 'And, sir, I'll need an officer's kit. Can you get James or someone to organise that? Ask him to make it second hand - one that looks as if I've worn it for sometime. I'd hate to look like a complete nozzer.'

'Nozzer! That's a saying I haven't heard since Ganges days... leave it to me. I'll get the back-pay sorted out as well.'

Anne came into the room, sat down by the bed and once more picked up where she had left off, she looked tired. 'Tell me what you said in the bunker... I want to hear it from you again... please tell me this moment, Sims.'

He'd pushed her far enough; he took her hand. 'Come closer.' Anne drew the chair as close as she could. 'Closer than that... I don't want everybody to hear, just you... I'll whisper it in your ear... this is our thing.' As she leant over him he lightly kissed her lips, her cheek, her ear, and into it softly said, '2nd Officer Anne Sherwood, I have loved you from the very first moment I saw you. I have never stopped loving you since, and I guess I shall love you as long as I live.'

She caught her breath. 'Then make sure it's for a very, very, long time,' she said. It was all too much for her. 'I thought you were going to die before I'd been able to tell you how much I love you too.'

She wiped her eyes and with her head resting on his shoulder lay quiet. Then stirred slightly, 'Sims?'
'Umm.'
'Did you still love me after I told you to fuck off?'
'Even *more* so.'
'More so?'
'Sure, I mean... come on... it was a high point in our relationship... you, with your diamond-cut, gilt-edged accent, swearing like that... I was so proud... a lifetime achievement... only wish I'd had a tape recorder.'

They lay quietly, Anne's head still resting on his shoulder.
'Okay,' he said, 'my turn for the questions... what happened?... what's the damage?... they're not coming forward with much info... you're doing fine... couldn't wish for better, come on, love... tell me... I want the lowdown.'
Anne sat up and looked at him seriously. 'You are going to be fine... that's the truth... I don't like to think of it... it was so awful... they shot you three times.' She broke down again, 'I really thought they'd killed you.'
'Well they didn't, did they?' said Sims, holding her as close as he could, waiting for her to calm down. 'Come on, honey, I want to know.'
'You have three bullet wounds,' she said, her voice breaking. 'One in the upper left arm, that one broke your humerus... that's why it's in plaster. The two others hit your right leg - one of them smashing your thigh bone,' again Anne broke down. 'Oh, Sims, you were lying there

all bent and broken... your blood was everywhere.'

'Steady love... take it easy. What about them?'

'You got them both... both dead... that's enough for now, darling, please ask Father for the rest... it was really the most horrible... terrible, terrible moment of my life... I don't want to think about it, Sims, my love.'

She visited him every day, practically living in his room. He progressed rapidly. One day the occasional vagueness left by the general anaesthetic had finally left him. He was on sparkling form. She decided to broach something that had been on her mind. 'Sims, what are we going to do when you come out?'

He leant over and whispered in her ear.

'Sims!' she said, rather shocked, 'I meant what are *your* plans when you come out?'

'Weren't you listening! I just told you. Actually, I've been trying to think about things quite a bit... still haven't managed to get past that first phase yet - planning comes later.'

'Is that what you think of most of the time?'

'Since I met you - all the time... how about this then?' and once more, he whispered in her ear.

If Sims could have seen her feet, he would have seen that she had slipped them out of her shoes and with her ankles crossed was rubbing the sole of one foot gently with the top of the other. 'Are you sure that's legal?'

'Possibly not... we may have to sail into international waters to stay completely in the clear... or perhaps French territorial waters, they allow just about anything there.'

'If we're doing that, who's going to steer?'

'For God's sake woman, if you're not careful, you'll

turn into a bloody accountant, and then where would we be?... stop worrying about the detail!'

Anne looked for a moment as though she was about to say something but then changed her mind.

'Now, where was I?' said Sims.

'You were at the point where you were just going to...'

The duty sister came in, interrupting things at a very interesting departure from what Anne had assumed was standard procedure for intimate couples on ketches or in private.

Sister left after checking his pulse, temperature, and given him his medication. Anne asked, 'How do you know about such things?'

'It's male intuition, love... *a priori* understanding... built-in knowledge. Women have a similar understanding, remember those Belgian chocolates? You knew intuitively, nay instinctively, that you had to fill your face with them; and you did too... both activities are perfectly normal, healthy behaviour.'

'Well, if we're going to be doing all that, it's a good thing the bullet that got you high up on your thigh, wasn't any higher,' she said, thoughtfully.

'Meaning?'

'We were very lucky,'

'We?'

'Yes... it must have passed very close to your... your, you know... your credentials,'

'*Credentials!*' he said, laughing. '*Credentials!* What the hell are my credentials?'

Colouring up, she said, 'You know very well what I

mean.'

'Anyway, how do you know?'

'I was checking you for more injuries... I noticed,' she said, rather weakly.

'Excuse me! can we just take a step or two back? Let's see if we can get this picture quite clear... so there am I, lying in a huge pool of my own blood, life rapidly ebbing from my body, and what were you doing in the meantime?... damn me, if you weren't rummaging around in my underpants - checking me out. This, from the woman who has just feigned shock at some of my quite innocent suggestions.'

'It wasn't like that at all. I was not checking you out... I was checking you over. And, for the record, I don't think some of your suggestions were entirely innocent.'

'Checking out... checking over, same thing,' he said, smiling at her.

'No it isn't. It was First Aid as taught; ascertain full extent of injuries.'

'Yeah, yeah, yeah, ... have it your way... actually, I'm quite impressed... shows a healthy, if not somewhat grubby and liberated attitude to things that matter most.'

*

'He's tough; recovering well. What would you like doing now?'

'I had a visit from the Commanding Officer HMS *Dolphin* - Commodore Sherwood. Our courier is expected to marry his daughter. Sherwood seems very fond of Reeves - thinks of him as his own son.'

'He *has* done well for himself,' said Stinton.

Billy Ruffian continued, 'He made it clear, and in no uncertain terms, that if in any way we harm Reeves, he will make life extremely difficult for NID. Sherwood is well respected, he's one of our foremost submarine warfare tacticians; his word carries weight... he will shortly be promoted to Rear Admiral. We have enough on our plate without dealing with an angry Flag Officer. So, we'd best leave Reeves as he is. We must also take this into consideration, if we reinstate Reeves to his original rank, MI5 will be on to it like a shot... best let things lie as they are.'

'Do you think he could still be useful?'

'Maybe - bring him in as soon as he's fit enough. We need to debrief him.'

*

Anne came into his room looking excited. 'Sorry I'm late. Pearl phoned to say Mo has had her baby, I just had to go and see her... I took some flowers from us both... a baby girl. She looks just like Mo, dark hair... so beautiful. Mo's going to call her...'

'Angelica,' he interrupted, smiling, 'she'll go for three children.'

'How did you know that?'

'Just male intuition... Mo's a smashing girl, she'll make a super mum.'

'Anyway, I gave her your love... she sends hers... she looked *so* happy, Sims.'

***

Chapter Twenty
The School Report.

They had removed the cast from his left arm much earlier. This though, was the day he had worried most about - the day they would remove the plaster from his leg. 'Not bad, not bad at all. It's all looking fine,' said the surgeon commander, looking at the x-rays and then prodding the scars and Sims' thigh muscle, 'We did a good job on you... plenty of trauma experience from the Korean war in our team... you were lucky. Lots of physio now for you, young man.' He turned to his attendant nurse, 'No time like the present, see that he's booked in straight away... you're healing very well.'

'When can he come home?' asked the ever-present Anne.

'A few day's physio and observation first, if everything goes well, he can go home for the weekend.' With that, he and the nurse left the room.

Sims leaned over to Anne. 'Did you hear that? I'm coming home... to a place I've never seen.'

'It's still your home. Mrs Calver's looking forward to meeting you so much, she's not stopped talking about you all week. Father's fussing around, checking this and that, I've never seen him so excited.'

'How about you?'

'I'll manage,' she said, smiling happily.

'Where's *Alice*?' he asked, as Anne drove him to Hell Head House.

'At the moment she's in Hell Head harbour... why?'

'I'd like to go there first if possible.'

'Okay, darling, but they'll be waiting at the house for us, you know.'

Anne drove as close as she could to *Alice*. 'There she is.'

'I want to go on board.'

'Are you sure you can manage?'

'I might need a hand.'

She helped him out of the car and down the steps to the pontoon where *Alice* gently swayed.

'Now for the hard bit, help me on to the deck, then go down into the cockpit and let me lean on you while I step down.'

Leaning forward with his hands on her shoulders, he stepped slowly and carefully into the cockpit.

A gentle zephyr blew through the calm of the small harbour: it rattled *Alice's* rigging against her mast. 'She's talking to you, Sims... she's missed you.'

Holding Anne by the waist, he said, 'I've dreamt of this for weeks; she's a lovely boat... if it hadn't been for her we might not have met.' She put her arms round him and held him very close. 'And,' he continued, 'I wouldn't have had this chance to properly ask you to marry me.'

'How on earth could I marry anyone else? Of course I'll marry you.'

'This seemed the best place in the world to ask; I hope

The School Report.

it's made your mum happy... now let's go home, I've got the fabulous Mrs Calver to meet.' The light breeze again sighed through *Alice's* rigging.

Anne wiped her eyes. 'You might be in breach of promise. You asked her to marry you, remember?... you wouldn't leave me for her, would you?'

'Not sure, depends how good your sarnies are.'

Commodore Sherwood and Mrs Calver waited as they drove up the drive to Hell Head House. Anne's father helped Sims out of the car. 'How are you, son?'

'Fine; I'll need the stick for a bit... but otherwise okay... you?'

'Never better... Anne's so happy... can't recall ever seeing her like this.'

With Anne on his arm, Sims went over to the woman waiting on the steps. 'Mrs Calver, it's so nice to meet you at long last,' and to her surprise, gave her a quite generous kiss. 'That's for those superb sarnies you sent down to *Alice*.'

'My god, it's a long time since I've been kissed like that.'

'Number one rule of any self respecting stoker: keep well in with the sarnie maker.'

'Anne, you've got yourself a good one, I think... Isn't he lovely?'

'*I* think so,' said Anne, linking arms with him.

Like this they went into the house. He looked around the hall. 'Some place.'

'Not place, *home*,' she corrected him.

'Let's all go into the library until lunch is ready,' said the commodore.

The School Report.

'Could I have a word alone with you, sir?'

The two of them remained in the hall while the others went into the library. 'I asked Anne to marry me this morning; she said, yes. How do feel about it now?'

'I'll say the same as I did in hospital, go to it, lad, you'll get no objections from me.'

'I proposed to her on *Alice* just before we came here... I thought you both might like that.'

'That was a lovely gesture,' he put his arm round Sims' shoulder and led him into the room with the others. Gravel crunched: a car drew up at the front door. Seconds later, Joss and James came in.

The hubbub of greetings died down. 'Mrs Calver, I'd like you to stay. James, give me a hand with these glasses please,' asked the commodore, opening two bottles of chilled champagne. Glasses filled, he said, 'Today, I am a very happy man. We have Sims up, about, and home. However, that's not all, I'd like you to raise your glasses for another purpose: I used the word home advisedly, Sims proposed to Anne today, and I know you will not be surprised to hear she accepted.'

Joss and Mrs Calver almost collided in their haste to get to Anne. It took several minutes of hugging, kissing and eye wiping before the commodore could continue. 'There is a slight dampener on the day... my Aunt Catherine is coming for lunch. The better news is, it is her custom to leave early, she will probably be gone by four o'clock. In the meantime, let us toast the future happiness of Anne and Sims.'

The sentiment *Anne and Sims* echoed round the old library.

The School Report.

James slapped Sims on the shoulder. 'Congratulations, she looks very happy. Come to that, so do you.'

'Thanks. I hear I should congratulate you too. What with everything, I forgot.' He made sure nobody was within earshot. 'James, I need to touch on a darker point... you did get their guns, didn't you?'

What Sims might be thinking demanded care, 'Yes,' replied James, cautiously.

'I couldn't get time to talk to you before - keep them, don't do anything to them. Are their magazines intact?'

'Yes, but for Christ's sake why?'

'It's important. Don't do anything to them. I want them here, don't give them to anybody, whatever the pressure. And my gun, have you got that as well?'

'Yes.'

'I want that too.'

'Sims, for God's sake *drop it*!'

'That suggestion suggests there's something to drop... something unfinished.'

James looked fixedly at him. 'It is *never* finished. Remember what Billy Ruffian said, it will *never* end.'

'I wasn't there at the time - but have it your way, let's not spoil the day.'

Anne did not care for Sims and James to be alone. She knew Sims wanted to talk to him in private. Their history: the spectre she feared most, might emerge into her present. In hospital, she wouldn't ever leave them alone together. Today, she was happy, though the shades of his broken body lay just below the surface. She guided Joss over to the pair. Hugging Sims, Joss said, 'I just knew this was how it would turn out. That day we sailed on *Alice*, I said, Anne, beautiful, isn't she? and you said, really gorgeous, I knew it then.'

'Did he really say that?' asked Anne, firmly retaking possession of Sims.

Commodore Sherwood tapped his glass for attention. 'On this special day I want Mrs Calver to dine with us... there's a lot to do in the kitchen, I suggest we all go in and lend a hand. Sims, you're excused duties.'

'I can peel spuds as good as the next man... I'm coming too... best room in any house.'

With the chores complete, Anne took him on a tour of the house. 'Do you think you can manage the stairs, darling? Mrs Calver's made a bed in a room at the quiet end of the first floor. In the morning you can stay there in peace, lie in as long as you like.'

'Let's give them a go.'

At the end of the long corridor she showed him into a comfortable, large room. Sims went over to the window. He looked across The Solent towards Fishbourne, Ryde and the little field in between them, he killed the dark memory that started to emerge.

'What do you think?'

'It's really very nice... remote. Do you think you'll be able to find your way here okay?'

'I will never *ever* need a map to reach you, John Sims Reeves,' she said, kissing him, 'never ever.'

Great Aunt Catherine Sherwood arrived: they returned downstairs.

She knew all but Sims and James; she inspected them both. 'Which one is yours, Anne?'

She resisted saying, the sexy one, 'This one, Aunt.'

The School Report.

The old girl looked Sims up and down, 'No doubt, I will speak to you later.'

'So looking forward to it... can't wait, ma'am.'

Anne sensed trouble.

'Is luncheon served yet, Robert? A lady of my age *must* eat.'

'To the dining room, everybody,' said the commodore.

They sat at the opposite end of the table from Great Aunt Catherine. 'Does she take solids or is it liquids straight from the neck?' he whispered to Anne.

'Please don't start, she's only here for an hour or two.'

Mrs Calver apologised to Sims and Anne, saying she would eat with the aunt's chauffeur in the kitchen. They had nearly completed the main course when the attack started. Anne noticed her aunt look at Sims, Please not now! she thought.

Great Aunt Catherine waited until there was a lull in the conversation - she needed to be heard: the focus. 'My nephew tells me you were once a stoker.'

'Yes, that's true. Sadly, all good things must come to an end, mustn't they?'

Anne nudged him under the table.

'And your family, they were working class too?'

'Really, Aunt!' exclaimed Anne, horrified by the complete lack of sensitivity of the question. She gripped Sims' hand tightly. He gave hers a squeeze in return that said: Don't worry, I'm not.

All but Sims and the commodore seemed acutely embarrassed. 'I do hope so, though we've always feared they might be disqualified for being classical musicians.' He leaned towards her end of the table. 'Us working class try to keep things like that quiet,' he said in a loud stage whisper. 'We also try to stay hush-hush about my grampy fighting at Jarama in the Spanish Civil War, and that my gran followed him there and idled her time away stitching arms and legs back on soldiers who had been stupid enough to get themselves blown-up fighting for something they believed in - unforgivable.'

Oblivious to the flaying Sims had delivered, she asked, 'Your father, was *he* a stoker too?'

'Aunt, that really *is* enough!'

Great Aunt Catherine was momentarily taken a back by the force of Anne's outburst.

'Don't concern yourself, love,' said Sims.

The old girl recovered some of her composure and was ready to restart the interrogation. 'I merely enquire, so that we know *what* we are dealing with here.'

Half standing, Anne shouted, 'Not WHAT, Aunt, WHO!'

'Steady, darling, let me answer her, we might just get some peace then.'

She was at last happy. She was the focus of all attention and ready to wield her power. 'The question was a simple one, was *he* a stoker too?'

'My father, in choosing not to be a stoker, demonstrated a complete lack of good taste.'

'What was he then... a seaman?'

'In a way, yes,' said Sims, stringing her along.

'My boy, how could he possibly be a seaman, *in a way*?' She was going in for the kill.

'Well, it depends somewhat on what you mean by seaman. If you mean someone who lives on a seamen's mess deck, then no, he was not.'

'Oh really... what *other* kind are there?'

He knew all the others were embarrassed on his behalf, he also knew he held the trump card. 'Those that live in the wardroom, ma'am.'

Anne looked at him. What did he mean?

Knives and forks stilled: nobody ate, the embarrassment and tension too much.

'I'm not sure I understand you.'

'Oh, I should have thought that with your nephew being a naval officer, you'd have known they are members of the wardroom... it's a place where officers live.'

'Young man, are you implying your father was an officer?'

It was time to stop playing her along. 'I'm not implying anything, my father was Lieutenant-Commander John Sims Reeves - 1st Lieutenant of HMS *Penelope*. He was on his way back to England to receive promotion to commander and take his first command of a destroyer. The *Penelope* was torpedoed - he was killed. It was very bad luck.'

'Is this true, Sims?' Anne said.

'Yes, every word.'

'But, you never said.'

'Anne, darling; I'm me... sink or swim, what you see, is me. What difference does it make what my father was?'

In front of the whole assembly she kissed him. 'None at all.'

'Hear, hear,' said her father.

The old girl attempted to take command once more, 'This is all very well, but why didn't you use your connection to better yourself?'

'Oh, come on now, surely even you can see history says there was no point in doing so, ma'am.' He then extended and qualified his point succinctly, 'I have met, and will be married to, the most intelligent, brave, beautiful, attractive girl in the whole world. Please, if you are able, tell me how I could have bettered that?'

Anne turned to him, and said, in a whisper - one that Joss and James sitting nearby plainly heard, 'Gosh, you really know how to turn a girl on.'

'And what would be the point of having a girl like you, if I couldn't do that?' he whispered, in reply.

This was equally overheard by Joss and James. Joss winked at James - James smiled back at her.

For the first time, Aunt Catherine looked rattled. And, as so many of her type react when exposed, she looked for someone to pass the buck to. 'Robert, why didn't you tell me his father was an officer and a gentleman?'

'I only recently found out myself, I didn't think it important at the time, Aunt,' he said, 'and I still don't.'

For the remainder of the meal she behaved relatively well, talking to Joss about James and his family, and talking to James about Joss's family. Finally, she announced, to everyone's relief, her departure. Her driver was summoned from the kitchen and her car brought to the front door. She stood up, the rest of the company did the same. In the hall, Great Aunt Catherine went to Sims. 'I suppose you had better kiss me,' she said, offering her face to him. Sims put his hand round her waist and dutifully pecked her on the cheek. As she turned away, he said, 'Take care ma'am,' and patted her on the behind.

The School Report.

The commodore led his aunt to the front door. Joss tried to convert a huge snort into a cough and clutched James who was failing in his struggle not to laugh. Sims looked at Anne, who whispered, with tears of laughter running down her face, 'Sims, you *can* be a bit of a sod, you know.'

Before going down the steps, she turned to Sims and said, with the very faintest hint of a smile, 'It's been a very long time since anybody has done that to me, young man.' Escorted by her smiling nephew, she got into her waiting car.

'Did she actually grin?' asked Sims.

'I think so... it's possible... I'm not sure... I don't remember seeing her attempt one previously,' said Anne.

*

She did not knock. Anne made her way noiselessly to his bedside. 'Darling, I can wait no longer,' she said, slipping between the sheets and lying next to him...

...in the early hours of the morning, and for the final time that night, she, sighed, stretched, and gave a long shuddering gasp.

*

He woke early and looked at Anne still sleeping. You are so beautiful, he thought, and resisted the temptation of telling her so. He carefully got out of bed, showered, dressed, and without waking her, went downstairs.

'Can I come in?' he asked Mrs Calver.

'Of course you can, my love... like some coffee?'

'Please... I like kitchens, always comfortable.'

'So do I, they smell right, don't they? Would you like some breakfast now?'

'Not right away, thanks, I'll wait till Anne comes down... I'll have a look round the house.'

Sims found and went into the study, sat at the desk, inserted a piece of paper into the typewriter and began to type. When he had finished, he carefully folded the single sheet and put it into an envelope.

He heard Anne's voice calling him from the dining room.

'Morning, darling,' she said, smiling, 'sleep well?'

'Like a top... you?'

'I've not slept like that for years... can't think why.'

He gave her a kiss, helped himself to some toast and scrambled egg, and sat on the opposite side of the table. Anne got up, went round to him and put her arms round his neck. 'Well?'

'Well what?'

She stomped back to her side of the table, sat down and pretended to scowl. She stood up again, went back to Sims; leant over him, and again, put her arms round his neck and kissed him several times on the cheek. '*WELL!*'

'Anne Sherwood, the idea of being married to you, took on a whole new range of possibilities last night... I'm glad to say, you're no accountant,' he said, smiling.

'Well that shows how much you know... actually, I am.'

'Come again?'

'I need to be a qualified accountant to do my job. What do you say to that?'

The School Report.

'That was really devious, Anne,' he said, looking hurt, 'you might have told me before I proposed... married to an *accountant!*... please say you're joking?'

'I wasn't going to tell you *beforehand*! that would have been really stupid... face it, John Sims Reeves, you're trapped with a pen pusher... for life.'

'*Jesus!*, I'm bleedin' doomed, a normal life blighted.'

With the previous night fresh in her memory, and thinking this a good time to change the subject, she said, 'Sims, how long do you think it will be before we can sail *Alice* to international waters?'

'I'm working on it, lots of exercise - night and day.'

He finished his breakfast, 'Got some physio to do,' he said, getting up. He handed her the envelope, 'Don't read this till you're on your own... it's private.'

Joss came into the dining room and found Anne giggling at the sheet of paper she was reading. Anne hurriedly put the note away.

Joss kissed her, and said, 'Well?'

'Well what?'

'Anne Sherwood, you're not going tell me you stayed in your room last night.'

She flushed slightly.

'There, I knew it... what was he like?'

'It was deeply personal - private.'

'Best friends should always share their most intimate secrets, everybody knows *that!*'

Anne hesitated for a moment. 'Thorough.'

'Thorough! THOROUGH!' exclaimed Joss.

'Yes, thorough; he even wrote me a report. Here, read this.'

The School Report.

The two girls sat side by side, laughing and giggling while reading the carefully typed paper:

Night School Report: Anne Sherwood, Hell Head House, Hell Head, Hampshire.

Subjects taken: Bouncing - Voice Development - Breathing - English Language.

Bouncing:
Anne has natural, vigorous and energetic bouncing skills. She demonstrates delightful enthusiasm for this subject. With a little extra tuition, she should be able to see the dust on the top of the wardrobe.

Voice Development:
Range: Mezzo/asthmatic.
Deranged: Often.
Summary - voice: In a word; operatic - only Callas, Tebaldi or Christa Ludwig come close.
Anne manages low notes with ease. She is, however, less controlled in the higher register, where she has a tendency to go all-to-cock and develop a frightening, ear-piercing shriek.

Breathing:
Sometimes erratic - often gasping. Here, high altitude training may be called for - a bed installed in the attic perhaps?

English language:
Anne must understand, that the English language is extremely rich, wide, and varied, and that it contains many more words and phrases than:

The School Report.

Oh God; yes; no; Christ that's wonderful, and eeek!

Summary - overall:
Her tutor says he has never actually seen her in overalls, however, he is looking forward to the moment he does with keen interest. He wonders what undergarments she is likely to wear when doing so. He also says, of the four subjects taken, she performed them all well above expectations. Her tutor declares he is hard pressed to see where she could improve, and suggests that even a trip to French National waters may only provide slight incremental benefits.

'You didn't tell me you were asthmatic... I'm a bit worried about your breathing,' said Joss, laughing, 'perhaps you make up for it by being, *energetic* though. Oh look, it's such a relief you have *natural ability* - that *is* nice to know, I was beginning to despair at one time. What's this about French National waters?'

'Never mind. That's too personal.'

'Sounds intriguing;... possibly obscene.'

'That's exactly what I said.'

'Oh come on, Anne, spill the beans, please!'

'No! Definitely not, and that, Joss Mortimer, is that.'

After they had finished their breakfast and had dissected the report a couple more times, they stepped out on to the terrace, linked arms, and met Sims coming the other way. He winked at Anne, and said to Joss, 'How are you this morning?'

'Oh, you know... a bit wheezy... a bit, how can I put it?... a bit mezzo-asthmatic,' she said, and turning to Anne, 'How about you, Anne?'

The School Report.

'Oh God; yes; no; Christ that's wonderful; eeek!'

Both girls hooted with laughter and walked on past him.

Sims watched them walk away. Anne half turned, gave him a slightly exaggerated sway of her hips and an almost obscene knowing smile.

'That's *completely* unfair, Anne.'

'No it's not. Why shouldn't I show my best friend, my tutor's report? She might learn something.'

'Not the report, I mean it's simply not fair for you to walk in that manner... ...there's gotta be at least twelve hours to bed-time.'

'Don't remind me,' she said, in her best mezzo-asthmatic voice.

Joss, smiling, looked at her friend: Anne Sherwood... alive at last. Mission accomplished.

***

Chapter Twenty One
Two Tokarevs and one Beretta.

'How did your weekend go?' asked the physio.

'Better than I could have ever have hoped for,' he replied, truthfully.

'And the leg, how do you think it held up?'

'Knees felt a bit shaky on Sunday morning. After a strong coffee and breakfast, I went for a walk and everything was fine.'

'And this morning?'

'More or less the same.'

'Keep up the good work.'

'I intend to... Is high altitude training okay?'

'If precautions are taken,' she said, feeling, oiling, and massaging his thigh. 'I must say, Anne looked pleased with herself today.'

This stopped Sims dead - his parallel patter had stalled. He stared at the smiling physio. 'I've known Anne for sometime, nice to see her looking *so* relaxed.'

The surgeon, satisfied with his recovery, judged him free of further surgery. 'I believe private arrangements have been made for your convalescence. As far as I'm concerned, there's no need for you to remain in Haslar. I shall need to see you once a week, unless that is, you feel something is not right. I want you here for physio three mornings a week. Happy with that, Lieutenant?'

'Absolutely, sir.'

'Nurse will make the arrangements. Well done... you're mending very nicely.'

*

Anne had returned to full duties that morning. Better than phoning, Sims decided he would go to *Dolphin* and tell her the news. He would call on James first.

3rd Officer Christine Harper was the first of quite a few people that day who thought him freshly risen from a watery grave. 'Never believe what you hear on the news, and especially what you read in the papers.'

She sat down looking quite shaken. 'Don't get me wrong... I'm so glad you're alive... it was a bit of a shock... what on earth happened?' she said, noticing the walking stick.

'Some other time. Can I speak with Lieutenant Fox-Eastleigh?'

'Yes, of course.'

'Sims, good morning, everything okay at Haslar?'

'Fine, they discharged me to convalescence at Hell Head.' Not waiting for James to ask more questions, he said, 'I want you to deliver my Browning, the two Russian guns complete with all magazines, and my three bullets to me at Hell Head House as soon as possible. Don't tell anyone, don't show them to anyone.'

'For Christ's sake.'

'Look, you weren't the one they shot... don't argue,' he said, bluntly.

Two Tokarevs and one Beretta.

Stealth required: Wren Pam Somerton did not hear him enter. 'Hi, sexy,' he called.

She stood there with her hand over her open mouth. Dropping her hand, 'Sims... *Oh my God*... is that really you, love?'

'Your very own hairy cupid, gorgeous... how's Ben?'

'He's lovely.'

'Do you think I could go in and see 2nd Officer Sherwood?'

'I'll go and tell her,' Pam said, looking as though she didn't quite believe he was real.

'Don't do that.' He took hold of her hand. 'We'll just go in and surprise her.'

Sims, followed by Pam gripping his hand, went in to the office where Anne and Joss were at their desks. 'They've given me my freedom, love. I'm all yours at Hell Head from now on.'

Anne leapt up from her desk, disengaged their hands, flung her arms round him and disregarding all admiralty regulations became intimately involved in kissing him.

'A bit different from the last time he was in here,' Joss said, to Pam.

Flip-flopping between pleased and dazed, Pam said, 'It's a very strange day today, I think I'll go and make some coffee.'

They sat drinking and chatting, Anne asked, 'Would you like me to take you home, darling?'

'That would be nice.'

'Don't be too long,' Joss said, winking at Anne as the two left.

Walking through reception, Pam called, 'Ben's going to be so pleased when I tell him... he was quite fond of you,'

'Tell him he's a poof,' Sims went and kissed her. 'It *is* really nice to see you again.' He kissed her again, 'When you see Ben next, can you ask him to bring over all my things from the office. Tell him, go careful with my records, they're very precious to me. Also my carved wooden box, that's precious as well... take care, sexy.'

Pam Somerton went into the office. 'How long ma'am?... how... ...I mean how?'

'Forever, Pam... ...it was written in the stars.'

*

After seeing the surgeon a week later, Sims decided it was time to visit some old friends. There was unfinished business to deal with. His first stop - Whale Island.

Coincidences do and often occur; on duty, his face-off guard from way back in January. Brandishing his stick, Sims said, 'Don't say anything, or I'll stick this so far up your arse your eyes will cross. I've come to see Sub-Lieutenant Hennerbury; I'm not late and I know where to find him.'

He walked into the armourer's workshop, 'I only deserve ninety seven percent.'

Sub-Lieutenant Hennerbury and Les Goodwin stood speechless. 'I've come to say thank you to you both. Without your bullying... I am sorry, *help*. I'd definitely be a goner.'

'Officially, you are, lad,' said Hennerbury. His appearance had presented the gunnery officer with a deep philosophical problem. *Officially,* Sims was late, and yet he was clearly in need of a haircut and his shoes polishing: ergo, he must still be alive. Les, in the meantime, remained opened mouthed and silent. Then, wits gathered, said, 'Fuck me, Sims, how did you manage to get out of that?'

'Can't give you too many details - combat range work was well worth it... I got both of them; they put three into me. Like I said, I only deserve ninety seven percent - a point knocked off for each bullet I took.'

'Jesus, I had this feeling the day you first walked in here, you... you were like a bad omen - a stoker with a *gun*!... like giving a mad woman a knife, *lethal*. From what you've just said it sounds like you were.'

Les Goodwin pointed to the stick. 'You going to be all right?'

'Yeah, Yeah, I'm coming on really well, thanks.' Then turning to Hennerbury, said, 'Really sorry about missing the comp.'

Gunnery officers are not known for bursts of sentiment. Sims put what happened next down to shock. What followed had probably never been exceeded by Hennerbury in the previous ten years. 'Dammit; sod the comp, there's always tomorrow... it's good to see you alive, lad,' he said, shaking Sims by the hand, with Les following suit.

'I'd like to be able to say I'll be available in the future, things are a bit uncertain at the moment... might be medically discharged... might not. No dates fixed yet... I'm getting married; I'd like you both to come with your respectives.'

'Count me in, who's the girl?' asked Les.

'Anne Sherwood.'

'I'll come too. Sherwood, any relation to Commodore Sherwood?' said Hennerbury, smiling at his joke.

'Yes, he's her dad.'

'Reeves, now you're taking the piss.'

'No I'm not, Commodore Sherwood's going to be my father-in-law - he's a really nice bloke. Now here's something else you might find just as unbelievable. I'm not a stoker any more. I'm now a lieutenant; a commissioned officer,' he said, showing them his identity card.

'Stoker, or not, I didn't do too bad, did I?' Not waiting for an answer, he said, 'Now to business. I need a favour... to do with this lot,' he said pointing at his leg and walking stick.

'What is it?' asked Hennerbury, cautiously.

Sims took out the three bullets the surgeon had removed from his body and laid them on the table. 'I need to know all... everything... absolutely everything you can tell me about these - comparative weights, calibre, even type of gun used if possible. They're a bit messed up... can you do it?... is it possible?'

Les picked them up. 'I can tell you straight away they're two different calibres, where are they from?'

'Me.' Not wanting to prime the pump, he added nothing more. What Les was going to reveal had to be from his expertise alone. He didn't tell them he had two of the guns from the shoot-out, both of which were the same type and calibre.

Hennerbury watched and listened to the exchange. He kept quiet, obviously, Sims was holding something back.

Sims turned to him, 'I've been in hospital for quite

some time, I'm a bit rusty, can I have a few sessions on the combat range? It'll have to be when I've got rid of this,' he said, waving his stick.

This request convinced Hennerbury that Sims knew more. 'Les has been working on another Browning, want to test it out on the target range?'

'Absolutely.'

So, he thought, limping across the causeway from Whale Island, as I suspected, there *were* three of them. This thought pushed back the satisfaction he felt from making a near perfect score on the target range. Hennerbury had said, 'Do try and get them to let you stay in, sir,' He had replied, 'For fuck's sake, don't call me, *sir*, sir.'

The following week, Sims, carrying a briefcase, returned to see what Les had managed to find out about the bullets.

'As you said, they were a bit mangled. These two... same calibre - 7.62 mm. Before they had hit you, going by their weights, I'd say they were twenty five millimetres long... at a push, I'd bet they were fired from two different Tokarev TT-33s. Ammo, probably Russian made 57-N-134S... you were a bit lucky there, lad, if they'd been made in Yugoslavia, you might not have a leg left to limp on... stacks more muzzle energy.'

This was technical detail Sims would have been happy to skip over. It made his stomach churn: things could have turned out so differently: he unconsciously rubbed his damaged thigh. Les continued. 'This one probably came from a Beretta M35 - bit of a show-off's piece... 7.65 mm by seventeen millimetres long. Whoever fired this one, might have chosen the 7.65 mm M35 over the 9mm M34, because it carried an extra round - eight in total... doesn't have as much stopping power, though.'

Sims picked up his briefcase; opened it, and pulled out the two Tokarevs. 'Ten out of ten so far... bit of a genius aren't you?' he said, smiling.

'It's my job,' said Les, modestly.

'Any idea who might use an M35? - someone from British Intelligence possibly.'

'Could be quite old, or new; could have been made in 1935 or yesterday; been going a long time... still in production... not much to go on,' said Les, thinking hard. 'Russians wouldn't use one... narrows it down to Europe and the rest of the world, if that helps.'

Sims smiled. 'So they're pretty common?'

'In theory, yes, but with service or intelligence personnel, you don't come across them that often - I've only worked on a handful... want me to check my records?'

'Please.'

'It'll take a couple of days... come back then... they'll be ready.'

*

He thought it time to visit the Seamanship School, in particular Lieutenant-Commander Maitland.

He met Ben coming out of their office, 'Whitley, you old bugger, how you doing?'

'You're up and about... come for your tot?'

'Not allowed... how are you getting on with the gorgeous Pam?'

'Spot on... thought you'd fucked it up at first... turned out well... I'll be a civvy in a couple of months, going for a job with Customs in Pompey... getting married soon, like to come?'

'Don't know... not sure... dabtoe's wedding? Beer supplied, or do we have to bring our own?'

'Fuck off, Reeves.'

Maitland appeared at his office door. 'Lieutenant Reeves, could I have a word when you've finished?'

'Won't be a moment, sir.'

'He's finally flipped, what's all this lieutenant business?

'He says it as it is, old son. Only don't call me sir... I just can't get used it... don't think it suits me.'

'Were you never a stoker, then?'

'Apparently not. I'd better go and see what he wants... catch up with you later, mate.'

Ben watched him walk to Maitland's office, Never been called 'mate' by an officer before.

Maitland shook his hand warmly, 'Come in, Reeves; It's so very nice to see you... heard about your exploits on The Island... you must have felt very lonely.'

Sims taken aback, 'You're only the second or third person to see it that way, sir.'

'What I'd like to know is why you didn't come to me when you first suspected something?'

'At the time things didn't stack up. I didn't trust anyone, and unfortunately, that included yourself. It wasn't a nice feeling.'

'No, quite,' Maitland said, fiddling with his pens on the desk, 'Do you think we were set up?'

'You, Lieutenant Fox-Eastleigh, and me: lambs for the slaughtering.'

'I feel a bit silly about all this... should have been quicker off the mark. You could have been killed... out of my depth... I am very, very sorry, Reeves.'

'We were all flung in the deep end... don't feel bad about it... we were all out of our depth, that's why we were chosen,' said Sims, feeling a little strange in having to comfort the conscience of a senior officer. 'I certainly don't bear you any ill-will, you were a damn good CO... best I ever had.'

'I thank you very much for that, Reeves, it means a lot, perhaps I can retire in peace now.'

'You're retiring? That's a shame.'

'Yes, at the end of the year. They're leaving me here till then. I shall go and look after my parents in the west country; I shall make fine furniture.'

Before Maitland could wander off into a world of dovetails, veneers and the importance of keeping chisels sharp, Sims reckoned it a good time to progress what he'd come for. 'I wonder if you could help me, sir? Have you ever come across anyone who uses a Beretta M35?'

'Intriguing question... is it one I should keep quiet about?'

'Definitely.'

'Firearms - not my cup of tea... supposed to keep up to scratch though. I would have done better with a shotgun I think,' he added, smiling.

Inevitably, Maitland was on the point of wandering off. Sims manouevred him back on track. 'So you never saw anyone use an M35?'

'Why are you so interested in M35s, Reeves?'

'One of the three bullets removed from me came from a Beretta M35. There were only two Tokarevs recovered -

Two Tokarevs and one Beretta.

I'm told Russians wouldn't use an M35. I think someone from British Intelligence set them on to me. I also think the route might have been from the cabal to NID, from NID to MI5, and then, from MI5 to the Russians.'

Maitland winced at the thought of being shot three times, he trawled through his memory. 'To answer your question, not a NID person, no,' he said, almost absent-mindedly. 'There was someone from MI5... I was transferred to NID from them... whether it was an M35 or 34, I wouldn't want to comment.'

'How do you know it was a Beretta, sir?'

'Oh, he flashed it around, said the Beretta was the best make in the world... a show-off.'

Sims leant forward - a possible lead. 'Have you got a name?'

'No... unusual I think... pompous; didn't like him... nobody did... in those days, everyone else on service revolvers.'

'What did he look like?'

'Average height, moustache, fair red hair... odd name... I'll do some thinking.'

The description sounded familiar. Much like the intelligence snooper at *Dolphin*. He wondered why Maitland had not also made the connection but decided he wouldn't push further. 'Thank you, sir, I'll have to be going shortly,' he lied.

Before he could leave, Maitland asked, 'Reeves, how did you escape being blown up?'

'I saw them plant the bomb... I'd been watching the freighter. I reasoned that if someone wanted me out of it that much, I was going to give them all the help they needed. I faked it, sir.'

'Were you scared?'

'Yes, sir, shit scared... if you don't mind me saying, these are odd questions.'

'No, they're not really, they are in a way in context. I have often wondered what I would do if I were called on to do something brave, something that required physical bravery.'

'You don't always have an option, it isn't a matter of choice... it's not a matter of being brave, you just react. In my case; I was really angry. Maybe being brave is when you've had a chance to think, are scared, but still act.'

'That *is* the very point I think, Reeves. I had suspected that things were not what they appeared. I did nothing... I'm not very proud of myself.'

'With all due respect, you're not a heavy, you're an academic.'

'Academia should *not* be a safe haven for cowardice, Reeves.'

Again, Maitland looked into some distant reach in the back of beyond. 'I didn't help Turing you know... I didn't support him... didn't stand up for him... a brilliant man in the process of being crucified by the ignorant. I didn't help him at all. No, Reeves, being an academic does *not* excuse cowardice. Give me a few days and I'll see what I can come up with... you'd better be off now.'

'Thank you,' said Sims, wondering what was going on in his boss's mind.

*

'What do you have for me?'

'Come on in... as I thought, just a small handful,' Les went to his desk and pulled a small tattered notebook out of the drawer. 'Four to be exact.'

Sims read the short list. 'Cresswell, Brand, Throagh, Mason... all M35s, Les?'

Les nodded, 'First, second and fourth, MI6... third, MI5.'

'One other thing, can you lend me a shoulder holster? If you've got one, I need it now.'

'What are you up to?'

'The less you know, the better. Yes or no?'

'Yes,' said Les, moving to a locker beside his desk. 'Come here, lad, let's make you comfortable.'

Sims took his coat off. Les adjusted the holster straps. 'Comfy?' he asked, sliding the Browning home. 'You didn't get this from me; okay?'

'Sure... can't stay, I have someone to show this little lot,' he said waving the list. 'You're a pal... thanks a lot... be seeing you,' he said, on his way out of the door.

*

'Any of these ring a bell, sir?' He asked Lieutenant-Commander Maitland.

Before looking at Les's list, Maitland said, 'I remembered his name... Throagh.'

'Well, well, do you think we have a suspect?'

'Possibly; not necessarily. I still have contacts in MI5; I'll have him checked out... see what his movements have been lately... can you come tomorrow?'

'I'll do my best.'

*

The following morning Maitland said, 'I have an address and a photo. Apparently, when not away, he's quite punctual, arrives home 1800 more or less on the dot.'

'If they know his movements that precisely, doesn't it imply he is being watched by his own gang?'

'Quite, yes, a good point... I think it does.'

'I need a bullet that's been fired from his gun. I'd prefer it if it didn't come out of some part of my anatomy this time.'

Maitland winced again. 'Do you think he always carries his gun with him, Reeves?'

'I think that depends very much on what job he's doing. If he's office bound he probably keeps it at home. If, on the other hand, he was going to be doing a bit of freelance work, he'd carry it with him.'

'Can you be sure of that?'

'No, but it's what I'd do in his circumstance.'

'Quite, quite,' said Maitland, deep in thought.

Sims waited a while for the old guy to resurface. 'Is there anything else, sir?'

'Now look, we have no proof at all, I don't want you doing anything rash. However, I was also informed that Throagh, by pure coincidence, is expected in Portsmouth today.'

'Where?'

'Not in Portsmouth exactly: Southsea, South Parade Pier. We need to know who he's meeting. He'll be there at 1300.'

'And so will I. He won't be expecting to see me. I'll check him out from a safe distance. If I think he's armed, I'll get his gun off him. If I think he's clean, we'll leave things until we can get him at home.'

Sims picked up the photo of Throagh, and copied his address. At 1230, he climbed out of the taxi directly opposite the pier and walked into the Royal Beach Hotel. He ordered a coffee, and sat waiting for Throagh to arrive.

After three quarters of an hour the waitress came and asked if he would like another coffee, 'Are you waiting for somebody, sir?'

'Yes, someone in the same line of trade as me... we go shooting together. Please don't call me sir, I'm quite ordinary really.'

The girl smiled. 'You don't look ordinary to me.'

'What do I look like, then?' he asked, not taking his eyes off the entrance to the pier.

'Nice.'

Sims thought, just a few months ago, I would have latched on to you so quick, you wouldn't have had time to notice your knickers were missing. She gave him another smile, and went to serve a couple sat a few tables away.

The clock struck, Sims looked up: 1400, and our Mr Punctual's an hour late. Shit, he's not coming. He paid the waitress, and took a taxi back to the Seamanship School.

***

Chapter Twenty Two
The Wet Deed.

Someone was blocking the driveway. Throagh parked his Lancia and walked the few yards towards his house. 'Move your car, I can't get in... this is my drive,' he snapped.

Maitland climbed out of his car. 'Good day. My name is Lieutenant-Commander Simon Maitland. I am a cryptanalyst with the Naval Intelligence Division.'

'Hmm, I know who you are,' said Throagh, recognising him. 'What do you want?'

'I need to talk to you, somewhere we won't be overheard. I have something to tell you. You will be very interested in what I have to say.'

'You'd better come in... it's clean.'

He led Maitland into a precise study on the ground floor. 'Well, what is it?'

'I have, for sometime, been engaged in research into patterns of human behaviour,' Maitland lied. It was a plausible lie. 'I have come up with a method for uncovering, or detecting, possible defectors, double agents and moles etc. I am able to do this by analysing personal attitudes, their movements, speech patterns, their habits even. I was posted to Portsmouth, in order to put my findings into practice.' He registered an uneasy shift in Throagh's composure. 'Using this technique,' he continued, 'I'm pleased to say we were able to accurately pinpoint an enemy agent; a Mrs Elizabeth Glass. She is now in our custody talking and, I must tell you, prepared to talk volumes more.'

'What has this got to do with me?'

'No doubt, you are aware of an incident on the Isle of Wight recently. You should know, you have been watched for some time. You were seen on The Island on the same day as a shooting, and among many other details, you are known to possess a Beretta M35. Incidentally, an M35 bullet was taken from the body of our agent. I would like to take your Beretta and have it analysed for elimination purposes. What do you think?'

This meeting was not what Throagh had expected. He reacted with a surfeit of pomposity. 'I think you've a damned cheek. I have served Her Majesty's Intelligence Agency for many years, there's not a single blot on my record. How dare you?'

'Quite, quite. That is why I was certain you would not object to handing your Beretta over for analysis.'

'Yes of course,' said Throagh, going to his desk.

'Just in case you are guilty, it is pointless trying anything... I have informed your superiors.'

Throagh bent down to get his gun from a side drawer. Maitland took the opportunity to level Sims' old Albion at him. But things happened too fast for him. Throagh moved quickly to one side and fired. Before he realised he'd been hit, Maitland got off a single shot hitting Throagh squarely in the chest. Throagh fell back against the wall: instantly and quite dead. Maitland looked down, saw blood pumping from a stomach wound, and sat waiting to die.

*

Sims limped into the Seamanship School as fast as he was able. He went straight to Maitland's office - it was empty. There was an envelope propped on the desk. It was addressed to him. He opened it and read...

My Dear Lieutenant Reeves,

I am sorry to have sent you on a bit of a wild goose-chase. I needed to buy a little time. My contact in MI5 confirmed that Throagh is being watched.

I am ashamed to say I have been so very slow off the mark. I failed to connect your description of Throagh after you reported his snooping at *Dolphin*. I fear I am getting too old for this job and am a danger to those around me. Having already put your life at risk, it is a fear I am not comfortable with.

It looks pretty certain he is a double agent. However, it is likely he is the protégé of someone much senior, and therefore, his treachery may never come to light. So, young man, I have decided to do some house cleaning, a *wet deed* I think the Russians call it in this awful trade of ours.

I am sure I know what would have happened if you'd met him. I cannot, as I have done in the past, stand in the margins and do nothing. I do not want to live with the knowledge that you might spend the rest of your life with a charge of murder hanging over your head. For murder is what it would be deemed to be - the evidence we have at the moment is too slim.

If things do not turn out well for me, be kind enough to tell my parents that their son had, at least, a little courage.

I wish you all possible happiness in the future. I am very proud to have known you.

God bless you, and your future wife.

Yours.

Lieutenant-Commander Simon Maitland.

'Shit, shit, shit,' spat Sims. Through the office window he saw Ben. He threw it open. 'Have you seen the boss?'

'He's not here... said he was going to London... couple of hours ago.'

'I can't drive that distance with this leg. Get the Land Rover, you're going to have to take me.'

'I can't, I've got a delivery.'

'Leading Seaman Whitley, I'm giving you a direct order, get the Land Rover now!'

'Yes, sir.'

Sims got into the passengers seat. Ben asked, 'Where to, sir?'

'Richmond Surrey - get going, and drop the fucking *sir* bit... do you know how to get there?'

'Yeah, Pam's parents live not far away.'

'When we arrive there, we'll ask for directions.' Sims, took out his Browning and slid in a full magazine.

'Are we going to need that?' said Ben, looking worried.

'I might... you won't.'

'Pull over by this post office,' said Sims.

'Just give me a few moments, please.' The post

mistress finished franking some envelopes. 'Now, which way are you facing?' she asked.

'That way.'

'Then turn round... it's second on the left.'

'Thanks.'

'There's Maitland's car,' said Ben.

'Stop here.' Sims got out, 'Now go straight back to Pompey.'

'I can't leave you here with your leg in that condition... *no way!*'

'Leading Seaman Whitley, this is another direct order: *fuck off!*... go back to Pompey!... *now!*'

He, hesitated.

'Please, Ben, go on mate... go back and take Pam out for a pint... this is not your problem.'

He reluctantly drove away as ordered. He wondered if he'd ever see Sims again.

Land Rovers are not built for speed. The journey had been agonizingly slow. At 1807, Sims walked down the road past a white Lancia Flaminia and towards Maitland's car. That's Throagh's house, he thought. He had not reached the gate when two shots blasted from inside. Sims automatically flung himself down behind a low garden wall. 'God, shit, that hurts,' he muttered out loud, clutching his thigh.

No noise came from the house. He got up and with his Browning made ready went to the front door. He quietly opened it - silence. Stealthily he went inside. He heard a faint noise coming from a door on his left. Sims pushed it open. 'For fuck's sake!' he saw Throagh slumped on the floor, obviously past help. At first, he thought his boss was as well. Maitland moved slightly. Sims went over to him. 'Sir...' he saw blood oozing out of his shirt.

'What service do you require?' asked the operator.

'Ambulance, a man has been shot,' he said, and gave her the address, 'You'd better send the police as well.'

He went back to Maitland. 'Hang on, sir, an ambulance is coming.'

'Reeves,' he whispered, 'he shot me in the stomach... it's quite painful being shot, isn't it?'

'Yes, sir.'

'I think I killed him.'

'Yes, sir, you did. It was a very good shot.'

'Quite, quite,' said Maitland, in his usual absent minded way.

'Don't talk, sir, save your energy for the nurses,' he said, holding his hand.

It was wasted advice: Maitland had gone.

'Oh Jesus *Christ!* You daft old cunt, why didn't you leave him to me?' Sims choked out.

The police and ambulance arrived within minutes of each other. Sims spoke to the plain clothes policeman in charge. 'You will need to inform MI5 for this one,' he said, pointing at Throagh. 'He was one of their agents, name; Throagh. It is more than likely he was a double working for the Russians. For this man, you will need to contact The Naval Intelligence Division, name; Lieutenant-Commander Simon Maitland. He had evidence that Throagh was a double and had come to take him into custody.'

'I'm Detective Inspector Adstock. And who are you,

sir?'

'Lieutenant John Sims Reeves. Also of The Naval Intelligence Division.' He showed the inspector his identity card.

'How did you come to be here, sir?'

'Lieutenant-Commander Maitland was my CO. I found a note addressed to me on his desk... his intentions were plain. I came as soon as I could to lend assistance. As you can see, I was too late, only by minutes, but too late,' said Sims, looking sadly at the old boy's body.

'*You* obviously thought he would need help, why do you think he tried to do this alone?'

'I wish I knew,' said Sims, not wishing to suggest it might have anything to do with ghosts from his boss's past, and long-term harbouring of guilt. 'It's possible, he thought Throagh would do a runner and he came to stop him. He was a very brave man, he would have known it was risky... he stood by his duty and conscience... a brave man, and a very nice one too.'

'You obviously liked him a lot.'

Sims nodded, and stood there for a moment. 'I think you ought to take possession of the weapons, and resist all pressure by the intelligence services to hand them over.'

'Why do you say that, sir?'

'Because, we'd like just a little of the truth, wouldn't we? And also, Throagh's Beretta may be implicated in another shooting,' he said not thinking it important at that time to mention the shooting in question was his.

'Point taken, sir, I shall need a statement before you leave.'

An hour later, Stinton arrived. 'Well, Lieutenant, what on earth's this all about?'

'Lieutenant-Commander Maitland and I were pretty sure that Throagh was among those who shot me on the Isle of Wight. We were not one hundred percent sure. We needed more evidence; I have reason to think he came here to see if he could get Throagh to panic.'

'It looks as if he managed that. Is the implication that Throagh was a double?'

'Yes, sir... almost certainly.'

Stinton was quiet for a moment. 'Well done, Lieutenant Reeves. I have a feeling Admiral Jessop is going to be very pleased to hear that.'

'A bit of revenge for Portland and Buster Crabb you mean. *Naval Intelligence exposes and eliminates an MI5 double agent...* might sound nice in the Sunday papers. I hope he'll be decent enough to mention Simon Maitland's contribution.' Sims said, sarcastically.

'We'll need to debrief you today, Lieutenant... at Tunworth House.'

'I'll get my statement done, and be with you.'

'In the meantime, I'll advise Admiral Jessop of Maitland's death.'

Sims sought out Inspector Adstock. 'I would very much appreciate it if a test firing could be carried out to prove that Throagh's gun was, or wasn't, implicated in the shooting I mentioned.'

'We would need the other bullet, sir,'

'That's not a problem, inspector, we have it.'

'How can you be sure it's the bullet from the shooting?'

'It's probably still got bits of my bone and blood on it, Inspector.'

'Is that what done your leg, sir?'

'No, *he* got me in the arm, my leg was buggered-up by his Russian mates.'

'Dangerous business you appear to be in, sir. Give me a call and we'll arrange things. Those guns will not leave the station,' he said, firmly.

'It will probably be in a few days. I have to go for a debriefing... I hear they can take an awful long time.'

'Not to worry, sir. When you're ready.'

'We had better be going, Lieutenant.'

Sims went over to Maitland's body.

'Don't touch anything,' said one of the scene of crime men.

He took no notice and patted his old boss's shoulder. 'Bye-bye, sir,' he said, affectionately.

'Did you not hear what I said, sir?'

'Fuck off.' Sims got up and walked to the door. 'Don't you want to say goodbye as well, sir?' Stinton did not answer.

He was angry. Maitland's killing; he wanted to speak to Anne; he was hungry; he knew they would keep him isolated until they had got what they wanted from him.

'Are we stopping anywhere for eats?'

'No, the admiral will have food laid on.'

'That's hours away, I haven't eaten since very early this morning, can't we stop for a sandwich... a pie.. anything!'

'No.'

'I want to make a phone call.'
'We're not stopping,' Stinton said, firmly.
'Shit.'
'Do you swear a lot, Reeves?'
'Only when I'm pissed off and hungry.'

An hour and a half later they drove up to the front entrance to Tunworth House. Admiral Billy Ruffian Jessop was waiting for them. 'Come inside... there's food waiting.'

Sims went straight to the table and helped himself to coffee and a substantial plateful of just about everything that had been laid out. Ignoring everyone, he sat down and started eating. They kept him hungry, now they could wait while he ate, and, while he inspected the brass plate set into the middle of the table.

'Well, Lieutenant Reeves, are you ready to start?'

He knew full well the admiral really meant; *you are* ready to start - it was not a polite enquiry.

For Maitland's sake, Sims was going to push the old bastard to the limit. 'Almost,' he said, taking another mouthful - might be my last supper. he thought, if I'm going to be crucified, might as well be on a full stomach.

Crucifixion was not on the cards. 'Reeves, you managed to clean-up a Russian cell, and get an MI5 double to boot. I can't say which one I'm most pleased with,' and without batting an eyelid regarding his unorthodox elevation from stoker to commissioned officer, said, 'You've really earned your promotion, Lieutenant.'

Admiral Billy Ruffian looked towards Stinton. 'If you

would fetch the secretary, we'll start the debrief.'

Stinton did most of the questioning. The secretary short-handing every detail down; the admiral listening closely. It took six hours to take Sims through the entire episode. They were thorough. When did he first become suspicious. Why did he keep the information to himself. The bomb planted on his launch, and its detonation. The shooting on the Isle of Wight, and finally the events of that day. Sims, during this time, careful in not implicating James Fox-Eastleigh in any way.

'That will be all,' Billy Ruffian said to Stinton and the note-taker, 'I want a private chat with Lieutenant Reeves.'

While the two were leaving the room, Sims asked, 'Do you mind if I help myself to some more grub?... shame to let it go to waste.' Without waiting for an answer he started carving thick slices off a large joint of beef and piling these between two huge hunks of bread, 'Any mustard or horseradish sauce?' He didn't say *sir* - he was still angry: fuck the consequences.

Billy had been watching him closely, 'In the sideboard, Reeves, and don't push your luck!'

Sims took a enormous bite out of his sandwich.

'That sandwich looks quite good. I might have one myself,' Billy said, hacking into the beef.

'How do you like your bread?' asked Sims. He and Billy worked together piling a plate high.

'You would seem to like horseradish, Reeves?' suggested Billy after seeing how much Sims had spread on his meat.

'My gran used to make our own - *Sauce au Raifort*

should make your eyes water, she used to say. All you need is a root of horseradish, a little thick cream, a pinch of salt and some French Dijon mustard - turnip is not necessary.'

'Raifort...turnip?' queried Billy.

'That's French for horseradish and the stuff you buy in English shops is about eighty percent turnip,' Sims took another bite. 'That's why it doesn't make your eyes water.' His anger lessened with each mouthful.

It painted an odd picture: this ex-stoker, who, not many minutes earlier had been revealing how he had eliminated a Russian spy cell and exposed an MI5 double agent to an admiral, was now discussing the merits of horseradish sauce with him. The two men seemed at ease with each other - making beef sandwiches can do this. It is quite a mystery how simple cooperation like this can shape the future.

Billy finished chewing and swallowing a particularly large mouthful. 'Reeves, how do you like your commission?'

The admiral was fishing for something, Sims angled back, 'It was a bit of a jump... takes a bit of getting used to. Considering the risks and the damage you can pick up on a job, money's not that good either... maybe when I get a full third ring on my sleeve, matters financial will improve... I've always fancied being a commander... things must get a lot easier then, I might even be able to afford some life insurance.'

'You'd have to be promoted to lieutenant-commander first.'

'I am the precedent that says that may not always have to be the case.' He watched the admiral's face closely.

'Are you open to a deal, Reeves?'

'Depends on the deal.'

'For the avoidance of doubt, let me speak plainly. With what you have achieved, we may be able to stay NID's execution. If you play along with our version of things, I'll organise your promotion to lieutenant-commander and then, even though you're a bit young, to full commander as quickly as it is possible.'

Sims remained silent for a few minutes. 'Okay. As long as I do not have to do any more dirty work for NID, it's a deal.'

'Done,' said Billy Ruffian. 'And for the record, I think you did a magnificent job. I didn't enjoy putting your head on the block, Reeves. How are the injuries?'

'Do you know? I thought you'd never ask, sir.'

Admiral Jessop smiled and shook Sims' hand, 'Thank you, young man. When you're ready, I've a driver to take you back to Portsmouth.'

'I'll take some of these sarnies with me for the trip home. And, if it's okay with you, I'd prefer to be taken to Hell Head House; it's near Lee-on-Solent.'

'Ah yes, you've made some useful contacts there I hear. Now, before you go, are there any questions you'd like to ask me?'

'Yes sir, how did Throagh know so much about what we were doing?... ...though thinking about it, I guess that's something for you to sort out, isn't it, sir?'

'Anything else, Reeves,'

'Yes, sir. If I may be so bold, not a question, more a little piece of advice,' not waiting to see if the admiral was going to allow him to be so audacious, quickly added, 'The next time you want to get at whatever it is you have hidden under that brass plate, make sure you refill the screw slots with fresh polish.'

*

Sims stood on the terrace watching Anne through the French windows. She saw him from the table, stood up and walked to him. She did not hurry. She was pale and angry. The image and prospect of him lying somewhere covered in blood had been all too easy for her mind to conjure during his absence. They stood facing each other: he, uncertain of the mood of the person stood in front of him. She raised her hand and slapped him hard on one side of his face. 'That's it! We've not had a single word from you,' she said. With her other hand she slapped him hard on the other side. 'That's it, it's over; it's all finished. do you hear me?... *finished.*'

The telephone rang, 'I must answer that - it will be Father, he phones every hour to see if there's news of you.' Before going inside, she turned and said, 'How dare you! After all we've been through. It's over, Sims, over.'

He stood there numbed. He had expected her to be upset, but not to this extent. After the events of the last twenty-four hours, he was exhausted and his leg giving him much pain after diving behind the wall. These things did not matter, they were insignificant compared to losing Anne. He was too exhausted to take it in. He needed to sleep. *Alice Alacrity* was the nearest place for this. He turned and walked down the drive towards Hell Head Harbour.

The Wet Deed.

Rounding the curve in the lane that led from Hell Head House, he heard her voice calling, 'Sims! Sims darling! where are you?'

Did she say darling? he asked himself.

He stopped - her calling getting closer. She saw him and broke into a run. When she reached him, she said, 'Where are you going?'

'You said we were over... we were finished.'

'Not us, silly... *never* us. Whatever it is, you think you're doing is over. Listen to me, Sims... ...my lovely, brave, man; you cannot take on the whole world. You've done your bit. From now on, *it* is over.'

'I wasn't trying to take the world on, I was just getting even with the git who would have been quite happy to shoot you on The Island.'

'And did you?'

'No, someone else did it for me.'

She kissed him, put her hand on his shoulder and looked him up and down. 'Are you hurt?'

'Not really... could do with some pain killers... a bit knackered... cheeks are still smarting,' he said, smiling.

'I'm sorry... I was *really* angry... I still am... not a word from you. Mind you, you'll get a lot worse if you ever do it again.' Her tone softened, 'Promise me you won't ever go away again, Sims.'

They stood in the middle of the lane holding each other tightly. 'I know you're bound to make me angry again one day, but understand one thing, it will never, ever, be over between us, John Sims Reeves; never, ever.'

They stood for a few more minutes just holding each other. Finally, she asked, 'Where have you been... what have you been doing?'

'Tell you later... sometime,' he said, yawning. 'It really *is* over Anne; all over. We can get on with whatever it is we're going to do with the rest of our lives now.'

'Come on. Come on home with me, Sims.'

Anne was still with him when he woke. 'Had a good rest, darling?'

'Now; let's get this clear,' he said, yawning. 'Don't for God's sake think I'm complaining, but with you in the same bed, rest seems to be at a bit of a premium. However, since you ask, yes, lots better thanks,' he said, sitting up and looking around. 'Is it my imagination, or are there more things in my room.'

'Our room,' Anne corrected him, 'I've moved in... I'm in drastic need of remedial English.'

For some time, they lay there quietly facing each other. Sims, gently stroking her face with the back of his fingers. 'You really are *so* very beautiful, you know.'

'I know you may have heard me say this before, John Sims Reeves, but, you *really* know how to turn a girl on.' She moved closer to him.

Commodore Sherwood joined Anne and Sims for lunch. 'You had us worried, son.'

'I am truly sorry about that.'

'Where did you go, and what were you doing?'

'Maitland decided to go after Throagh alone.'

'I've not heard of him, who's Throagh?' asked Anne.

'He was the third person shooting at us on the Isle of Wight: an MI5 double.'

'How long have you known this?' asked the commodore.

'On The Island, I was pretty certain there were three of them. It took a bit of research to find out who the third one was.'

'How did you know it was Throagh? How could you be sure?' Anne asked.

'He drove a white Lancia Flaminia - we were followed by one on The Island. Also, James picked up two identical Russian guns and gave them to Dad. But, of the three bullets taken from me, one was a different calibre. The odd one was from an Italian Beretta M35.'

The commodore smiled at being called *dad*. 'But why did Maitland pre-empt Throagh's exposure?'

'Because he was a good bloke,' said Sims, handing Anne the note Maitland had left him. She read it and handed it to her father.

'I didn't know him, I wish I'd met him,' said Anne, 'He must have been a nice man.'

'Too nice; too gentle.'

'Do gentle people often kill?'

'If they believe it is really necessary, yes.'

'There are still a few things to clear up,' said Sims.

'Such as?' she asked, looking worried and clutching his arm.

'Nothing dangerous, love. Maitland's funeral, I have that message from him to give to his parents, and there's a ballistics test to do that will prove Throagh's culpability one hundred per cent. Also, I'd like you to come with me to visit my parent's and grandparent's houses, we need to sort out their effects - what you'd like to keep or throw out.'

'Your parent's and grandparent's *houses!*'

'Yes, I have them rented out. I reserve one room in each, an apartment in one and in the other, one to store things... one of the tenants at least, will be pleased to have the extra room - they've just had their second child.'

'Are you telling me you own properties?'

'Yes. Is there a problem with that?'

'No, of course not... you just didn't say. What else don't I know about you?'

'Christ, I don't know. Will you come on these jobs with me or not?'

'Of course I will. I can't trust you on your own, *can I?*'

'You two sound as if you're married already,' said the commodore, laughing. 'Sims, I'll attend the funeral as well.'

'I think that would mean a lot to his parents.'

'Joss and James will come I'm sure,' said Anne.

'So will Ben and Pam, and I'm bound to be able to rustle up a few more from the Seamanship School. We'll give the old boy a good send off.'

Anne asked, 'How do you like being called, *dad*; Dad?'

'I think I can handle it very well; I accept the role, Sims.'

The easy change from sir to dad and father to dad, set the future solid. They were a family now, comfortable in each other's company.

***

Chapter Twenty Three
Anne's Favourite Game.

Anne drew back the double curtains of the large bay window. She looked back into the room. Sunlight flooded onto the furniture neatly stored there. She walked over to a chest of drawers. 'This is really beautiful.'

'I know, my grampy said it was George IV. He said you could tell by the partly hidden dovetails on the side... a giveaway, he used to say. I think Maitland would have loved it. There's some really nice porcelain stored in those chests... Sevres, Worcester, Caughley, a bit of Derby, and a nice Sitzendorf candelabra that will look fine on the dining table at Hell Head.'

'The houses are much larger than I thought they'd be,' she said.

He looked troubled at being there: she moved closer to him.

'Some of this stuff is beautiful... some of it just stuff... warp and weft of memories: coloured threads of good people's lives,' he said, quietly,

Anne slipped her arm through his. Warp and weft of memories, Mo was so right, he must be made to write. 'Did you come here often?'

'Now and again... when I could.'

'What did you do?'

'Mainly just sat and listened to my gran and gramp's voices - I don't remember mum and dad's.'

'Oh, Sims,' she said, hugging him close.

Suddenly, 'Look, love, some of this stuff is just tat. It really shouldn't clutter up your house.'

She took his hands in hers. 'All these things are part of your past... part of your history. And you must get this into your head, it's not my house, it's *our home.* Our children will want to know your past as well as mine.'

'We're having children, then?'

'Don't you want any?'

'Yes, of course I do.'

'Come on, Sims,' she said, softly. 'What's the matter?'

'I really fancy having kids, but I guess I'm a little scared of leaving them like you and I were.'

Anne put her arms round him and rested her head on his shoulder, 'I think that's a fear every parent has to face, darling.'

*

It was late March, and the long lawn leading down to the ha-ha that looked over lush pasture running down to the edge of the glittering Solent, had been given its first trim of the year. Anne and Sims pulled a sofa up to the open French windows and sat there quietly looking at the view. He had Anne and a home - his life was now complete.

Anne's favourite game had no strong intellectual foundation. It was a simple pleasure gained if the right components were all together. Those right things were; Sims;

somewhere quiet; somewhere comfortable. The game's structure was constant. Its course varied, the outcome always understood. Like reading a good book that has a good story, a happy ending, and has been read and enjoyed many times, Anne felt safe, happy, and comfortable playing it.

Sitting close to him with his arm around her, and with all the pieces in place, the game usually started with Anne asking something along these lines: 'When did you first know you were in love with me?' Sims knew just how far to stretch his response: sufficiently drawn out to make her impatient, though answered well before he spoilt the moment.

'More-or-less straight away.'

'Not immediately then?'

'No, you must have been two hundred yards away when I first saw you. You were obviously female, and therefore, I was naturally interested. It was at twenty five yards I fell for you - totally... completely... utterly.'

She loved this bit. Someone could fall in love with her at twenty five yards distance.

'Like my old Albion, that's your deadly range. Outside that, shots can go a bit wild.'

'What was it that first got you?'

'Oh definitely your bum.' Then he would add, 'Your legs as well.'

'Anything else?'

'Not really, I was quite focused on your bum.'

Around this point in the game, Anne would nudge him in the ribs - just hard enough to get the game going in the direction she wanted it to.

He would vary his answers. One day it might be her

bum, another, her moustache,

'Hmmm, what in particular about my moustache attracted you.'

'That's a difficult one... mainly, I think the way you waxed the tips with mayonnaise,' he once said.

'What was the next thing?'

'Well at twenty five yards I couldn't see your eyes, but you called, and on hearing your voice, I fell in love all over again - twice in two minutes, seeing that I was sober, that was a record.'

'How many times a minute when you've a belly full?'

Sims knew this was time to change tack. 'When you were close enough for me to see your eyes, I knew there was no going back. There would never be anyone else. If you wouldn't have me, no one would.'

'So, you really love me then?' She would never tire of hearing him say it out loud.

Sims would consider his answer just a little too long. 'I think you know only too well.'

'I want to hear you say it. Tell me *now!*'

He would go into such a description that left her in no doubt. She would then turn to him and kiss him. She was in no doubt how much he loved her. He was in no doubt what the kiss meant, and what was going to happen next.

It was a game of contentment. A game played by two people very much in love. Played by these two experts, it was a game that would last for eternity.

The End

Appendix
Two Short Stories for Mo.

During their happy six months together, Sims made up many stories for Mo. *The Golden Mace* was Mo's favourite. It is told, more or less in its entirety within the pages of this book.

Two other stories, mentioned: *The Hoopoe* and *Felicity* were both written by Sims from memory long after he had originally told them. To avoid annoying the reader in having mentioned, but not told them, I decided to include both in this appendix.

In later years, Sims allowed that Mo's memory of *The Golden Mace* was probably more accurate than his own. They both agree *The Hoopoe* and *Felicity* are pretty much word for word as they were during their first telling.

Walter Gunn - 2016

The Hoopoe.

He only ever wrote on hand-made paper of the finest quality: the words laid down were always written with a goose feather quill carefully dipped in cuttle fish ink.

'Poetry cannot be written with a Biro,' he claimed.

In the summer, he rose just after dawn, made two cups of coffee and two slices of toast and jam - although sometimes, for a change, he would have toast, olive oil, garlic and gherkins.

One morning as he sat at his desk, nibbling a crust of toast, taking a sip of his coffee, and looking across his study through the open French windows that led to the lawn, a Hoopoe stepped out from underneath a rhododendron bush. It busily probed, then stepped, then probed its way across the damp grass.

Though he had seen one the previous year, Hoopoes were very unusual in his area. The Hoopoe occasionally raised its crest and stretched its wing to the ground. The man watched its every move, fascinated by its beautiful colours; fawns, blacks, whites, and a colour that people in a hurry might call *salmon pink.*

It is with this colour, such a description can only be excused when one realises there is no adjective in the thousands of languages, dialects, patois or creoles dreamt up by man, that by itself, or with a large paragraph of assistance, could do more than dull its true beauty.

The Hoopoe.

The Hoopoe probed its way closer, looked up, raised and lowered its crest, and flew to the threshold of the French windows. It cocked its head to one side and appeared to be studying the man and his desk. The poet could not stop himself uttering, 'How very beautiful.'

With a quick flap of its wings, the fabulous bird flew to the desk, dipped its beak into the ink pot, and with an action so deft, wrote on a scrap of hand-made paper the poet used for jottings: *Thank you, we are rather handsome aren't we; I prefer handsome to beautiful by the way - it's a male thing...*

The poet, not sure if this was the incipient phase of a new and possibly violent creative period, played safe. In case his wife had slipped some inappropriate substance into it, he sniffed his coffee cup, 'No, just coffee,' he said to himself.

...It's so nice to taste real sepia ink and to write on real paper - Hoopoes should refuse to talk to humans on anything else.

If this was some kind of trip, the poet was not going to impede its course. 'Where on earth did you learn to write?'

You've misphrased the question, you should have said; How long have you been able to write? I would have answered; always, in fact, we taught humans.

'Supposing I accept this as gospel, why are you here writing to me today?'

I have a message for you. I came last year, but I wasn't sure if I'd got the right address.

'You had a message for me *last year!* Perhaps it's a little out of date now.'

Is that really important! wrote the Hoopoe, with an irritated flourish.

'Well, these days, it can be, yes.'

Hmmm, perhaps that's why we lost out to Wells Fargo and the Penny Post... mind you, we're often still more reliable than the postal system in France.

'So, it's not urgent then?... wait a moment, did I hear correctly, you mentioned Wells Fargo and the Penny Post, are you in business?'

Yes, of course. Hoopoes were originally designed to be messengers - quite nice livery isn't it?

The poet, who believed in nature rather than a God asked, 'Designed by whom?'

Oh I don't know... personally, I think it's a presumption too far... we are just messengers; it's what we do. Perhaps not the most efficient, I grant you, but we get there in the end... got any more paper?

'If you don't mind me asking, you don't seem to be carrying a post bag, so where's the message?'

In my head... we remember them, some are hundreds of years old.

'Oh come on, even I know Hoopoes don't live that long.'

No! Of course they don't, don't be so bloody naïve. Messages are handed down from generation to generation; they are embedded in our minds - humans call this 'instinct', but hey, what do they know?

'If that's the case, you must accumulate lots of messages, your head must be full of them.'

No, no, no! wrong again! At this point, if the Hoopoe had been structually capable of sighing, it would have done so. *When we've successfully delivered them they're erased... this ink is rather good,* it wrote, smacking its beak.

'I really don't wish to be a bore, there seem to be some possible flaws in the system, What happens to the message if a Hoopoe doesn't breed?'

It's hard luck for the Hoopoe - know what I mean, hard luck for the message, and, I dare say, hard luck for the person supposed to receive it.

'Okay, let's just cut to the chase. What's the message for me?'

Yes, of course. That's why I'm here isn't it? Now let me see... she must be your great, great, great Aunt, I think. She says she will be arriving on the four o'clock train at Granborough Road Station from Aylesbury - can you arrange for a pony and trap to pick her up. PS. she'll only be staying a few weeks. There; message delivered - no tip necessary. I'll sit here for a moment if I may, it always makes me a little dizzy while erasing is going on.

'Oh do come *on!* She must have been dead at least eighty years. I take it it's not possible for you to send a message back in time?'

Sod off, wrote the Hoopoe, *I've got breeding to do...* he flew back to the lawn, probed, stepped, raised his crest, stretched his wing to the ground, and muttered to himself, *the bloody cheek of it... you deliver a message and they're never satisfied... no wonder they lost the ability to think rationally... what's the next message?... oh no! not bloody Austria again... mind you, this is quite interesting... ...Archduke Franz Ferdinand is going to be assassinated... better get there quick!*

***

Felicity

Felicity, the vicar's daughter, was just seven years old, and for the first time she was allowed to walk unaccompanied down the lane past the witch's house.

Her mother's pace had always quickened passing the small gate set into the Cotswold stone wall. Today, Felicity stopped and looked through the wooden bars. 'Hello,' said a voice above her; Felicity had not noticed the witch leaning over the wall and watching her.

'Christ! you made me jump,' she said. 'You're a witch aren't you?'

'A bit of a generalisation,' the witch replied, 'but, yes, I am.'

'I'm not sure I understand.'

'It's a bit like calling people who come from abroad, foreigners... there's many different kinds; some good - some bad... it's the same with witches too.'

'Well, what kind are you, then?'

'Basically, white... I think... I've had my off days though... especially during the warlockopause.'

'I don't know much about witches, my father's sunday school never seems to touch on the subject, what other colours are there?' asked Felicity.

'Oh, let me see... crimson; they tend to work with sailors in Rotterdam... in the Vatican there are purple ones;

known for their chanting and misleading the innocent. And, I suppose I shouldn't forget the black and white ones.'

'What do they do?'

'Get mistaken for badgers and zebras, mainly.'

'Yes, I think I can understand that.' Felicity paused and took a closer look inside, 'Your garden is very nice, it must take a lot of work keeping it so tidy.'

'Oh it's quite easy really, I just wave my wand at the weeds and tell them to sod off... usually works... I don't like killing things, so the slugs I just bung into next door's vegetable patch. Now, how would you like something to drink? I've got some very nice potions... really fresh... make your hair stand on end, some of them.'

'Sounds good to me,' said Felicity, who, now having reached her seventh birthday, had been worried that illicit substances were just not going to happen for her.

They walked up the narrow stone path to the open front door, and looking down the corridor that led to the kitchen, she could see it was bathed in a beautiful soft green light. To her complete surprise, there, hanging over the table was a large glowing cabbage. 'How the hell does that work?'

'It's simple,' said the white witch, 'there's a switch on the back with *on* and *off* written on it... things are a lot more straight forward than people realise. Mind you, they are a very special cabbage, one has to grow them from bulbs, you see.'

'Well, bugger me,' said Felicity, 'science made clear at last.' It was her moment of enlightenment. And so, from the age of seven, Felicity's future was determined

Felicity.

- her life's mission would be to bring clarity to all things unknown. To the educationally unlit, she would bring light. She would re-label the mislabelled and reclassify the misclassified. In The British Library, for instance, the well thumbed title, *'Wan King - a voyage of self-discovery'*, she had moved from *'Travel'* to the completely new category of *'Adult Friction.'* She would clarify the unclear - she would explain that foot lockers weren't something you keep your feet in, and pitchforks were absolutely useless for eating tar with.

Naturally, many honours were bestowed upon her. But the one she was most proud of, even above the Nobel Prize for Clear Carton Labelling - awarded for her tireless work in that field... it's well worth mentioning here, that Felicity completely overhauled the nation's nutritional health, by having *'open here'* printed on breakfast cereal packs... but let's get back to her proudest moment, she was invited to be a guest on *'Desert Island Discs'* - she knew she had made it, there was no higher honour.

As usual, towards the end of the programme, Roy Plomley asked, 'If you could only take one of the eight records with you, which one would it be?'

She answered unhesitatingly, 'The men's 100 yard hurdles.'

'And what book?'

'I always like to keep myself busy,' she replied, 'so I'll take that seminal work; *365 completely vulgar things to do with a young sailor.*'

'And the luxury?'

'I would have thought that was bleedin' obvious... a completely vulgar young sailor, of course,' she spluttered.

The sole dark mark on her otherwise unblemished life was never proven: in her mid-nineties, during a particularly turbulent menopausal crisis, it was said there were irregularities in the accounts of her *'Clarity Charity'* - the logo of which was a large glowing cabbage. It was claimed that funds had been misused for licentious purposes. Naturally, she vigorously denied the allegations saying that the apartment she shared with Mother Theresa had been paid for out of their own pockets and the fifteen members of the SAS found unconscious on the floor had obviously broken in and been overcome by fumes from a faulty hookah.

Her death at 105 remains a mystery. She was found barely conscious in a lorry park next to Mac's cafe near Aldermaston and died at the scene. Theories surrounding her demise are manifold. The coroner wrote in his report: "Never before, have I seen a corpse wearing a look of such complete ecstasy." The pogo stick laying alongside her body was never satisfactorily explained.

***

Important
Ranks of the Royal Navy

Stokers:
> *Junior Stoker   JM(e)*
> *Ordinary Stoker   M(e)1*
> *Leading Stoker   LM(e)*
> *Petty Officer Stoker   POM(e)*
> *Chief Petty Officer Stoker   CPOM(e)*

Officers:
> *Midshipman*
> *Sub-Lieutenant*
> *Lieutenant*
> *Lieutenant Commander*
> *Commander*
> *Captain*
> *Commodore*
> *Rear Admiral*
> *Vice Admiral*
> *Admiral*
> *Admiral of the Fleet*

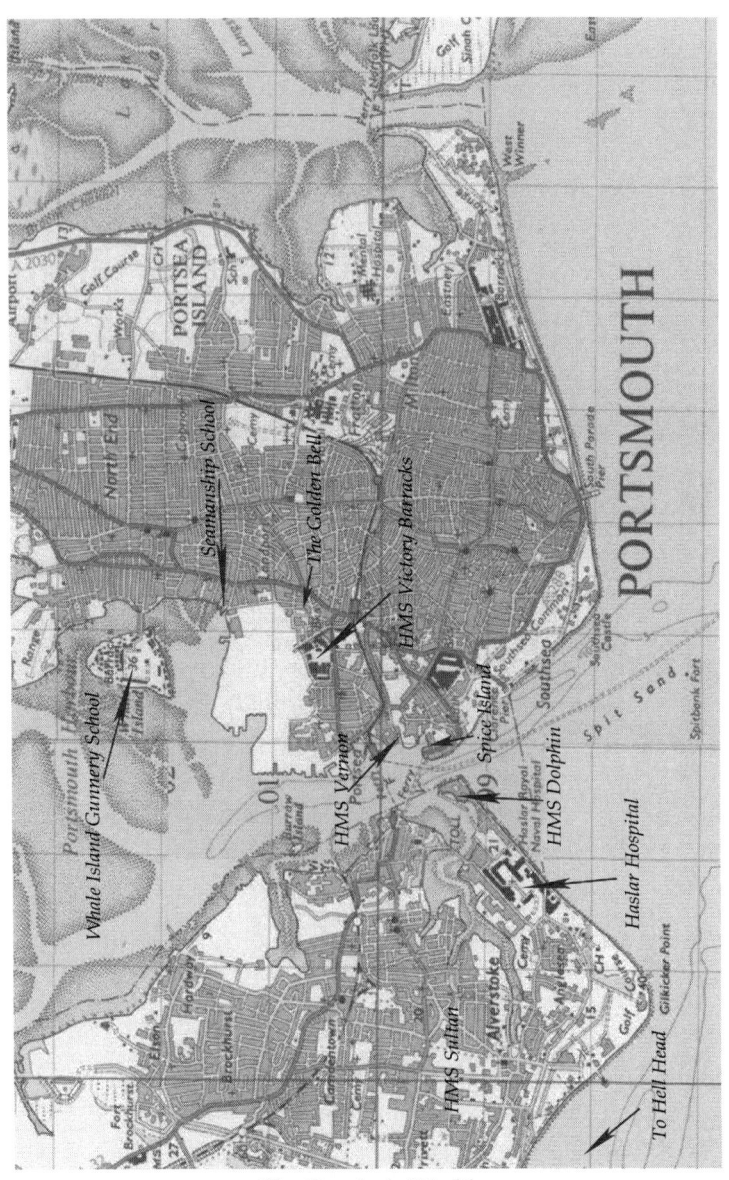

The Courier's World
Portsmouth and Gosport

The Courier's World
The Solent and Isle of Wight

Glossary for both Rites of Passage and Hawkshaw.

45th Commandos	Royal Marine Commandos - The author advises not to play rugby against them - dismemberment being a strong possibility.
Admiralty House	Administrative home of the Royal Navy - based in London.
Admiralty Regulations	Regulations covering every aspect of Royal Naval life.
Admiralty Standing Order	A single Admiralty Regulation.
Aide	An officer appointed to assist high ranking officers - personal secretary.
Albion	One of many types of service pistol. It was a variant of the Enfield Mk1 revolver with a spurless hammer and therefore requiring a full pull through to fire. It was manufactured by Albion Motors, Glasgowhence its name.
Annie Oakley	Semi-fictional American gun-toting cowgirl.
A priori	Knowledge independent of experience. According to one American philosopher, independent of fact.
Arethusa	A training ship moored in the Thames. It primarily trained orphans for future service in the merchant and Royal Navies. It was a terribly hard life for those lads. It is not to be confused with HMS Arethusa.
AWOL	Absent without leave.
Big Sylvie	Notorious Portsmouth prostitute.
Boat	Submarines are always called boats in the Royal Navy.
Boiler maker	The universal tipple for matelots in Portsmouth at the time of Billy Ruffian's Courier. A half pint of bottled brown ale mixed with half a pint of mild ale from the barrel.
Boom	A spar running along the lower part of a fore and aft sail.
Bosham Castle	Does exist. Though, it is in fact, a cottage.
Bow	The front, or sharp end, of a boat.
Bowsprit	A spar extending forward from the bow

Glossary for both Rites of Passage and Hawkshaw.

	to which the forestays and, therefore, the foresails are attached.
Brigantine	A sailing vessel with two masts. The foremost being square rigged, and the mainmast rigged fore and aft.
Bulgogi	A delicious Korean beef and vegetable dish. The author first made this in the UK and later had the pleasure of eating it in Korea. The UK version was a good match.
Bulkhead	Wall.
Bull	Centre of a target.
Bunting tosser	Signalman.
Button (The)	Small wooden cap on the very top of the 143 ft mast at HMS *Ganges*.
Butts	Originally a safe area at the target end of a shooting range from where the targets could be raised and lowered, and the scores recorded.
Celadon	Denotes a type of ceramic as well as its greyish green colour - also known as jade green.
Chandlery	A shop or company dealing in ship's supplies - ropes, sailcloth, rigging equipment etc. Originally the room in a house where candles were stored.
CIA	Central Intelligence Agency - USA.
CO	Commanding officer.
Coxswain. (1.)	Senior seaman rating on board ship responsible for discipline.
Coxswain (2.)	Helmsman of a motor boat or small sailing vessel. A coxswain's certificate proved one's ability to pilot such vessels.
Cryptanalyst	Essentially, a code breaker.
Cutter	In the Royal Navy a cutter was a two sailed sloop rigged unpowered sailing boat of between 30 and 35 feet in length.
Dabtoe	Stokers' slang for a seaman.
Deck	Floor.
Deckhead	Ceiling.
Dockyard maties	Dockyard workers.

/ Glossary for both Rites of Passage and Hawkshaw.

Ensauté	Neither myself or my French friends think there is any such word - it's another word Sims made up. Sauter does exist and means to jump!
Fanny boats	Tourist boats taking holiday makers around the dockyard waters.
Fathom	Six feet - approx two meters.
Fenders	Protection pads suspended over a vessels side to protect against chafing and impact and damage when berthing. In the Royal Navy they were hauled inboard as soon as the vessel was underway. To not do so was considered sloppy behaviour.
Firing squad	Execution squad.
Flag Officer	Term applied to those holding the rank of admiral.
Flag Papa	Blue Peter. A square blue background with a white square at its centre. The white square is approximately one third of the flag's height and width.
Flotsam	Floating debris as opposed to Jetsam which is rubbish thrown overboard.
Fore and aft Springs	Mooring lines running from the bows running rearward and from the stern, running forward to the shore. Their purpose is to restrict fore and aft movement of the boat. They are used in addition to normal bow to shore and stern to shore mooring lines.
Frigate	There's little point in looking at a Royal Naval ship and trying to distinguish some particular feature that determines it as a Frigate. They may come in different sizes and carry different armament. The term describes the ships role rather than its shape - anti-submarine; convoy escort etc.
Gaff	A spar to which the head/top of a fore and aft sail is attached. It is tensioned upwards by a 'topping lift' or 'Gaff Halyard.
Golden Bell (The)	No. 60 Charlotte Street, a public house in Portsmouth loved and frequented by

Glossary for both Rites of Passage and Hawkshaw.

	Sims and also, coincidentally, by the author. It, and the quaint street it sat in were bulldozed down and now lie under a car park! Happy memories buried in the name of progress - may the Portsmouth town planners responsible, rot in hell.
Grog	Rum 95.5 proof - 54.5% Vol diluted 2 parts water to 1 of rum. Named after Admiral Vernon who introduced the dilution in 1740 - Vernon's nickname was 'Old Grogram' after the grogram boat cloak he habitually wore.
GRU	Russia's largest intelligence agency.
Gunwale	The upper edge or planking of the side of a boat.
Haslar	The Royal Naval hospital in Gosport.
Hell Head	The original name for what is now called Hill Head.
Helm	Whoever's at the helm is steering the vessel whether it be by tiller or wheel.
HMS *Alacrity*	A fictional frigate based on HMS *Alert*.
HMS *Arethusa*	Leander class frigate.
HMS *Bellerophon* (1)	An Arrogant class, 74 gun, ship of the line. This *Bellerophon* is the ship on which Napoleon surrendered to the British. The French still believe that Napoleon actually won the battle of Waterloo and that the British cheated!
HMS *Bellerophon* (2)	Admiral *Billy Ruffian's* first ship. This ship fought at the battle of Jutland.
HMS *Bellerophon* (3)	Also the name of the gunnery school at Whale Island Portsmouth. To avoid confusing matters too much, the author decided to use only its common name: Whale Island.
HMS *Dolphin*	Home base of the Royal Navy submarine service.
HMS *Dreadnought*	Britain's first nuclear submarine.
HMS *Ganges*	A shore based training ship situated on a spit of land at the confluence of rivers Stour and Orwell opposite the mouth of Harwich Harbour. HMS *Ganges* was

Glossary for both Rites of Passage and Hawkshaw.

	conveniently situated there, enabling it to take full benefit of the freezing winter time winds coming straight off the North Sea. Boys from the age of fifteen and three months were subjected to a year of brutal training there. During the Author's time at *Ganges*, it was not unknown for deaths to occur when under punishment. It was so cold there.
HMS *Pembroke*	Royal Naval barracks in Chatham.
HMS *Salisbury*	A *Salisbury* class type 61 aircraft detection frigate.
HMS *Scarborough*	Type 12 Anti submarine, *Whitby* class Frigate.
HMS *Start Point*	A fictional submarine depot ship based on HMS *Rame Head* and HMS *Hartland Point*.
HMS *Sultan*	Engineering and nuclear engineering training establishment in Gosport.
HMS *Vernon*	Torpedo and Anti-submarine depot in Portsmouth close to Spice Island.
HMS *Victory* (1)	Nelson's famous ship. Too many honours to mention.
HMS *Victory* (2)	Shore base barracks in Portsmouth.
Home on the Range	A truly awful 'saddle song' of the West.
Inner	The second circle from the centre of a target.
Jack	Civilian term for a Royal Naval sailor. Especially Portsmouth and other naval bases.
Jarama	A famous battle in the Spanish Civil War. It took place in February 1937 to the east and close by Madrid. Estimates vary between 6000 and 25000 dead.
Jetsam	Rubbish thrown overboard as opposed to Flotsam which is either wreckage, lost cargo or naturally occurring floating debris.
Jib	A sail forward of the main mast - usually triangular.
Jibing	Changing on which side of the sails the wind is acting. There is an important difference between jibing and tacking.

Glossary for both Rites of Passage and Hawkshaw.

	Because the wind passes around the stern, jibing requires extreme care as it is possible for the mainsail to violently slam over from one side of the boat to the other and in doing so break the mast and rigging. (See also tacking and wearing).
Keel haul	An old naval punishment whereby a rope is tied the wrists of the offender, then passed under the keel of the ship and then tied to his ankles. He is then hauled under the barnacle encrusted ships bottom. Depending on the severity of his crime, this may have been carried out more than once.
Ketch	A sailing boat with two masts - the main mast being larger than the rear or mizzen mast.
KGB	One of a number of Russian Intelligence agencies. The KGB operated mainly from Russian embassies and consulates. Therefore, its members were afforded diplomatic immunity.
Killick	Leading hand.
Lanchester	A submachine gun used by the Royal Navy. Dangerous, in that it was prone to accidental discharge if dropped.
Lee Enfield .303	Service rifle.
Lee on solent	During the period the books are set in, the Royal Naval air station, HMS Arial was located there.
Life story	Service record.
LM(e)	Leading stoker.
Magpie	The third circle from the centre of a target.
Marking time	Marching on the spot.
Marline Spike	A pointed rod especially used for parting the strands of rope when splicing.
Martini Mk3	A .22 target rifle - lever action as opposed to bolt action. the lever fitted snugly to the front and extending below the grip, and was operated by being pushed forward which opened the breech.

Glossary for both Rites of Passage and Hawkshaw.

Master at Arms	Senior Regulator. Think naval policeman.
Matelot	Sailor - from the French, matelot meaning sailor!
Mess deck	Living quarters for ordinary matelots.
MI5	Military Intelligence responsible for internal security in the United Kingdom.
MI6	Military Intelligence responsible for intelligence matters outside the United Kingdom.
Mizzen	The lowest or sole sail on the mizzenmast.
Mizzenmast	The rearmost mast on a sailing vessel.
NAAFI	Naval, Army and Airforce Institute. This acronym rather impolitely referred to as meaning: No Ambition And Fuck-all Interest.
Neaters	Pusser's rum without water added.
NID	Naval Intelligence Division.
NKVD	Soviet law enforcement agency. Its duties included: espionage and political assassinations abroad.
Nozzer	The first six weeks at HMS Ganges were spent by new recruits in the Annexe - they were known as Nozzers.
Onslaughted	A word fabricated by Sims.
Orwell	A river flowing from Ipswich to its confluence with the river Stour inside Harwich harbour and then flowing immediately into the North Sea.
Outer	The fourth circle from the centre of a target.
Pompey	Portsmouth.
Pontoon	A floating platform often used as a dock.
Port	Left hand side. See also Starboard.
Postie	Postman.
Pusser	Admiralty approved.
Pusser's rum	A potent spirit made in heaven.
Ratings	Sailors of the lower deck.
RDF	Radio Direction Finding - pre-GPS stuff.
Rosyth	Royal Naval dockyard Scotland.
Roy Rogers	One of those excruciatingly awful Hollywood singing cowboy heroes. The

Glossary for both Rites of Passage and Hawkshaw.

	line, 'before I get those dirty rats who shot your little girl and labrador, let me sing you a little song', may not have ever been spoken. It does however, sum up the entire genre of the Singing Cowboy.
RPO	Regulating Petty Officer - not generally liked. Pathologically hated by Sims.
Sally Port	The defensive door in Old Portsmouth through which crews left for their ships anchored in the Solent.
SBS	Royal Naval version of SAS.
Sheets	Confusingly, these are not the sails but the ropes that control their fore and aft tension.
Ship	Surface vessel. Submarines are not ships, they're boats.
Shotley Point	The spit of land at the confluence of rivers Stour and Orwell opposite the mouth of Harwich Harbour. HMS Ganges was conveniently situated there enabling it to take full benefit of the freezing winter time winds coming straight off the North Sea.
Slack water	Tide neither ebbing nor flowing - still.
Sloop	When used to describe a sailing vessel, it means a vessel with one mast, one mainsail, and one jib, both rigged fore and aft.
Spice Island	An area of Old Portsmouth. Its name carried from the old days and so called by sailors because the 'spice of life' was to be found there - namely, whores and booze. It had nothing to do with spices.
Spithead Mutiny	16th April to 15th May 1797. Sailors mutinied for better food, pay and treatment.
Starboard	Right hand side - a corruption of the word Steerboard from the time when a ship was steered with a rudder device fixed to the side of the vessel. Naturally, to place a vessel steerboard side to the dock wall would have been to invite damage. Hence the Port side went to the

Glossary for both Rites of Passage and Hawkshaw.

	dock wall. As most people are right handed, the steerboard was placed on the right hand side of the vessel thus allowing the helmsman to be on the inboard side of the rudder.
Stern	Rear end.
Stour	A river flowing from Manningtree to its confluence with the river Orwell inside Harwich harbour and then flowing immediately into the North Sea.
Tacking	Changing the direction of a sailing vessel with the wind passing around the bows. (See also jibing.)
Tannoy	As Hoover is to vacuum cleaners, Tannoy is to ships' loudspeaker and broadcast systems.
Tiffy	Artificer.
Tiger Tops	Tiger beer topped off with a drop of lemonade.
Topping lift	This term is usually applied to the device that raises and lowers a crane's derrick. Rightly or wrongly, the term was often used for the gaff halyard.
Tot	Daily rum issue of 'grog' for all ratings over the age of twenty - 3/8ths of a pint.
Twelve Bore	A shot gun.
Wearing	Royal Naval term for jibing. (See Jibing)
Whaler	In the Royal Navy this describes a three sailed, two masted sailing vessel of between 25 and 27 feet long.
Woods metal	Also known as Lipowitz's alloy - melts at 70°C.
Wren	Member of the Women's Royal Naval Service. Also known as Jenny Wrens.

Printed in Great Britain
by Amazon